Being Cut

A Rumination on Relationship Cutoff

Arwen Spicer

Cover Design by Glenn Peters

Published by Arwen Spicer, LLC

ISBN-13: 979-8-9912076-0-7

To my dear friends, Z. A. and "Anna,"
for your steadfast support and understanding,
and to "Ryan" for the grace of second chances.

Content Warnings

This book discusses relationship cutoffs: one person refusing contact with another. While it validates the right to cut someone off, it is also critical of how our culture addresses cutoffs. The book discusses trauma. It touches traumatic issues including domestic violence, rape, misogyny, abuse, transphobia, addiction, stalking, internet rage, racism, politics, colonialism, climate grief, and more. My stance is leftwing, but I critique several stances that are mainstream in certain segments of left-leaning culture.

Yet each man kills the thing he loves,
By each let this be heard,
Some do it with a bitter look,
Some with a flattering word...

–Oscar Wilde,
The Ballad of Reading Gaol

Contents

Introduction 1

Part 1: Why Cutoff Culture Exists

Chapter 1: Why People Cut Others Off 23

Chapter 2: Why We Valorize Cutoff 32

Chapter 3: The Right to Cutoff 46

Part 2: The Destructiveness of Cutoff Culture

Chapter 4: Six Tenets of Cutoff Culture 71

Chapter 5: Cutoff as Ethically Neutral 78

Chapter 6: Cutoff as a Responsible Way to End a Relationship 95

Chapter 7: The Duty of No Contact 109

Chapter 8: The Advice to Ignore or Rebuff Transgressors 125

Chapter 9: The Advice to Reprimand Those Who Question Cutoff 138

Chapter 10: The Advice to Begin by Accepting 159

Chapter 11: Impacts Equivalent to Abuse 182

Part 3: An Alternative Approach to Interpersonal Conflict

Chapter 12: A Relational Approach to Cutoff 190

Chapter 13: A Relational Approach to Forgiveness 213

Chapter 14: A Kemetic Response to Cutoff Culture 233

Conclusion 237

Self-Help Extras:

Appendix A: Tips if You Wish to Cut Someone Off 244

Appendix B: Surviving Cutoff 246

Afterword 260

INTRODUCTION

Four years after my dear friend cut off contact, I was reading my eight-year-old a bedtime story—*Batman*, I think—and doing my best to blink back tears.

After a while, my daughter said, "Why are you sad, Mama?"

I said, "Because my friend is mad at me and will never speak to me again."

She said, "I feel sad for her. And you."

When my friend cut off contact with me, few in my social circle acknowledged the pain I was going through. They shrugged it off with a joke or a quick "that's sucks" and changed the subject. Sometimes, they said my pain was unreasonable; I just needed to learn from my mistakes and do better. Sometimes they lectured me: "People have a right to choose who they have in their lives," as if I'd said they didn't. Sometimes, they said nothing. I find it telling that one of the few who accepted my pain—who accepted the sadness of the situation—was a child. She had not yet learned to ignore the obvious: feeling thrown away by someone you love wounds you.

Relationship cutoffs are defined by disconnection: disconnection between the cuttee and cutter, often disconnection between the cuttee and cutter's whole social circle. But perhaps the most damaging disconnect is between the reality and social narrative, the disconnect that occurs when you are cut to your core and others say nothing much happened.

That's the disconnect that kept me crying four years later.

I'm a lucky person. I never experienced a specific, overwhelming traumatic event until I was thirty-nine. That's not to say I carried no trauma. I had been psychologically wounded, both by acute circumstances, like relationships failing, and chronic factors, like a lifetime of negative social messaging about my personhood as a woman. But I never experienced the kind of psychological wound that produces significant post-traumatic-stress symptoms until my friend abruptly and permanently cut me off.[1]

She had her reasons, and this book is not about judging her. I cannot overstate, however, the damage that experience precipitated in my psyche. Now, let's look at those two sentences again. They sound disingenuous, don't they?

I don't intend to judge her.

The action she took toward me catalyzed deep trauma.

It sounds like I'm trying to deny responsibility for the fact I am judging her, doesn't it? There is a piece of that, of course. She hurt me, and I sometimes think (and say) unfair things in return.

Yet I deeply mean both of those statements, and being able to sit with both of them is crucial to the purpose of this book. It is not my place to say what action she should have taken. Only she can make that judgment. Yet the action she chose ignited a catastrophe in my life. Both things are true. She may have done right.[2] A person can make the right choice, and that choice can have damaging consequences. Those consequences matter, even if the choice was right.

My cutoff trauma began in 2014, and since then, I have healed significantly, not completely. If the final stage of grief is acceptance, I have not reached acceptance yet, not completely—maybe 85 percent. In flashes, I am still very angry. That anger is natural, but it is not productive, and I have worked to keep this book largely free of it. Nonetheless, it's there, and in some of these pages, it will show. In a few places, I choose to let it show because it is a piece of my reality, and I want to keep it real.

The crucible of this cutoff has been so unlike anything else I have experienced that it became a revelation, a death and a rebirth.

---

[1] The shade of difference might correspond to what Gabor Maté calls "capital-*T* trauma," typified by "automatic responses and mind-body adaptations to specific, identifiable hurtful and overwhelming events" (21) vs. "small-*t* trauma," which describes, "long-lasting marks seemingly ordinary events... can leave on the psyches of children." (22) He calls small-*t* trauma "nearly universal in our culture" (22). Gabor Maté, with Daniel Maté, *The Myth of Normal: Trauma, Illness, and Healing in a Toxic Culture* (New York: Avery, 2022), 21–22.

[2] My mother asks what makes a choice "right." That's the question, isn't it? In this case, what I mean is a choice a person could reasonably defend as the best according to their own moral system.

I am not an exception. Being cut off by a loved one is an intensely traumatic experience for many people. Cutoffs can protect people from untenable situations, and we cannot and should not eliminate them, but as a culture we can do much better in supporting all people in ways that minimize relationship breakdown and trauma. Honestly examining how cutoffs work is one piece of that cultural healing.

Cutoffs matter. They have psychological weight; they do psychological damage. They are also often the best choice. I have personally been on both sides of this chasm.

I have cut someone off too, another dear friend, in 2007. I, too, had my reasons, and if I were in exactly the same place, I would probably do it again. That cutoff—first by my choice and then, for a brief time, by his—lasted until 2014. Indeed, it was my later experience of being cut off myself that led me to reach out to him in 2014, and with grace, he allowed me to reconnect. That story is part of this book as well.

Both these stories hurt. Now multiply that by millions of people worldwide who go through events like this. For personal relationships to end in absolute severance is very common. It isn't always traumatic, but it is traumatic far more often and deeply than our society recognizes. The aims of this book are twofold: first, to validate the psychological weight of cutoffs. Second, to propose a different kind of cultural awareness to mitigate the harm associated with cutoffs. Although this book includes some self-help suggestions, it is not a self-help book; it's more a help-each-other book, an invitation to reinvest in relationship with others.

What I Mean by a "Cutoff"

As used in this book, "cutoff" is any circumstance in which one person totally breaks off contact with another.[3] This covers a

---

[3] As far as I am aware, the only clinical definition of "cutoff" in current use in psychology is in Bowen Family Systems Theory, where "emotional cutoff" refers to "how people manage their unresolved emotional issues with parents, siblings, and other family members by reducing or totally cutting off emotional contact with them." This definition is more restrictive than mine in that it only refers to families and less restrictive in that it encompasses limited contact without complete severance. "Emotional Cutoff," The Bowen Center for the Study of the

wide range of situations. My focus is permanent (or indefinite) cutoffs between people who have been in an emotionally significant relationship. Such relationships include marriages, romantic or life partnerships, significant dating relationships, family, and friendships, as well as any other relationship of mutual emotional depth. They do not include relationships in which the emotional investment has clearly been one-sided, for example, consistently rejected unrequited love. They do not include relationships that have been quite short-term or superficial, for example, cutting someone off after two or three dates or blocking a friend we never knew well on social media. These other types of cutoffs are also complex and worth discussing, but this book will focus on permanent cutoffs in significant relationships. Unless otherwise noted, I will use the word "cutoff" as a shorthand for this kind of permanent or indefinite cutoff.

A permanent cutoff happens when we communicate to someone (explicitly or implicitly) that we will never contact them again and/or they are not allowed to contact us. Permanent cutoffs are common. Odds are you have experienced one, as the person cutting (cutter), the person cut (cuttee), or a closely connected bystander. Yet you may not have heard the word "cutoff" much, even though it is the most common word for this action. That's because, as a culture, we don't talk much about cutoffs. In fact, conversations about them are somewhat taboo: not completely unacceptable, but uncomfortable and marginal. If we mention divorce or breakups, people know what we mean. If we mention cutoffs, without context or definition, we're likely to get puzzled looks. Cutoffs don't register as significant, but they are.

Terms Related to Cutoff

Though this book focuses on permanent cutoffs, it is useful to distinguish a cutoff from some related terms and concepts.

Family, accessed June 29, 2024, https://www.thebowencenter.org/emotional-cutoff.

No Contact

The popular dating practice of "no contact" refers to temporarily cutting off a partner after a breakup in order to get some emotional distance. "No contact" practice usually recommends at least a few months of no contact.[4] It is often not a permanent cutoff but a mechanism for getting some space to heal. However, because there is little literature discussing cutoffs and, thus, no widely accepted vocabulary, many use "no contact" to refer to permanent cutoff, and many use "cutoff" to refer to temporary no-contact.

The Silent Treatment

The silent treatment typically refers to a practice of refusing to acknowledge someone while currently in a social relationship. For example, a person might not respond when someone speaks to them. It is generally understood to be an unhealthy practice, used as a means to express hurt and anger. It differs from a cutoff in that it is not used to end all contact but to communicate feelings within an ongoing relationship.[5]

In the work of Kipling D. Williams on ostracism, cited in this book, there is some slippage between the silent treatment and cutoffs. He does not use the term "cutoff" but uses "silent treatment" broadly enough that it might refer to cutoffs as a subset.

Ghosting

Ghosting is a type of cutoff in which a person stops communicating without any explanation or warning. It can occur in a superficial relationship, such as disappearing after the first date, or

---

[4] For example, Wendy Rose Gould, "Why the 'No Contact' Rule Is So Important after a Breakup," Verywell Mind, Reviewed by Sabrina Romanoff, PsyD, June 12, 2023, https://www.verywellmind.com/no-contact-rule-after-a-breakup-7501465.

[5] In the only message I wrote to my friend's husband about her cutting me off, I incorrectly referred to the action as "the silent treatment." If I had the opportunity to talk with her about what happened between us, I would own this misstatement and the misunderstanding of her action it implied. Since that conversation is unlikely, I will at least own it here.

in a serious relationship, such as breaking off contact with a fiancé. Because ghosting involves no prior announcement of breaking contact, it can be hard to tell if ghosting in a significant relationship is intended to be temporary or permanent. Being ghosted is often a psychologically traumatic experience,[6] and in this book, I consider ghosting in serious relationships to imply an emotional significance at least as weighty as an explicitly permanent cutoff.

Abandonment

Abandonment has different definitions depending on context. There is legal abandonment, as in abandoning a minor child or a patient under one's care. Emotional abandonment, however, is defined as a *feeling* of being abandoned, regardless of the external events. Being cut off can trigger feelings of abandonment, but we can also feel abandoned in ongoing relationships if, for example, they feel disconnected or unsupportive. In fact, many people cut others off because they feel abandoned by them.

Canceling

Canceling someone refers to ceasing engagement, typically on social media and/or through economic interactions, as a means of censure. This most often occurs in the context of members of the public agreeing to cancel a person with some degree of social platform who has said or done something considered objectionable. As a public, socioeconomic act, canceling is different from relationship cutoffs, but it is culturally related.

Ostracism

Ostracism usually refers to a social practice in which an individual is systematically excluded by a group.[7] However, Williams

---

[6] Gili Freedman, Darcey N. Powell, Benjamin Le, and Kipling D. Williams, "Emotional Experiences of Ghosting," *Journal of Social Psychology*, May 17, 2022, https://doi.org/10.1080/00224545.2022.2081528.

[7] Richard J. Crisp, "Love and Other Attractions," in *Social Psychology: A Very Short Introduction* (Oxford Academic: Very Short Introductions,

expands the meaning to include exclusion by individuals.[8] Ostracism is effective as a tool of censure because a sense of social belonging is a fundamental human need. Ostracism has been practiced by many societies since the distant past. In our current world of numerous interlocking communities, many online and ephemeral, it is often comparatively invisible. For example, a person treated normally at work, in town, and by certain friends may be systematically excluded from the social network of an ex-partner. No one beyond that network may be aware of it. Yet this is an act of ostracism with potentially significant psychological consequences.

Cutoff Culture

This book uses the controversial phrase "cutoff culture" to describe a set of cultural practices that validates relationship cutoffs and makes them likely to occur. The term was coined by Jeff Reifman in his 2013 essay, "Shining Light on Relationship Cutoff."[9] He subsequently apologized for using it, following critiques that it made an inappropriate comparison to rape culture, implying that cutoffs are like rape.[10] Let's be clear: cutoffs are *not* in the same category as rape. To cite just one crucial difference, there is almost always a right to cut someone off. There is never a right to rape.

That acknowledged, I don't think Reifman had anything to apologize for. This book uses his term, and I find it an appropriate one. In his apology, Reifman conceded it was an improper use of the word "culture."[11] I don't concede that. "Culture" can mean many things, but in the sense of "rape culture" or "cancel culture," it means a set of practices that work to make something common

---

2015), https://doi.org/10.1093/actrade/9780198715511.003.0006, p. 96.

[8] Kipling D. Williams, *Ostracism: The Power of Silence*, (New York: Guildford, 2001), 8.

[9] Jeff Reifman, "Shining Light on Relationship Cutoff," *Breakup Lessons*, November 19, 2013, https://breakuplessons.com/shining-light-on-relationship-cutoff/?r=medium.

[10] Jeff Reifman, "Shining Light on Internet Rage," *Activism: Theories of Change*, August 21, 2014, https://medium.com/activism-theories-of-change/shining-light-on-internet-rage-37269f75d1c7.

[11] Reifman, "Shining Light on Internet Rage."

or accepted.[12] It also connotes a significant, negative trend. We have a set of practices that make cutoff common and accepted, and I do contend that the normalization of cutoff has, on the whole, been negative. Thus, I argue, we do have a cutoff culture (and a rape culture and a cancel culture). As to the idea that the phrase "cutoff culture" creates a false equivalence with "rape culture," the fact that two troubling issues both have cultural practices associated with them does not make them equivalent.

In fact, I'd argue that cutoff culture is connected to rape culture and to cancel culture. They are all outgrowths of the same dominant culture. Cutoff culture, rape culture, and cancel culture, though the terms focus on very different phenomena, are all enabled by a larger culture that promotes dehumanization and disconnection. In many ways, cancel culture and cutoff culture emerged as defenses against rape culture. We should be talking about these cultural phenomena together, and not as a competition over which is worst. Rape culture is worst. We should talk about them together because they are entangled, and to heal ourselves, we must address the root causes that perpetuate all of them.

If the term "cutoff culture" is triggering for some in ways another phrase might have avoided, I regret that. Nonetheless, at the time I am writing this, I feel the benefits of this useful and concise term outweigh the detriments.

A Relational Ethics Approach to Cutoff

"Ethics" is a term with a lot of uses. We often use it to describe standards for appropriate conduct within a profession, such as "business ethics" or "medical ethics." We may also use it in everyday speech as a synonym for "morality," but these two terms are not the same. "Morality" commonly refers to principles for judging right and wrong. "Ethics," in the philosophical sense, refers to the structured study of such principles. In this book, I use

---

[12] I find it ironic that Reifman apologizes for an improper use of the word "culture" in "cutoff culture," while linking to a *Merriam-Webster* page that includes exactly the definition of the term he seems to use: "the set of values, conventions, or social practices associated with a particular field, activity, or societal characteristic." "Culture," *Merriam-Webster.com*, accessed October 8, 2021, https://www.merriam-webster.com/dictionary/culture.

"ethics" to describe a structured defense or questioning of principles for making decisions about right and wrong actions. I am not a trained ethicist, and I do not rigorously evaluate different philosophical schools. Rather, I put forward some broad suggestions for mitigating suffering in our society, based on my experiences, observations, and research.

A Relational Approach Is Systemic

The ethics I advocate are fundamentally systemic, and this puts them at odds with dominant American ethics, which are individualistic. A systemic approach is based on looking at how different factors interact. Systemic solutions seek to channel those interactions in the desired direction. Dominant American ethics, in contrast, are based on personal choices with little attention to the larger social and cultural factors that drive those choices.

For example, Americans are famous for unhealthy eating. Dominant American ethics says, "I'm going to educate you about good nutrition, and then you need to make good dietary choices."[13]

A systemic approach says, "There are many factors in American society that drive unhealthy dietary choices: lack of time to plan meals and cook, the cheapness and ubiquity of unhealthy food, advertising, stress eating due to overwork and precarity. To support better dietary decisions, we need to address these factors: provide more rest; provide more security and emotional support; make healthier food the cheaper, easier option, etc."

Dominant American ethics tend to respond to systemic ethics by saying, "You're coddling people who make poor choices. You're not expecting them to be adults and be responsible. That's ethically wrong."

In this book, I argue for more compassion on human failings. From the dominant culture perspective, I may appear to be saying that people do unhealthy things, and our society should accommodate that rather than expecting them to be responsible grownups. But here's how I'd frame it: people do unhealthy things, and our society should accommodate that *so that* they can be

[13] An indication of the dominance of this view is the sheer volume of student essays I have read that argue this.

responsible grownups. We are all imperfect. If our society cannot tolerate imperfection, we cannot function. We all want people to be responsible, but shouting at someone desperate, afraid, and exhausted to be responsible will rarely work. Most times, it will drive them deeper into unhealthy behavior, increasing the sum total of our social problems and decreasing the sum total of people acting as responsible adults. Supportive structures (that include accountability) work better to help people live well. That is why this book prioritizes a systemic approach.

Rights and Duties Ethics

In broad strokes, our dominant culture prioritizes what we might call rights-and-duties ethics.[14] That is to say, our standards for good conduct toward other people, animals, plants, ecosystems, and things in general are dominated by our conceptions of rights and the duties they imply. A right, as we conceive of it in modern democratic societies, is a type of social power someone (or, rarely, something) inherently possesses and which cannot justly be denied, except, in some cases, through due process of the law. For example, liberty is a widely recognized right, but nation states generally argue that it can be denied to certain criminals by imprisonment with due process. In the United States, we know this concept chiefly through the Declaration of Independence. We have "unalienable rights," Jefferson taught us, including, but not limited to, "life, liberty, and the pursuit of happiness." Duties are obligations we have to respect and uphold the rights of others. Human beings have a right to life; therefore, we have a duty not to kill them, except, arguably, in some special circumstances, such as war or self-defense.

Rights, moreover, are not always limited to humans. In recent decades, we have broadly accepted that some animals have some rights. We generally accept (in theory) that they have a right not to be tortured, at least not more than is necessary for what is considered a higher purpose, such as testing medical treatments. Thus, pet owners have a duty not to abuse their pets, and those found

[14] For a succinct explanation of rights and duties in ethics, see Jethro Lawrence, "Ethics Explainer: Rights and Responsibilities," The Ethics Centre, June 2, 2017, https://ethics.org.au/ethics-explainer-rights-and-responsibilities/.

to have failed in that duty may have their pets removed from their care. In Western Civilization, the 1970s saw a serious flirtation with the idea that rights should be expanded to encompass plants, ecosystems, and the Earth.[15] However, these movements largely failed to take root (so to speak), and today our dominant discourse still discusses rights almost exclusively in terms of human beings and, to some extent, other animals.

With regard to cutoffs, our dominant culture holds that we have a right to cut someone off. There are a few exceptions, such as a parent's duty to provide for minor children or the necessity of interacting professionally with a coworker. Outside of these exceptions, however, we can cut someone off for any reason; it's our prerogative, our right. That person, in turn, has a duty to us: to stay out of our lives, to respect the right to cutoff. In contrast, once we cut someone off, we have no duty to them beyond our duties to strangers: not to kill them, rob them, etc. As far as rights-and-duties ethics go, this statement is valid and makes sense.

As a means for fostering a healthy culture, however, it is insufficient. If we let our overarching sense ethical responsibilities to other people end here, we promote a cold culture, one in which we agree that almost all of our emotional supports can justly be yanked away without notice at any time. Such a culture makes it difficult to trust, to commit, or to provide a space for the universal fact of human weakness. If any mistake may justly be answered by the complete removal of an important relationship at any time, we do not dare to make mistakes. Unfortunately, being human, we cannot avoid doing so. Catch-22. Such relationship precarity can easily cause trauma, and when we are in the grips of trauma, we are less likely to behave in a balanced, healthy way. Under this relationship precarity, harmful behavior becomes more likely. This cultural current needs to be reversed.

A Relational Ethics Alternative

As an alternative to these isolating and rigid ethics, I propose a *relational ethics* approach to cutoffs. Relational ethics is a loose term that touches numerous different practices and movements, from care ethics to transformative justice to many traditional

---

[15] See, for example, Christopher D. Stone's 1972 book, *Should Trees Have Standing?* and Arne Næss's work on deep ecology.

Indigenous perspectives. The core of all relational ethics, however, is a recognition that we live in relationship with others: other people, lifeforms, systems, etc. Because we are in relationship, we affect each other, and because we affect each other, we have some ethical *responsibility* to act in a way that supports each other's well-being and minimizes harm.

Duty and *responsibility* are terms with overlapping meanings, but for clarity, I will distinguish between them in this book. I will use *duty* or *obligation* interchangeably to refer to a mandate we are required to perform to uphold someone's rights, in the Western Enlightenment sense of natural rights, such as our right to free speech or right not to be murdered. This is a culturally specific usage, different from other concepts of duty, such as a duty to one's parents in many Asian cultures or the Hindu concept of *dharma*, sometimes inadequately translated as "duty." I am using this specifically Western definition because I am primarily addressing Western cultures, which place a high priority on natural rights within an individualistic frame of reference.

I use *responsibility* to refer to an ethical consideration we should weigh in our decision making but are not required to act on in every circumstance. For example, we have a *duty* not to rob someone; there are few, if any, exceptions. However, we have a *responsibility* to be respectful to others; that is, we should generally strive to be respectful. In some circumstances, however, other requirements, such as warning off an attacker or speaking the truth to power, might legitimately take priority over respectful behavior.

A relational ethics response to cutoff recognizes that cutoffs in significant relationships are psychologically weighty and highly contextual. Such ethics resist a one-size-fits-all approach, preferring to examine each cutoff as a unique social situation. While respecting the necessity of some cutoffs, a relational approach also recognizes that cutoffs are often psychologically devastating and promotes practices to foster healing for all involved: the cutter, the cuttee, and bystanders. Because cutoffs can be traumatic, relational ethics resist their use when less extreme boundary setting will serve the same purpose. The goal of such ethics is to minimize harm.

Relational ethics recognize contextuality and nuance. They are inherently systems-oriented and foster connection over disconnection. They are premised on the notion that our actions are rarely truly neutral in their effects. In most cases, they will generate some good and/or bad. Thus, in our ethical decision making, we should strive to maximize the good. I advocate a relational ethics that recognizes rights and duties but regards them as the ground floor of ethical decision making, not the whole house.

My Positionality (or Where I'm Coming From)

I've said relational ethics are contextual, and by that token, my own context as the author of this book matters. Here I'll provide some information on the perspective I bring to these issues.

My Professional Background

I am a writer and English professor with a background in utopia studies and degrowth ecology and economics,[16] all of which informs my perspective. I am not a mental health professional, and nothing I say should substitute for professional mental health services. I am also not a lawyer, and nothing I say should be construed as legal advice.

My Cultural and Personal Perspectives

I am a white, middle-class, American, cis-leaning woman from Generation X. Almost everyone I've personally experienced cutoffs with is also a white, middle-class American, which shapes my perspective. While I draw on ideas and practices from other cultures, I attempt to do so respectfully and without appropriation, recognizing myself as an outsider. My sources for this book are wide-ranging, including scholarly papers, popular articles, social media posts, and personal accounts from diverse individuals. In the course of this research, I have come to believe that many of the trends I discuss are common in much of the present-day Global North. As an American, however, I focus on the English-

---

[16] Degrowth is an eco-social stance that advocates a planned downscaling of unnecessary production and consumption in order to meet all humans' needs for well-being within the Earth's biophysical limits, using democratic governance. Many degrowthers also propose the extension of rights to the non-human world. Degrowth should not be confused with negative population growth movements; degrowth does not advocate population reduction policies.

speaking world and particularly the United States. When I refer to our "popular" or "everyday" culture, I refer primarily to United States mainstream, especially left-leaning culture, often as expressed through social media, with a sense that most observations apply more broadly.

My own politics are left leaning, and though I hope this book is useful to a broad range of people, it primarily addresses the American left, including some degree of critiquing the left from the inside. I also make some social assumptions that align with the left, for example, an acceptance of LGBTQ+ identities, the need to address systemic racism and other inequities, and the existential importance of far-ranging socioeconomic change to address the climate emergency.

Because this book is about personal relationships and draws considerably on my own life experience, it is also relevant that my own sexual orientation is non-dominant. While I consider myself on the asexual spectrum with a heterosexual orientation, I identify as a "friendship bonder," a term I invented to describe a person whose primary emotional attachments are based on friendship rather sexual attraction or romance. [17] (Even the term "sexual orientation" is a misnomer because, for me, it's not really about sex.) As a consequence of my orientation, this book foregrounds the emotional importance of friendship to a degree unusual in our society. Most of the published sources I cite address romantic or family cutoffs. Friendships are often not considered a relevant category. They are relevant, however, and not just for friendship bonders. Loving attachment can be sexual, platonic, familial, collegial, etc. Wherever it occurs, there exists the potential for trauma when a relationship catastrophically fails.

My Experience of Being Cut Off

The catalyst for my writing this book was being permanently cut off by Sophia (not her real name), a person I considered a beloved friend. This book focuses on my post-cutoff experience, yet the fraught status of cutoffs in our society begs the question of

[17] Being a friendship bonder is different from being queer platonic because the latter suggests relationships are not sexual. For a friendship bonder, primary relationships may be sexual or not; sex is not a defining consideration.

why she cut me off in the first place. As the concept of cutoff is linked to escaping abuse, the question arises: did I abuse her? Because this question is connected to my credibility as an author, I want to provide my best understanding of what happened between us. This is, of course, my version, and I expect Sophia's would differ, but I do not have access to it.[18]

Sophia and I met in 2008 and worked at being friends for six years before she cut me off. At moments, we had a joyful connection unlike any other I have known, but in retrospect, I suspect our friendship was doomed by the incompatible attachment styles we had at the time. I don't mean that we could never have been friends under any circumstances. People grow and change, and attachment styles are tendencies, not prophecies. But at the time, Sophia had what I would describe as an *avoidant* attachment style, one typified by emotional withholding and anxiety about commitment. On the other hand, I had a *preoccupied* or *ambivalent* attachment style, one characterized by insecurity and a need to be loved and accepted.[19] This is a train wreck of a combination: I needed her to commit to being my dear friend; she could not. The fact that we were both highly sensitive to criticism and prone to internalizing shame intensified our vulnerability to each other.

An early nail in the coffin of our friendship occurred when she moved to a different town around early 2010. I already had experience of relationships breaking for lack of face-to-face

---

[18] If that last jab sounds like passive-aggressive snark, it is to a degree. But I'm going to harp on it throughout this book. *Cutoffs cut off communication.* That action impedes understanding and healing. That is important and bears repeating.

[19] Stephanie Huang, "Attachment Styles and How They Affect Adult Relationships," SimplyPsychology.org, January 23, 2024. https://www.simplypsychology.org/attachment-styles.html. I had a secure attachment to my parents, so how did I end up with this anxious attachment style? I believe it's because I had a secure attachment *only* to my parents. With no siblings, little time spent with extended family, and no community that filled the role of family, I grew up feeling like I was on a lifeboat with my parents, and, if anything happened to them, I would be truly alone. I think the fact that psychology texts (including Huang's article) often discuss attachment styles purely in terms of parenting underscores the extent to which our individualistic society has forgotten that, even with excellent parents, it does take a village to raise a mentally healthy child.

contact. Out of my half dozen or so relationships that have had significant conflict, only one had conflict face-to-face. The others—including my cutoff of Ryan—all cracked under the weight of physical absence, trying to express deep caring through writing. Many more simply faded away. When Sophia told me she was moving, I remember thinking, "Our friendship is over." But she had every right to move, so I wished her well and did my best to stay friends because I loved her. For a while, that worked. We had a voluminous, enjoyable email friendship.

Then, in late 2010, in the wake of a romantic breakup, I went through a life-altering crisis[20] and shared some vulnerabilities with Sophia, hoping for emotional support. She tried to provide it through sympathetic and thoughtful words. Yet I felt her to be standoffish and to subtly reinforce that she saw me as unimportant and inferior. Our first conflict occurred in a phone conversation in which she assumed I wanted her to break up with her partner to be with me. I didn't want to be her partner, but even if I had, I would never try to break up a happy couple. I was offended that she thought I would stoop to that, and I said so. She apologized, and we ostensibly moved on. But after that, plagued by low self-esteem, I lashed out at her intermittently for what felt like her low opinion of me. Once, I harangued her for not replying to an email more promptly. More than once, I accused her of writing subtle digs at my expense in her fiction.[21] It was that sort of thing, snapping over imagined slights. Of course, these outbursts distressed her and drove her to withhold even more.

From my vantage point, this rough patch spiked in late 2010 and early 2011 and then rapidly improved, in step with own psychological healing. I owned progressively more responsibility for my outbursts, and my angry messages became more infrequent and then ceased. However, on both our sides, the overt conflicts were replaced by self-protection and distance. We became cordial while keeping each other at arm's length. We shut each other out

---

[20] As to why I went through this crisis, the short answer is misogyny, or see Joanna Russ's *The Female Man*.

[21] Was this true or in my head? I don't think any such "digs" were conscious or intended to be cruel. I do think I may have identified a tendency in her fiction to lionize romantic monogamy and sideline other relationships. In that, she replicated our society at large, which hit me hard as a friendship bonder. Though I didn't want to be her partner, I did want to be significant in her life.

from important events in our lives, not even mentioning them until well after the fact: her living abroad for months, my bringing home my adopted kids.

Throughout this period, however, I was making significant strides toward healing my psyche and, thus, also my feelings toward Sophia. By October 2014, my emotional life was much healthier, and I had no resentment against her to speak of. I missed being friends with her. Pained by the ongoing strain and distance, I wrote her an email in which I fully owned responsibility for my own bad behavior, explained my evolving state of mind, and invited her to move forward with me in rebuilding a more sincere and open friendship. She replied very politely that she would never communicate with me again. She did not explicitly tell me not to contact her, but it was clear that was what she wanted.

Since then, I've contacted her five times. The first, three months after the cutoff, was a couple of paragraphs of florid assurance that our friendship would one day recover. I said I didn't expect a reply and got none. The second, a year later, in January 2016, was a couple of lines saying I missed her and wanted to make peace. Again, I did not ask for a reply and got none. The year between those two messages was the hardest year of my life. I was in intense pain almost every day, and when she did not reply, I broke. A couple of weeks later, I sent her a nasty, judgmental letter, the gist of which was that I knew we were no longer friends. It was an invasive, arrogant outburst I deeply regret. I didn't regret it at first though. At first, giving her a piece of my mind felt good. It wasn't until three months later, under the kind straight-talking of a staunch friend, that I began to realize how traumatic my letter likely was for her. I asked my friend if he thought violating the cutoff to send a short apology would be warranted. He said, under the circumstances, yes, and I sent a postcard apologizing. I asked for no reply and got none.

The following year, 2017, Sophia ended up working in the same building as me. (I suspect she didn't know I worked there when she took the job.) Though we never ran into each other, it made me—and I suspect her—distressed and anxious. At one point, each of us had flyers associated with our activities on the wall. Her flyer was also in the restroom stalls, so I was confronted with her face every time I used the restroom. Eventually, with my therapist's blessing, I sent her a page-long email, which said I hoped we could work cordially together and that I was open to being friends again in the future, but if she was never able to communicate with me again in this life, that was all right. I believe I also said I might contact her at some point in the future, just to see if anything had changed. For the first time, I explicitly asked her to reply, saying it would be healing for me.

She did reply, with three emails over about thirty-six hours. The first was one line saying she wanted no contact. The second was a brief, kind message, reiterating that she wanted no contact but saying she wanted us both to feel comfortable at work and would be cordial if we had to work together. These first two messages were, as I predicted, very healing. The third, however, angrily demanded I never contact her or approach her again for any reason. It undid the healing. I take her wild veering in tone as evidence that she herself was writing out of triggered trauma, as I was in 2016. I brought her tirade on myself with that letter. She referenced it, so I know she saw it. That was our last contact.[22]

Why Cutoff Affected Me So Strongly

One morning when I was in kindergarten, I made the critical error of sitting near the back of the school bus, the space unwritten law reserved for the big kids. A few stops later, the seats around me were crammed with rollicking eleven-year-olds. I knew they would demand why I hadn't changed seats. I knew I would tell them the truth (I had nothing else to tell them). I knew they would misunderstand what I said, and I knew exactly how they would misunderstand it. I knew I'd try to correct them but they wouldn't hear me. I knew there was nothing I could do about it.

"Why don't you change seats?" one big kid leaning over the back of a seat asked.

"Because my mom said the bus driver said we're not allowed to."

The kid guffawed. "She says her mommy says she's not allowed to!"

[22] My editor asks if I could quote Sophia so the reader can better judge the situation. Our communications were mostly emails and copyright protected, so I probably legally can't, and if I could, I expect she would consider it a violation.

"No," I said. "My mom said the *bus driver* said I'm not allowed to." (The bus driver, you see, was higher authority; that was my point.)

But the laughing and shouting drowned me out.

As a child, I was often unheard or misconstrued. Because I was shy, because my voice was soft, because I had trouble articulating my thoughts, I was routinely overlooked or misunderstood. A version of that still happens today. In a meeting I was leading just the other day, I interjected, "Well, I...," and was talked over a good four times before anyone noticed I was attempting to speak!

Being unheard or being misunderstood are foundational wounds of my childhood. Cutoff does both. In my relationship with Sophia, I will likely be unheard for the rest of my life, and there is no space for unwinding the miscommunications that surely exist between us. That hits me where I am most vulnerable. While cutoff is traumatic for many, this is a large part of why it tore into me so ferociously.

Yet as expert in stress and addiction Gabor Maté observes, in our toxic culture, almost all of us are living with trauma.[23] Almost all of us are vulnerable to retraumatization, even by events others may not perceive as traumatic. We all have "school bus" stories.

Representing Subjective and Fragmented Voices

To tile together a mosaic of our culture's views of cutoff, I cite a wide variety of sources from scholarly articles to angry tweets to my mom. I want to be clear that my citing someone's advice does not mean I endorse it; in fact, I often question it. Having a blog on relationships, for example, does not automatically make the blogger a credible expert on relationships, and even some expert advice I question in light of my own experience and research. I invite contextual, critical reading and forming your own conclusions.

In researching this book, I also interviewed a number of people about their cutoff experiences. Other stories are drawn from published sources and my own recollections. These accounts are necessarily partial, both in the sense of "non-objective" and in the sense of "incomplete." I have sometimes found myself (and

---

[23] Gabor Maté, with Daniel Maté, *The Myth of Normal*, 22.

readers) inclined to jump in and say, "I bet what's really happening is..." or "But the other person probably thought..." That sort of extrapolation is natural and can be useful to critical thinking, if tempered by the reflection that we do not know the whole story. I don't even know the whole story about the events in my own life. I don't intend any story in this book as the last word or the total truth. I do believe, however, that these stories capture pieces of reality: real emotions and experiences. Those realities are worth being open to and sitting with.

One of those realities comes from my marvelous editor, Jennifer Brennock. Footnote readers may have noticed that I explicitly refer to some of her editorial comments. Cutoff silences; the opposite of silence is putting voices in conversation. Jennifer offers insights, some of which, with her permission, I'm transmitting in her own voice because cutoff should be a multivocal issue.

Cutoff should also be a temporal issue. Too often, it is used as an unchangeable solution to a changing situation. To illustrate how my own cutoff journey has evolved, I've stamped a number of my observations with dates: when something happened, when I first wrote about it, etc. Like most, I change over time, and I hope this book captures some of that reality too.

Naming Conventions

In creating aliases for contributors, I have favored Anglo names (ex. Mary) or names I intend to sound culturally non-specific (ex. Jana). I have resisted the urge to assign ethnically non-dominant names in situations where I may miss nuances relevant to those ethnic experiences. In some cases, I have avoided names from an acquaintance's home culture in order to better anonymize their contributions. The result is that my naming conventions are somewhat more ethnically homogenous than the actual population of contributors. Where a person's ethnic or racial background seems relevant, I have attempted to indicate that in a way that preserves their anonymity.

The Structure of This Book

This book is divided into three sections.

Why Cutoff Culture Exists examines the diverse reasons people cut each other off and positions cutoff culture as an understandable, but not always productive, reaction to the misogyny and other oppressions of our dominant culture. The section closes with an examination of what the "right to cutoff" means.

The Destructiveness of Cutoff Culture comprises my central critique of our widespread cutoff practices, identifying six tenets of cutoff culture with a separate chapter on each of the six.

An Alternative Approach to Interpersonal Conflict suggests a different orientation toward cutoff, one rooted in relational awareness with a goal of minimizing the total harm of relationship conflicts. Because cutoff in African American culture has its own set of social dimensions, the section concludes with reflections from clinical social worker and Kemetic teacher (*sbA*) Ray Shellmire on cutoff in the African American community and a Kemetic path back to connection.

Appendix A provides a short list of suggestions for minimizing the harm of cutting someone off.

Appendix B provides some "self-help" thoughts for those who have been cut off.

PART 1

WHY CUTOFF CULTURE EXISTS

Chapter 1

Why People Cut Others Off

Carolyn jolted awake to find her brother standing in her bedroom. She was in her sixties and lived in her own home, which he had entered without permission. She told him to leave, and he did—and proceeded to tell his wife, untruthfully, that Carolyn had sent him packing with screams and curses. After decades of boundary violations, lies, and misrepresentations of her character, this was the final straw. Carolyn ghosted her brother, resolved to cut him off for life. Now, she is done with listening to him blame her for parental abuse they suffered as children, done with providing fresh fuel for accusations of her hatefulness.

She likens her brother's conduct to having lead bullets slowly fired at you over the years until you die of lead poisoning. "I love my brother," she says, "and he's important to me, but over fifty years [of harm] is enough."[24] Carolyn asserts that if she dies before him, she will ban him from her funeral. When I asked her why, she said, "Because he would stand there and tell lies," just as she saw him do at their mother's funeral. She says she didn't cut him off sooner, in part, because he said he loved her, and she wanted to give him the benefit of the doubt. But as the years went by, it became clear that his words were not going to match his actions. Ultimately, she decided, "I'm not willing to harm myself in order to be in relationship with him."

Carolyn's situation speaks to the intense wounding that often drives permanent cutoffs: the need to escape abuse, the inability to find any other way to establish the necessary boundaries.

Tricia understands this well. As a young adult, she cut off her mother. Since her childhood, her mother struggled with drug use,

---

[24] All quotes from Carolyn in discussion with the author, November 21, 2021.

poor choice in men, and low self-insight that led to stresses for her children. A running theme was expecting Tricia to invest energy in helping her while simultaneously blaming her for various problems in the family. Eventually, Tricia decided that their unhealthy dynamic was too great an energy drain, so she ended it. After more than a decade out of contact, she approached her mother on social media, reasoning that time might have led to changes in her attitudes. Perhaps they could develop a healthy adult relationship. With her mother's very first response, however, Tricia saw things had not changed. The litany of blame and self-pity resumed, and Tricia responded by rapidly dropping out of sight again. She has not spoken to her since.[25] I've heard Tricia talk about her mother several times. She always speaks with calm and understanding; she often mentions her mother's strengths—her frugality, her cooking skill. She doesn't hate her mother, but she feels her own life is more positive without her.[26]

The need to protect oneself from abuse or dysfunction is an all-too-common reason for cutoff, and one our culture understands pretty well. We have an established discourse, for example, around setting boundaries to exclude what we call "toxic" people.

But protection from toxic behavior is not the only reason for cutoff. Triggers cited in popular media include:

- Power and control
- Exhaustion
- Loyalty to others
- Perceived slights
- Money
- Abuse[27]

---

[25] Based on various conversations with Tricia. She confirmed the accuracy of this passage, February 13, 2023.

[26] Tricia's attitude reminds me of a dear friend who passed away in 2016. Reading an early manuscript of my unpublished novel about cutoff, she told me—I've never forgotten—"Your pain has meaning." She also said she needed to cut off her mother, even knowing cutoff can do harm. She was a deep-feeling, deep-thinking person, and her conviction of the rightness of her decision was absolute.

[27] Barbara Greenberg, "10 Reasons Why People Get Cut off from Their Family," *Psychology Today*, July 6, 2017,

- Not being happy around someone
- Someone being negative
- Someone taking more than they give
- Lack of trust
- Lack of support[28]

- Single outrageous actions
- Frustrations over time
- Being made to feel inadequate
- Coercion from others to cut someone off
- Nothing[29]

So why do people cut others off? It depends. Here is a small illustration of the diversity of cutoff situations.

Cutoff to Unambiguously End an Incompatible Relationship

Author Deirdre Saoirse Moen writes about cutting off a man who was her former partner and friend.[30] She explains that she and this friend, whom she calls X, had incompatibilities that led to an unhealthy relationship: X was looking for a woman to be dominant in a relationship. Moen had no desire to be that woman, but her tendency to "chew him out" when annoyed enabled him to lean on her to fill that space in his life. With numerous tensions in their beliefs and expectations, she increasingly wished the friendship to end, even as he wished to rekindle a romance. Finally, she decided that cutting him off would not only free her from a

---

https://www.psychologytoday.com/us/blog/the-teen-doctor/201707/10-reasons-why-people-get-cut-their-family.

[28] T.D. Jakes, "5 Reasons It's OK to Cut Someone out of Your Life," *TDJakes.com* (blog), accessed November 29, 2021, https://www.tdjakes.com/posts/5-reasons-it-s-ok-to-cut-someone-out-of-your-life.

[29] Deborah Tannen, "Why Friends Ghost on Even Their Closest Pals," *Time*, May 16, 2017, https://time.com/4779713/friendship-ghosting/.

[30] Deirdre Saoirse Moen, "Exes and Cutoff Culture," *Sounds Like Weird* (blog), May 14, 2014, https://deirdre.net/2014/05/14/exes-and-cutoff-culture/.

relationship that had become distressing but also send a clear signal to him that they would not get back together as a couple. Thus, she cut him off both to spare herself pain and to communicate that he should move on. As my wise mother observes, there can be multiple motives for the same act.

Moen's account is an excellent illustration of the complexities that can surround cutoffs, including years of miscommunications, incompatibilities, growing apart, and mutually flawed behavior. As Moen puts it, "[A] flaw in my character exploited one of his needs, and he also took advantage of that." Moen states that she regrets not cutting him off sooner and, thus, hopefully sparing both of them wasted energy and suffering.

Cutoff to Appease Jealous Family

In her insightful discussion of ghosting for *Time* magazine, Deborah Tannen discusses being cut off by her close friend Susan in high school. When she tracked Susan down *fifty-four years later*, Susan explained that she cut Tannen off due to pressure from an older brother. Tannen writes that the brother "had insisted she stop seeing me, because he felt I had too much influence over her. But looking back, [Susan] said, she thinks he was just jealous. And it broke her heart at the same time that it broke mine."[31] In this case, Tannen notes, the cutoff was not a sign that Susan didn't care or wanted to get rid of her. If anything, it occurred because Susan cared so much that the friendship left her brother feeling jealous of it. A cutoff, Tannen observes, "might, in fact, be a testament to how important the friendship was."[32]

Cutoff to Ease Emotional Pain

Cole had been friends with Biva for forty years, ever since high school.[33] They had a deep, emotionally intimate friendship, which never tipped into romance, despite some romantic yearnings on Cole's part. Over the years, their warm friendship sustained some periods of conflict, including about a year and half when Biva fell out of contact. When the two got back in touch,

---

[31] Tannen.

[32] Tannen.

[33] Cole in discussion with the author, August 17, 2022.

however, Cole quickly found that while much of the familiar intimacy remained, something would have to change to reignite the relationship for him. "There has to be a phoenix aspect," he told me. The old relationship was dead, but maybe something could arise from the ashes.

Biva had recently gotten divorced, and while Cole was not necessarily looking for a conventional romance, he realized he wanted Biva to be "his person," the primary emotional partner in his life. He was looking for a "*When Harry Met Sally* type of thing," he told me, in reference to the famous 1989 romcom about old friends finding love. About a month after sharing these feelings with Biva, she told him gently that she wanted to try pursuing a relationship with an old flame, not him. He understood her right to make that choice.

"I get that," he said to her. "But I can't be part of that." Emotionally, he couldn't go back to being a secondary presence in her life. His feelings were too deep to allow it.

She said she understood, and they amicably broke off contact.

Then he blocked her number, "not necessarily in a punishing way," he said, "but in a protecting way." He added, "I won't make any attempts to reconnect with her."

He loves her, but he cut her off. He cut her off because he loves her. He told me it gave him a sense of relief and liberation.

Cutoff to Find Focus and Clarity

Ironically, some time before Cole cut Biva off, Biva cut Cole off.[34] Like so many friends and families in the past few years, they'd had some political disagreements, and then she stopped responding to his messages. She ghosted him. Cole figured that was what she needed and accepted it. Then, about a year later, she texted him out of the blue, wanting to talk, and they had a phone call.

"I figured you knew why I cut you off," she said.

He said, no, he didn't.

She explained. At the time she cut him off, she and her husband were making the painful journey toward their eventual divorce. "I just couldn't have your voice in my head while I was going through this," she said.

---

[34] Cole.

She cut him off because it helped her focus her thoughts and feelings.

Cutoff by Accident

When I was in college, I effectively cut someone off without even realizing it. It was only when writing this book over twenty years later that it occurred to me it might be considered a cutoff. Larry was a newish friend and someone I had a crush on. In the midst of confused and intense feelings, we had a brief but ugly spat by email. Feeling terribly guilty about my part in it and sure I'd made a mess of everything, I wrote to him that I thought it would be best if we dropped contact. He agreed. While I never told him he was not allowed to contact me again, I did effectively say contact should not continue, which, I suppose, is a cutoff. In 1999, however, long before our current cutoff discourse, it never even crossed my mind that this might actually be a cutoff, a word that was not in my vocabulary. It never occurred to me that he might feel prohibited from ever trying to reconnect with me. I had no investment in permanently blocking him from my life; I simply wanted to stop bothering him. Thus, if this was a permanent cutoff, it was a purely inadvertent one based on miscommunication.[35]

Cutoff out of Altruism

I have encountered one example of a purely altruistic cutoff, a cutoff based solely on the welfare of the person being cut. My dear friend Anna is a political activist involved in activities that, by her own account, could be considered subversive in some parts of the world. (I do not know any details as she believes it is safer for

---

[35] Actually, Larry did speak to me again. It was a year later, and as I was walking on my college campus, I heard a voice call, "Hi, Arwen." I looked up and there he was. At the time, I still felt terribly guilty about our fight and, in a state of panic, I smiled, waved, and hurried off. I never saw him again. But the fact that he *chose* to say hi to me (I obviously hadn't seen him) proved extremely healing. It told me I hadn't wounded him as badly as I'd feared. It assuaged my guilt and helped me move on. It allowed us both to end our acquaintance on explicitly friendly terms. If he had believed he had no right to speak to me because I had cut him off, none of this could have happened.

me not to.) Anna is also a fan of Japanese popular culture and once formed an online friendship with a fellow fan; let's call the friend Bright_Bird. The two were corresponding about their interests and beginning to share details about their personal lives when Bright_Bird mentioned where she was living. It was a region where the government practiced punitive surveillance of its citizens, and Anna was afraid that Bright_Bird might suffer political consequences as a result of being connected with her. So to protect her friend, she ghosted her: "I hoped that not explaining who I was would have given her some shot at plausible deniability. (Which was actually true: it's not like she was a willing party, merrily socializing with a known enemy of the state. She was just a clueless kid who met someone online.)"[36] The predictable hurt followed, messages asking why Anna had broken off contact. Had Bright_Bird done something? Was Anna angry? Anna never replied and eventually Bright_Bird gave up. They never spoke again.[37]

---

[36] She elaborates on why she felt ghosting was safest: "[B]oth me and her come from societies that lived under communist oppression, where much of a person's life was defined by their 'cadre profile,' meaning basically where on the scale of sympathizer vs. dissident they were. The common practice was that guilt was also ascribed by association, so even just having a friend or a relative who was active in the dissent, or who emigrated to the West, meant you were blacklisted to some degree. Now, while having a bad profile... might not get you prosecuted or imprisoned straight away, the regime had numerous softer ways to put a pressure on you: you couldn't get a normal job, you couldn't get decent housing, your kids couldn't get into schools, you could have your property confiscated, co-workers would be asked to inform on you, you wouldn't get permission to travel abroad, some relatives would cut ties, some friends would turn away, etc. These kinds of big and small annoyances permeated your whole life and their cumulative effect was pretty destructive." Anna, email message to author, January 29, 2024.

[37] Another case of "cutoff" due to altruism might be the traditional story of the Buddha and his cousin, Devadatta, who attempted to murder him. Prudently, the Buddha avoided contact with this person who wished to kill him. But being the Buddha and, thus, fully enlightened, this avoidance arose from compassion for Devadatta. By avoiding him, the Buddha spared him the karma of committing murder, thus facilitating Devadatta's own spiritual journey.

Cutoff Is Formally Complex

Like human life, cutoffs are contextual. They grow out of moment-to-moment details among unique human beings. They happen for all sorts of reasons, from life-rending pain to trivial misunderstanding, and some reasons we might never guess. Yet our society, which loves pat answers, often attempts to impose one best practice for navigating cutoffs. This approach is doomed to failure because cutoffs are *complex*, in the formal sense of the word.

In everyday English, "complex" means complicated, not simple. But here I'm using the term more precisely. Developed by Dave Snowden, the Cynefin Framework (pronounced "cuh-ne-vin") has outlined four types of situations where humans need to make decisions:

- Known (also called Simple, Obvious, or Clear)
- Knowable (also called Complicated)
- Complex
- Chaotic[38]

These types often overlap, and we cannot always be certain which domain is most applicable to our problem solving.[39] That said, the framework provides a useful guide for how to address various situations.

Known situations are those in which the relevant information is already understood; it is the domain of established best practice. An example might be building a working car engine. *Knowable* situations are those in which we can apply a set of good practices to determine a course of action. An example might be a game of chess. Complex and chaotic situations, however, defy traditional analysis. In *chaotic* situations, cause and effect are unclear, the situation evolving moment by moment: an example would be the 9/11 attacks and their immediate aftermath.[40]

---

[38] Simon French, "Cynefin: Uncertainty, Small Worlds, and Scenarios," *Journal of the Operational Research Society*, 66 (2015): 1638, https://doi.org/10.1057/jors.2015.21.

[39] French, 1638.

[40] "Cynefin Framework," *Wikipedia*, accessed December 1, 2021, https://en.wikipedia.org/wiki/Cynefin_framework. As an English

Complex situations, in contrast, are the domain of emergent wholes, the nebulous zone where cause and effect can be somewhat understood but only provisionally or retroactively. They are the domain of ecosystems, of brains, and of human sociality. As a human social phenomenon, cutoffs are *formally complex*. Thus, they cannot be adequately addressed through one best practice or even a set of good practices. They exist in the realm of *emergent practice*, requiring continual probing, exploration, adjustment—guesswork. Just as there is no single reason for cutoff, there is no single answer for it.[41] Yet we can observe broad themes.

Cutoff has probably always existed within human relationships and probably always will. In many cases, it is the best available choice. Culturally specific factors, however, determine the ethics for how cutoff should work. In the 21st century, the sweeping cultural transformation caused by the internet has made it emotionally far easier to cut people off and, I suspect, far more common. A cutoff announced by text or email places the safety of a screen between the cutter and the cuttee's reaction. Ghosting can be achieved by literally doing nothing, not replying. Blocking communication, though a prudent step in many situations, allows a cutter to enforce a cutoff without even thinking about it. We have automated ostracism.

To combat this digital coldness, we need compassionate ethics. Though there is no single "right approach," broad principles can and should apply. Foremost among them is to minimize harm, but to do that we must be sensitive to both the harms of cutoff and the harms it seeks to address.

---

teacher, I feel like I should apologize for citing *Wikipedia*. Still, its article on the Cynefin Framework is the most comprehensive and comprehensible of any readily available, public source.

[41] I wish to thank my Clark College colleague, emergency management specialist Jeff Kaliner, for his excellent presentation on the Cynefin Framework, which first introduced me to it.

Chapter 2

Why We Valorize Cutoff

Despite the harm cutoff can cause, our culture often valorizes it. Some are thinking, no we don't. We *criticize* people who cut others off. "We live in a culture where the only happy ending is a reconciliation," asserts Rabbi Elliot Kukla, noting that this social narrative can stoke feelings of guilt and shame in those who don't wish to reconnect.[42] While I don't agree reconciliation is our culture's *only* happy ending, it is undoubtedly a prominent theme that can read as shaming those who don't reconcile.[43] Brittany Christopoulos describes in detail some of the negative messages cutters may receive:

> By cutting someone out of your life, you will look like the bad guy. You can explain it to everyone in the world until you are blue in the face, but *not everyone will understand the reason.* And in terms of the person you are trying to be set free from, they will tell a different story, forcing people to pick sides or change their opinion of you....

---

[42] Elliot Kukla, "It's Okay to Forgive, or Not: Grieving When You're Estranged from Your Family," *The Body Is Not an Apology*, December 2, 2019, https://thebodyisnotanapology.com/magazine/when-theres-no-hollywood-ending-how-do-i-grieve-the-dying-when-i-am-estranged-from-family/. As of the publication of this book, this link appears inactive, but Rabbi Kukla can be reached at ElliotKukla.com. He was very kind in supplying with a copy of this essay.

[43] As to our story tropes, I think it depends on who's reconciling. In the movie, *Frozen*, for example, the happy ending shows sisters Elsa and Anna reconciling but evil Hans getting kicked to the curb. Indeed, it's normative to show no reconciliation with the characters framed as villains.

Being Cut

> People outside of your core group of people won't fully understand or relate to your reasoning… [emphasis in original][44]

Our culture, especially these days, is quick to judge, and it has plenty of condemnation for just about anyone, including those who cut others off. To be clear, we should *not* shun or shame a person for cutting someone off. Many times, it is a necessary step for them. This is all true; it's also true we valorize cutoff.

When I say we valorize it, I don't mean we always do. I mean there's a significant cultural tendency to do it. We see it in the social media firestorm against Jeff Reifman for critiquing what he then called "cutoff culture." (He has since retracted the phrase.)[45] We see it in a plethora of self-help sources, from popular articles[46] and online videos[47] to advice from mental health professionals[48] encouraging cutoff, sometimes very appropriately—and sometimes maybe not.

I have seen this valorization in my own friends' lockstep support of someone they don't know deciding to cut me off over conflicts they knew almost nothing about. Out of dozens of people I have talked to about being cut off by Sophia, only one suggested that she might have made a poor decision, while several lectured me for questioning her. In contrast, when I cut my friend

---

[44] Brittany Christopoulos, "What Actually Happens When You Cut Someone out of Your Life," *Unwritten*, April 9, 2018, https://www.readunwritten.com/2018/04/09/what-happens-cut-someone-life/#google_vignette. My editor adds that even members of the core group may not understand, "but they will still support you because they trust your judgment or trust that you are doing that best thing for you.... There is a lot about trust in cutoff culture. Dividing those you trust and those you don't." Editorial comment, September 26, 2023.

[45] Reifman, "Shining Light on Internet Rage."

[46] For example: "5 Reasons It's OK to Cut Someone out of Your Life," *TDJakes.com*.

[47] For example: Hassan Campbell, "You *Have* to Cut People off *without a Warning*," YouTube. August 11, 2019, video, https://www.youtube.com/watch?v=fmv7uiBMjsA.

[48] For example: James Macintyre, "Cut Toxic People out of Your Life, Says Christian Psychiatrist," *Christian Today*, November 9, 2017, https://www.christiantoday.com/article/cut-toxic-people-out-of-your-life-says-christian-psychiatrist/118186.htm.

Ryan off, not one person challenged my decision, including mutual friends very fond of him. I am grateful for that. Passing judgement on me as a cutter when I was in so much pain would have harmed me, as, indeed, passing judgment on me as a cuttee did. My point is, though the pattern is not set in stone, there is a cultural current, perhaps especially on the progressive left, that demands unquestioning support of those who cut others off.

Why? Where does this come from?

Punching Up Against Oppression

This strong cultural push to support cutoff is a response to oppression. We live in a misogynistic patriarchy. We also live under oppressions based on race, ethnicity, LGBTQ+ status, ability, socioeconomic status, country of origin, immigrant status, religion, and more. But I will focus on misogyny, partly because, for me as a privileged white cis-spectrum woman, it is the major category of oppression I have experience of bearing and, thus, some personal authority to speak to—but more importantly because the oppression of women, in particular, is a prominent factor in the development of our current cutoff culture.

To discuss these issues, I have to invoke male-female gender binaries. I recognize that trans, non-binary, intersex people, and others who do not fit these binaries are often erased from our social discourse, and I do not wish to further that erasure. However, that erasure exists due to millennia of cultural tradition assuming a binary view of gender and a view that privileges maleness over femaleness. Indeed, LGBTQ+ oppression is rooted in misogyny. Same sex relationships and gender crossing trouble the normalization of male dominance over women. Patriarchy is facilitated by a gender binary, heteronormative worldview. As trans activist Natalie Wynn puts it, "Misogyny is the most universal prejudice, and trans people are not immune."[49] We cannot understand how misogyny works without invoking a male/female binary—so here goes.

I could write a whole essay on our culture's misogyny. In fact, in drafting this book, I did. But to keep the focus on cutoff, I'll restrain myself to highlighting the most salient aspect of misogyny

[49] Natalie Wynn (ContraPoints), "J. K. Rowling," YouTube, January 26, 2021, video, https://www.youtube.com/watch?v=7gDKbT_l2us.

in our patriarchy: violence against women. According to the National Intimate Partner and Sexual Violence Survey's (NISVS) Report on Sexual Violence, 1 in 4 women in the United States (26.8%) reported being the victim of completed or attempted rape in her lifetime; for men, the figure was 1 in 26 (3.8%).[50] For contrast, 1 in 9 men reported being coerced to enter someone in his lifetime.[51] One in 3 women reported being sexually harassed in a public place, while 1 in 9 men reported this.[52] While men may underreport sexual victimization more than women do, [53] underreporting alone seems unlikely to account for this massive gender disparity in experiencing sexual violence. Intersectional oppressions intensify the chances of being victimized by sexual violence. For example, of Non-Hispanic American Indian/Alaska Native women, 43.7% reported being raped in their lifetime, the next highest number being Non-Hispanic Black woman at 29.0%.[54] The NISVS found 47.3% of women and 44.2% of men reported physical or sexual violence or stalking by an intimate partner in their lifetime.[55] These are appalling figures for both female and male victims. However, when Intimate Partner Violence (IVP) *impacts* are factored in, 41% of women experienced IVP with impacts while the figure for men dropped to 26.3%.[56] Impacts include, but are not limited to, fearfulness, injury, needing medical care, missing work, needing housing services, and PTSD

---

[50] National Intimate Partner and Sexual Violence Survey, *2016/2017 Report on Sexual Violence*, June 2022, p. 3, accessed 20 July 2022, https://www.cdc.gov/nisvs/documentation/nisvsReportonSexualViolence.pdf.

[51] NIPSV, 3.

[52] NIPSV, 5.

[53] For particular stigmas against male victims, see, for example, Matthew Martinez, "Underreporting among Males Likely due to Gender-Based Stigma," *Marquette Wire*, February 27, 2018. https://marquettewire.org/3988006/news/underreporting-among-males-likely-due-to-gender-based-stigma/.

[54] NIPSV, 5.

[55] *National Intimate Partner and Sexual Violence Survey: 2016/17 Report on Intimate Partner Violence*, October 2022, p. 3, accessed April 6, 2024, https://www.cdc.gov/nisvs/documentation/nisvsreportonipv_2022.pdf

[56] *National Intimate Partner and Sexual Violence Survey: 2016/17 Report on Intimate Partner Violence*, 10–11.

symptoms.[57] Overall, woman are considerably more likely than men to experience sexual violence and negative impacts from intimate partner violence.

Stalking, which I'll discuss more in the next chapter, also differentially impacts women. The NISVS found that about 1 in 3 women reported being stalked in her lifetime vs. 1 in 6 men.[58] In addition, female victims were almost twice as likely as men to be followed and watched, a particularly threatening stalking tactic (60% vs. 36%).[59]

Yet one study found that only 41% of female stalking victims reported being stalked to the police.[60] Many factors doubtless influence this underreporting. Bethany L. Backes, Lisa Fedina, and Jennifer Lynne Holmes (2020) note that stalking cases are considered difficult to evidence and prosecute, so police often resist pressing stalking charges in favor of a domestic violence misdemeanor.[61] Backes, Fedina, and Holmes also found that police often lack a clear understanding of what stalking entails[62] and that few interventions exist besides arrest, leaving little space for restorative methods of accountability and repair.[63]

As with sexual violence, impacts are greatest on people from marginalized groups. Research shows that individuals from racial, gender, and sexual minorities are more likely to be stalked.[64] Yet systemic discrimination makes it more difficult for people from marginalized groups to get help. Undocumented immigrants, for example, are often afraid to call the authorities out of fear of

---

[57] *National Intimate Partner and Sexual Violence Survey: 2016/17 Report on Intimate Partner Violence*, 2.

[58] *National Intimate Partner and Sexual Violence Survey. 2016/2017 Report on Stalking*, accessed August 19, 2022, p. 3, https://www.cdc.gov/nisvs/documentation/nisvsstalkingreport.pdf.

[59] *National Intimate Partner and Sexual Violence Survey. 2016/2017 Report on Stalking*, 3.

[60] Bethany L. Backes, Lisa Fedina, and Jennifer Lynne Holmes, "The Criminal Justice System Response to Intimate Partner Stalking: A Systematic Review of Quantitative and Qualitative Research," *Journal of Family Violence*, vol. 35, 2020, p. 666. https://doi.org/10.1007/s10896-020-00139-3.

[61] Backes, Fedina, and Holmes, 671.

[62] Backes, Fedina, and Holmes, 674.

[63] Backes, Fedina, and Holmes, 675.

[64] Backes, Fedina, and Holmes, 675.

deportation. American Indian and Alaska Native women have been especially likely to be victimized by stalking.[65] Yet Native Americans residing on tribal land have faced additional barriers in the form of restrictions on the legal rights of tribal governments to prosecute crimes committed by non-Indians.[66] There is no question that stalking victims need access to a wider range of more effective interventions to promote safety, accountability, and healing.

Within this context of a society that is oppressive and dangerous for women and all marginalized people, cutoff culture has developed to empower the oppressed. When the individuals and social structures around you are often threatening or demeaning, one means of self-protection is to say, "Go away." Setting this boundary can be an act of taking back power for women, who are often socialized from childhood to take on the role of pleasers, placing others' feelings ahead of their own needs. Cutoff is an extreme form of ostracism, and as Lisa Zadro et al. (2017) observe, ostracizing someone gives the source of the ostracism a sense of control; in fact, control is what people engaging in ostracism most consistently report experiencing.[67] Cutoff can rebalance power.

Cutoff culture amplifies the power of marginalized people by creating a social norm that supports the choice to cut others off. Instead of a marginalized person telling someone to leave her alone and being ignored (which very often happens), cutoff culture develops a social enforcement of her cutoff. Ideally, according to cutoff culture, friends, family, therapists, strangers—everyone—would stand behind this marginalized person, forming an impenetrable wall to support her in forcing her oppressor away. The goal is to decrease the psychological and physical threat that

---

[65] "Stalking Victimization in the United States," *Bureau of Justice Statistics Special Report.* U. S. Department of Justice, Jan. 2009, p. 3, https://www.justice.gov/sites/default/files/ovw/legacy/2012/08/15/bjs-stalking-rpt.pdf.

[66] "Ending Violence Against Native Women," Indian Law Resource Center, accessed October 9, 2021, https://indianlaw.org/issue/ending-violence-against-native-women.

[67] Lisa Zadro, Alexandra Godwin, Elena Svetieva, and Nisha Sethi, "Creating the Silence: Ostracism from the Perspective of the Source," in *Ostracism, Exclusion, and Rejection*, edited by Kipling D. Williams and Steve A. Nida, (New York: Routledge, 2017), 137–38.

marginalized people face when more powerful people disregard their boundaries.

This orientation goes a long way to explaining why Jeff Reifman's essay critiquing cutoff culture received such immediate and vocal backlash, particularly from feminists. One of his critics, whom Reifman does not name, states the goal explicitly:

> The thing about "cut-off culture" where a woman says "Hey don't talk to me anymore" and a man says "ok" and then processes his feelings privately is something I am actively trying to support and create with this blog [supporting women's empowerment]. Because we live in the opposite kind of culture, and when you're the one being leeched on by someone who won't let go it's terrifying and exhausting.[68]

QED. According to this commentator, cutoff culture validates women in setting boundaries to protect themselves from the terror and exhaustion of living under a misogynistic system in which male entitlement too often leeches away women's lives.

My editor, Jennifer Brennock, muses along similar lines. Because women have been acculturated to please others, she reflects,

> You have to be a truly violent soul for me [i.e. cis-women, in general] to say ["go away"] to you, which highlights the extreme case necessary for [a cis-woman] to be able to control what is in her own space. Bringing it back to we [cis-women] are not taught to express our needs and desires. The relationship gets more power than we do as individuals. What I mean is we don't say "go away" with the same everyday choice as we would with "Would you like sugar in your coffee?" We have to be pushed to an extreme. Men can certainly more freely say "go away" without even blinking about it. They don't have to wonder if it was the right thing to do. They just express their desire. All these thoughts are very cis and binary, of course.[69]

---

[68] qtd. in Reifman, "Shining Light on Internet Rage."

[69] Editorial comment, September 26, 2023.

This line of reasoning articulates a central logic of cutoff culture: because women are trained to serve men, rejecting a man with the intensity of cutoff must be a response to sustained, outrageous behavior; if the behavior were not outrageous, women would accommodate, not cut off.

This process undoubtedly describes many cutoff situations: as a generalization, women are trained to be accommodating and men to expect that accommodation. This is, however, a generalization, not an absolute. While it describes many cutoffs, it also does not describe many (see chapter 1). Yet though this narrative is far from universally applicable, cutoff culture is characterized by the assumption that this is the only plausible explanation for a cis-woman cutting off a cis-man.

While cutoff is often discussed in the context of a woman cutting off a man, people of any gender can use cutoff, and cutoff culture resists numerous oppressions in addition to misogyny. Kukla notes that people in the trans community and people who experience intersectional (multiple) oppressions often suffer trauma that necessitates cutting off families of origin to protect their health and safety.[70] Clinical social worker Ray Shellmire, who specializes in culturally sensitive counseling and education within the African American community, notes that cutoff is a common means of defense in African American culture, a development he sees as a response to the intergenerational trauma of cultural colonization.[71]

The goal of using community support to amplify the power of marginalized people is a good one. In many cases, there is no question that concerted support of cutoff is exactly what a person needs to be safe and healthy, physically and/or psychologically. However, cutoff is advocated far more broadly than this. From dating blogs that advise always cutting off an ex, to the cavalier advice to cut off anyone who isn't actively making us feel happy,[72] to the common use of ghosting as a (seemingly) no-cost way to avoid an uncomfortable social situation, cutoff has become a widely accepted response to even minor interpersonal conflict or discomfort. This invites a culture of disconnection.

---

[70] Elliot Kukla, "It's Okay to Forgive, or Not: Grieving When You're Estranged from Your Family."

[71] Ray Shellmire in discussion with the author, January 1, 2022.

[72] T.D. Jakes, "5 Reasons It's OK to Cut Someone Out of Your Life."

To be sure, cutoff culture does not deny that humans need connection and relationship, in general. But it advocates an ethics in which any particular relationship (even significant love relationships) should be revocable at a moment's notice: "Never speak to me again"—and it's over. The inviolable boundary is set. This undercuts general interpersonal connection in two ways: 1) by advocating this instant revocability of all commitment, it supports a culture in which no relationship (between adults) can assumed to be dependable, a recipe for profound psychological insecurity; 2) it assumes that one relationship is substitutable for another: your partner cuts you off; find another, no deep harm. You may, indeed, find another; deep harm can still be done. We bond with individuals, not relationship categories. Framing enduring relationships between two particular individuals as unimportant—or even as immoral to ask for—invites an unhealthy culture filled with suffering people.

Oppression is the offspring of disconnection. The Global North derives its material prosperity from Global South (usually) without a pang of conscience because we do not *see* the Global South. We do not experience connection with the many thousands of people whose lives, homes, and ecosystems are threatened by copper mining for our electronics[73] or cultivation of the palm oil[74] used in almost half our packaged food products.[75] We don't know the people who allege they were enslaved as children to harvest our chocolate.[76] The recurrent failure of corporations and governments to heed the Water Protectors of Standing Rock, instead pushing through oil pipeline projects that threaten the land and

---

[73] "Environmental Conflicts on Copper," Environmental Justice Atlas, accessed April 6, 2024, https://www.cevreadaleti.org/commodity/copper.

[74] "Environmental Conflicts on Palm Oil," Environmental Justice Atlas, accessed April 6, 2024, https://www.cevreadaleti.org/commodity/palm-oil.

[75] Michelle Pugle, "Palm Oil: What's the Verdict?" Verywell Health, December 1, 2023, https://www.verywellhealth.com/palm-oil-8406451.

[76] Oliver Balch, "Mars, Nestlé, and Hershey to Face Child Slavery Lawsuit in the US," *The Guardian*, February 12, 2021, https://www.theguardian.com/global-development/2021/feb/12/mars-nestle-and-hershey-to-face-landmark-child-slavery-lawsuit-in-us.

water[77] while dangerously delaying climate action, occurs because the people making the decisions, by and large, do not *know* the humans and other-than-humans affected. They are not connected to the culture and history of these places. They do not *love* them. Thus, they can write off the damage they cause because they don't (yet) feel its impacts. Stereotypes such as houseless people being lazy or African Americans unable to sustain marriages are driven by people who don't *know* these communities, who have not spent much time interacting with them. The self-described "incel" Reddit user who confidently asserts, "Women are not complex in their mating behavior they want the best genes they can find and [environment] to raise the baby in (looks and money),"[78] has not spent a great deal of time in deep conversation with women. He isn't connected to women as human beings. Disconnection enables disrespect and dismissal.

To use disconnection as a key strategy in fighting oppression is to use the tactics of oppression. Cutoff culture fights fire with fire: silencing with silencing, disregard with disregard, and often harm with harm. And while in many specific cases, this is clearly the lesser evil, as a general social position, it replicates the same cultural assumptions it seeks to oppose. To cite the famous dictum of intersectional feminist Audre Lorde, "*[T]he master's tools will never dismantle the master's house.* They may allow us temporarily to beat him at his own game, but they will never enable us to bring about genuine change."[79] Lorde made this assertion in the context of

---

[77] "US Regulator Issues Notice to Dakota Access Pipeline over Safety Concerns," *Reuters*, July 22, 2021, https://www.reuters.com/business/energy/us-regulator-issues-notice-dakota-access-pipeline-over-safety-concerns-2021-07-23/.

[78] qtd. in Winnie Chang, "The Monstrous Feminine in the Incel Imagination: Investigating the Representation of Woman as 'Femoids' on /r/Braincels," *Feminist Media Studies*, 2020, p. 10, https://doi.org/10.1080/14680777.2020.1804976. "Incel" stands for "involuntarily celibate" and is a label taken on by young men who feel aggrieved by what they view as shallow or unfair rejection by women.

[79] Audre Lorde, "The Master's Tools Will Never Dismantle the Master's House," (1984) *Sister Outsider: Essays and Speeches* (Berkeley: Crossing Press, 2007), 112 (emphasis original). "Intersectionality" refers to the phenomenon in which having multiple marginalizations creates unique oppressions not experienced outside that combination of

academia, arguing against the pretense of empowering intersectionally marginalized women by demanding they participate in the very forms of scholarship that marginalize them. My use is broader but, I hope, in a similar spirit: we cannot fix a harmful culture by recapitulating that culture's harms. If the goal is to dismantle oppression, our value system must not cultivate disconnection but connection.

The Thing Contains Its Opposite

Throughout this book, I'll argue that certain aspects of our culture tend to replicate the ills they seek to cure. Borrowing loosely from Carl Jung, I'll gloss this tendency as *the thing containing its opposite*: an extreme response tending to fall toward the extreme it opposes. For Jung himself, the idea of *opposition* was fundamental: he argued that psychological energies, such as value systems, all contain innate oppositions—for example, freedom and security—and a person will achieve the greatest psychological health by understanding and accepting these inner tensions rather than rigidly refusing to see them. The tendency to slip into replicating the actions or views of the opposition is one consequence of the refusal (or inability) to see the internal tensions in one's own belief systems.

For Jung, the concept of opposition explains a tendency in some people to swing from one extreme to another. A person who had been a devout Christian, for example, might swing to adamant atheism. Jung argues that such a move occurs when a person becomes aware of inconsistencies in their prior value system. The devout Christian might come to notice that Christianity has often sanctioned un-Christ-like oppressions. Unable to navigate such perceived threats to their value system, they may respond by rejecting the entire system, declaring that God does not exist and so on. Though there is nothing inherently unhealthy about switching from one belief system to another, for Jung, this process of disillusioned recoiling marks an absence of psychological balance, an inability to recognize the intrinsic oppositions in a system, for example, that Christianity can be both forgiving and judgmental. In "The Personal Unconscious," Jung writes,

---

marginalizations. For example, Black women experience oppressions distinct from those faced by white women or Black men.

> Obviously it is a fundamental mistake to think that when we recognize the non-Value in a value, or the falsehood in a truth, the value or the truth then ceases to exist. It has only become relative. Everything human is relative, because everything depends on a condition of inner antithesis.... There must always be present height and depth, heat and cold, etc., in order that the process of equalization—which is energy—can take place. All life is energy and therefore depends on forces held in opposition.[80]

Jung advocates embracing oppositions in order to come to a more harmonious experience of the energy that is life. He contends, "The solution of the problem [of anxiety over oppositions] lies not in a conversion into the opposite, but in the retaining of the former values together with a recognition of their opposites."[81] To return to the example of Christianity, a person might come to recognize that a drive to teach Christian values has sometimes led to coercing obedience. This does not mean the values or the desire to promote them is necessarily wrong, but an awareness of this potential for coercion may help the believer balance their desire to share their values with sensitivity to others' experience.

In terms of cutoff culture, a person who supports cutoff as a means of empowering the marginalized might come to recognize that this support can sometimes cause unnecessary harm to cutoff people. This does not mean the desire to empower the marginalized through supporting cutoffs is necessarily wrong, but an awareness of this potential for harm may help the support giver balance their desire to empower the marginalized with an awareness of the damage cutoff can do.

I have purposefully used one example (Christianity) that reads as conservative and one example (support for cutoff) that reads as progressive. Both right and left political wings are capable of doing

---

[80] C. G. Jung, "The Personal Unconscious," *Two Essays on Analytical Psychology*, translated by H. G. and C. F. Baynes, (London: Baillière, Tindall, and Cox, 1928), p. 79, Internet Archive, accessed June 20, 2022, https://archive.org/stream/in.ernet.dli.2015.218694/2015.218694.Two-Essays_djvu.txt.

[81] Jung, 79.

harm through lack of balance. I do not mean to make a false equivalence between Right and Left. They are not equivalent, and to avoid a digressive quagmire, I will leave it at that. But any system of thought, if sufficiently univocal, by definition refuses to hear other points of view and, thus, loses its ability to perceive its own failings—and every system has failings. That's human.

The desire to resist oppression contains the seed of oppression. This fact is nothing to be afraid of. It's true of just about anything if taken to an extreme. Jung emphasizes the harmony and reconciliation of opposites, embracing what is relative, because this helps us find wholeness. It helps inoculate us against being trapped in the fiction that one rigid view is the entire truth. In the context of cutoff, this reconciliation of opposites creates space to see cutoff as sometimes necessary and empowering within a broader system that prioritizes healing through human connection.

Transforming Structures of Oppression

What might a world that uses non-oppressive tools to dismantle oppression look like? That's a massive question, but for now, here is a quick sketch. A culture that resists oppression with non-oppression would, by default, view all participants in a conflict as people in need of healing: victims, perpetrators, and third parties. It would support victims and third parties, including any expressed need for separation from those who have harmed them. But it would also support perpetrators, seeking to understand their maladaptive actions and mindsets and to help them heal, grow, and become safer to be around. Such a culture would also recognize that many conflicts cannot be reduced to a victim and a perpetrator. In many cases, both parties have harmed each other, though often not equally. Both, therefore, would be treated as victims and perpetrators, both comforted and held accountable for harm they've committed. Such a culture would prioritize ensuring that all people have community supports. This does not mean a perpetrator necessarily gets to talk to the person they've harmed or that person's loved ones. It *does* mean the perpetrator is not required to "process their feelings privately," as Reifman's critic puts it. Rather, by default, they would be surrounded by friends, family, and professional supports if needed, and generally treated with kindness within their community. Kindness would be the norm.

We are, of course, a long way from this world, whether we're speaking of cutoff or a raft of other issues. But because this book focuses on cutoff, that is where I'll begin. Cutoff can be intensely harming. Nonetheless, it is often the path of least harm. I firmly uphold the principle that people have a right to cut others off. However, the deceptively simple assertion is a shorthand for a dense net of ethical issues.

Chapter 3

The Right to Cutoff

In 2007, I cut off contact with my friend, Ryan. I didn't say it was permanent; I hoped it wouldn't be. But I did say it was indefinite, that I didn't know when or if I would be able to speak to him again. At the time, Ryan and I had been friends for fifteen years, ever since meeting in our freshman college dorm. For most of that time, I had considered him one of my best friends. We were roommates our sophomore year, and after I transferred to a different university, we stayed in touch, exchanging long emails on the state of our lives and supporting each other through the pangs of young adulthood.

But in the early 2000s, our lives went in different directions. Ryan had more or less found his rhythm: he was in a prestigious graduate program with a good group of friends and a girlfriend he adored (and is now married to). I was lost. I was also in grad school, but socially I could not connect. My friend group was small and somewhat tenuous, my dating life a mess, with my most promising relationship ending right around the time Ryan began to sing the praises of his new girlfriend. I felt ashamed. In comparison to Ryan's successes, I felt like a failure. Because the gulf between our experiences of life seemed so great, I felt I could no longer turn to him for commiseration. I don't know if this was actually the case; I was too embarrassed to seriously try. Our email correspondence dwindled, his brief and sunny, mine terse and distantly polite.

I loved Ryan. He was one of the most important people in my life, and for years I could not conceive of giving up on our friendship. Infrequently, I tried to open up a conversation about how our friendship needing tending. I expect I did this ham-handedly.

In some moments, I was testy, and he was testy back. Once when he was back in our home state visiting, I gave him a card attesting to how much his friendship meant to me. He glanced at it quickly and then spent much of the evening on the phone with his girlfriend, finally leaving the card behind at my parents' house. This is a small thing, but it hit me hard. She had replaced me, I felt. I didn't matter anymore.

But I held on to a semblance of polite contact, hoping for the day that my own life—and my own self-esteem—would catch up, that I would feel whole enough in myself that I could speak to Ryan again without shame and without expectations, and perhaps we could really be friends again.

Then, in 2007, my then-partner and I broke up a couple of weeks before Ryan was set to get married. The straw on the camel was the wedding invitations: he'd forgotten to send them, and so he sent out email invitations instead, hurriedly inviting everyone to the upcoming wedding. I had been steeling myself to smile through his wedding, as friends are supposed to. But the combination of a sudden rush into what promised to be a very painful situation, the stress of making instant travel plans (I'm an anxious traveler), and what I perceived as the offhandedness of his not even sending proper invitations: that combination did me in.

For years, every time I'd seen his name in my inbox, it had caused me pain. I was out of reserves; I could not keep up the pretense. Evaluating my psychological state, I realized there were only two choices I was emotionally capable of at that time: I could cut him off while I was still capable of polite words, or I could start shouting I hated him. I reasoned that the former was less destructive. I still believe that's true. So I emailed him and said that I had to indefinitely break off contact, that it was simply too painful to be in touch. We didn't get back on mutual speaking terms for seven years.

But what did Ryan actually do to me? Get caught up in a new romance and write shorter emails? Forget to take a greeting card with him? Send wedding invitations by email instead of paper? Be clueless about emotional pain that I myself was working hard not to reveal? If all this sounds trivial, it is. Or to be more accurate, for my psyche it was catastrophic, but his actions themselves were, at most, slightly insensitive. He did almost nothing wrong. And it wounded me so badly that for years I honestly didn't know if I could ever overcome my hate for him. That's on me. It comes almost entirely out of my own insecurities and psychological problems.

Ryan is not—and never was—abusive, toxic, narcissistic, immature, or even especially callous. He was none of the things that cutoff culture assumes we cut people off for. He was always a good and caring person. He did virtually nothing objectionable.

I still had to cut him off. I was not wrong in my assessment of my own needs. I had to cut him off or start spewing venom at him. That's where I was. Those were my choices. That is as good an illustration as I can think of for why cutoff must be an absolute right, not just a right to protect ourselves from harassment or abuse or threats, but a basic right we can exercise at almost any time for almost any reason. As Ryan put it when I told him I was breaking off contact, "Pain is pain." People feel it for all sorts of reasons, and each person must be the arbiter of their own psychological capacity. If they judge they cannot maintain contact, they must have the right to make that call.

When I say we have a "right" to cutoffs, I'm using the word "right" precisely and in a Western cultural context, referring to those unalienable rights Thomas Jefferson invoked in the Declaration of Independence. Among them are life, liberty, and the pursuit of happiness, but that isn't the whole list. I'm referring to the Enlightenment idea that human beings have these things called *natural rights* that are inherently ours as individuals and which no one can justly take away, at least not without due process of the law.[82] This is the tradition that gave us human rights and civil rights and the Bill of Rights in the US Constitution. It's a way of understanding our most basic, inalterable freedoms and responsibilities within a social contract.

A Right That Is Often Violated

Not everyone agrees that cutoff is a right. Particularly in family contexts, there can be considerable pressure to stay in contact, and depending on specific cultural factors, some contend that

---

[82] Personally, I find it unlikely that natural rights actually exist as Platonic essences out there in the ether. I regard them as a social construct—but as a useful one I recommend we cling to for dear life because it prevents immense abuse and suffering.

family members do *not* have a right to cut family off. Family is sacred, the reasoning goes; thus, family bonds cannot be broken.

Even in family contexts, however, Western societies increasingly accept that people do have a right to cut others off for their own physical or psychological safety. Few today would argue that a person being abused is required to stay in contact with their abuser just because they are biologically or legally related. In non-familial contexts, most in our mainstream culture accept that cut-off is a right. It is widely understood that this right is essential to both physical and emotional self-protection. But when we start to unpack the social dynamics of cutoff, we uncover a byzantine cultural tangle. We agree the right to cutoff—like rights in general—should not be violated. But we do not agree on what the right to cutoff actually is.

What Is the Right to Cutoff?

People sometimes violate cutoffs egregiously—and sometimes by doing almost nothing. They may violate a cutoff by incessantly following someone or by sending one polite email once. But do all these acts violate a right?

We generally agree that we have a right to choose who we have in our personal lives. We cannot always choose if we bump into them in the store or have to see them at work, but we can choose whether to actively socialize with them or not. We agree we have this right. Yet we have no consensus on what this right entails. We agree that incessant texting over a long period of time is a violation of the right to cutoff. But does a flurry of texts right after a breakup violate that right? How about one email in three years? Saying "hi" as you accidentally pass in the street? The cutter might find these actions unpleasant, but do they *violate a right*? Are they ethically impermissible, tantamount to a moral crime? Views on these questions differ widely, yet we often behave as if they didn't, as if common ethics were self-evident. This haze masquerading as moral certainty covers a slurry of problems that can intensify psychological injury to multiple parties involved.

At one extreme, one could argue that a person who has been cut off can legitimately engage in any degree of pestering short of actual definitions of harassment or stalking. Perhaps pestering, like rude speech, is not good behavior but is also not a violation of a right. This view, however, is complicated by the fact there is no consistent definition of harassment or stalking.

I'll take stalking as a case in point. It should be noted that not all instances of stalking occur after a cutoff. For example, someone may be stalked by a person who was never an acquaintance to begin with. However, terminated romantic relationships are the most common catalyst for stalking,[83] and they often involve cutoff. As previously noted, stalking is a significant social problem. The National Intimate Partner and Sexual Violence Survey (2016/2017) (NISVS) found that 6.9% of American women and 4.1% of American men reported being stalked in the year preceding the survey.[84] Even more worrying, these numbers are growing exponentially. In the 2015 NISVS, 3.7% of American women and 1.9% of American men reported being stalked in the preceding year.[85] From 2015 to 2016–17, the figures approximately doubled. Why?

This growth may be attributable to a few different factors. Over the past decade or so, social media has made cyberstalking easier.[86] It's unclear, however, how big an impact this has year to year. Our society is also becoming lonelier.[87] Increased loneliness

---

[83] William R. Cupach, Brian H. Spitzberg, Colleen M. Bolingbroke, Bobbi Sue Tellitocci, "Persistence of Attempts to Reconcile a Terminated Romantic Relationship: A Partial Test of Relational Goal Pursuit Theory," *Communication Reports*, 24, no. 2 (2011): 101, http://doi.org/10.1080/08934215.2011.613737. p. 101.

[84] Sharon G. Smith, Kathleen C. Basile, and Marcie-jo Kresnow, *The National Intimate Partner and Sexual Violence Survey (NISVS): 2016/2017 Report on Stalking – Updated Release*, Atlanta, GA: National Center for Injury Prevention and Control, Centers for Disease Control and Prevention, 2022, p. 3, https://www.cdc.gov/nisvs/documentation/nisvsstalkingreport.pdf.

[85] Smith et al., *The National Intimate Partner and Sexual Violence Survey: 2015 Data Brief – Updated Release*, Atlanta, GA: National Center for Injury Prevention and Control, Centers for Disease Control and Prevention, 2018, p. 5, https://stacks.cdc.gov/view/cdc/60893.

[86] Simon Chandler, "Social Media Is Fostering a Big Rise in Real-World Stalking," *Forbes*, October 11, 2019, https://www.forbes.com/sites/simonchandler/2019/10/11/social-media-proves-itself-to-be-the-perfect-tool-for-stalkers/?sh=5715ef43d79e.

[87] Talia Lakritz, "7 Reasons Why We're Much Lonelier Today Than Ever Before," *The Insider*, June 21, 2018, https://www.insider.com/why-do-i-feel-lonely-2018-6.

might exacerbate some people's drive to force connection with others. Increased isolation during pandemic lockdowns, for example, has been linked to higher incidence of stalking.[88] At the same time, our cultural sense of what actions constitute stalking has also become broader. The 2016–2017 NISVS considers someone a victim of stalking if they experienced multiple instances of stalking tactics and

> [they] felt fearful, threatened, or concerned for their own safety or the safety of others as a result of the perpetrator's behavior.[89]

In contrast, the 2015 NISVS report considered someone a stalking victim if they experienced multiple instances of stalking tactics and

> [they] felt *very* fearful, or believed that they or someone close to them would be *harmed or killed* as a result of the perpetrator's behavior.[90] [emphasis mine]

Between 2015 and 2016, the NISVS broadened its definition of stalking by removing explicit language about physical harm and changing "very fearful" to just "fearful." It is likely this change in definition is a factor in the jump in reported stalking incidents.

This slippage around what defines stalking is not limited to the NISVS; it typifies our culture's discourse around stalking. *Merriam-Webster* offers the following legal definition of stalking:

> The act or crime of willfully and repeatedly following or harassing another person in circumstances that would cause a reasonable person to fear injury or death especially because of express or implied threats.[91]

---

[88] Ahmed Saeed Yahya, and Shakil Khawaja, "Stalking and COVID-19: Consequences of a Pandemic," Psychiatrist.com, August 6, 2020, https://www.psychiatrist.com/pcc/covid-19/stalking-and-covid/.
[89] Smith et al., 1
[90] Smith et al., 5.
[91] "Legal Definition of Stalking," *Merriam-Webster*, accessed September 25, 2021, https://www.merriam-webster.com/legal/stalking.

The Free Legal Dictionary, however, states that stalking must have an "intent to instill fear or injury,"[92] a provision absent from *Merriam-Webster*'s legal definition. These are more restrictive than either of the NISVS definitions. Traditionally, legal definitions have delimited what constitutes stalking by the provision that it must "reasonable" fear of harm, itself a subjective judgment.

Other definitions do not claim to legally define stalking as a criminal act but rather as a damaging social behavior. Understandably, these definitions are broader. *Merriam-Webster* offers this one:

> A crime of engaging in a course of conduct directed at a person that serves no legitimate purpose and seriously alarms, annoys, or intimidates that person.[93]

According to this definition, even repeated acts that "seriously annoy" someone can be stalking. This is a far cry from reasonable fear of injury or death. Writing for Verywell Mind.com, however, Ariane Resnick states, "Stalking involves behaviors towards a person that make them feel unsafe," and says of repeated contact, "Whether you've told someone not to contact you repeatedly or just once, if they continue to reach out, it can be considered stalking." In other words, after someone says, "Don't contact me," sending them two emails (repeated contact) could be considered stalking if it makes them *feel* unsafe. The feeling need not rise to a legal standard of "reasonable" fear; what sparks the fear is irrelevant; intent is also irrelevant.[94] However, in their 2004 book, *The Dark Side of Relationship Pursuit*, William Cupach and Brian

Spitzberg provide a more restrictive description: "Stalking represents the extreme boundary of pursuit persistence that easily qualifies as excessive."[95] Shelley Carolyn Taylor observes that

---

[92] "Stalking," *The Free Legal Dictionary* (Gale, 2008), https://legal-dictionary.thefreedictionary.com/Stalking.
[93] "Legal Definition of Stalking," *Merriam-Webster.*
[94] Ariane Resnick, "What Is Stalking? How to Know If You're Being Stalked," Verywell Mind, June 28, 2021.
https://www.verywellmind.com/what-is-stalking-5114376.
[95] William R. Cupach, and Brian H. Spitzberg, *The Dark Side of Relationship Pursuit: From Attraction to Obsession and Stalking*, (Mahwah, New Jersey: Lawrence Erlbaum Associates, 2004), 41. Cupach and Spitzberg's assertion that stalking "easily" qualifies as excessive may speak to

even scholars who research stalking have no agreed-upon definition. She cites several, including:

- *one* use of an unwanted pursuit tactic,
- *two or more uses* of an unwanted pursuit tactic,
- two or more *uses of a tactic* that produces fear,
- two or more *weeks of pursuit* that produces fear.[96]

In short, definitions of stalking are so diverse it is difficult to extract a standard from them.

Let me offer myself as an example. A commonly cited "stalking tactic" is sending unwanted messages. Sophia cut me off in 2014. Between the start of the cutoff in 2014 and 2017, I sent her five messages against her stated wishes. The first two were brief and polite; the third a short, angry rant; the fourth a brief apology for it; and the fifth polite and intended to reduce tensions. Does this mean I stalked her? I am not a lawyer, so I will not hazard a guess as to whether my actions rose to a legal definition of causing "reasonable" fear. I did not, however, threaten her, damage property, etc. I certainly did not intend to physically injure her or instill fear. On the other hand, if stalking is defined by a minimum of one or two acts of unwanted contact, then I stalked her. So did I? It depends on which definition you consult. The upshot is I don't know if I committed stalking.

Many people attempt to address this fuzziness by offering a single clear standard for how to respond to cutoff: once a person says, "Never contact me again," those words are sacrosanct and any further attempt at contact for life is a violation of a fundamental right. Our culture has an odd relationship with this view. In my experience, few people explicitly defend it if pressed. Indeed, to do so seems ridiculous. For instance, say hypothetical Belle cuts off hypothetical, non-abusive Terry, and then they bump into each other thirty years later and Terry says, "Hello, Belle. It's nice to

---

the age of the book. Since 2004, our cultural concept of what constitutes stalking has become significantly broader.

[96] Shelley Carolyn Taylor, "'How to Win My Ex Back?' A Qualitative Exploration of Online Forums of Persistent Unwanted Pursuers of Former Romantic Partners," Dissertation, Northcentral University, San Diego, June 2018, 30–31.

see you again." It would be bizarre to say that Terry has stalked her or, indeed, violated her fundamental right to cut him off.

Few would argue this, even among those who vigorously affirm the right to cutoff. Rabbi Kukla, for instance, speaks strongly against pushing people to reconnect with family who have cut them off, even on a deathbed, but he stops short of asserting this should *never* be attempted, instead offering cautionary advice about its advisability.[97] I myself once got a verbal lashing from an online friend, Delia, when I suggested I might try to contact Sophia, whom Delia does not know. When I asked her about this tongue-lashing a few years later, she stated that she had given me a "wake-up call" to leave the matter alone in part because "I saw potential that if you just left it there for a year, five years, ten years—perhaps one day, [Sophia] would find she was ok with being in contact again, even if she was 100% against it now."[98] Even behind a heated defense of the right to cutoff, there was, in this case, a belief that as little as another year might make unsolicited contact acceptable. When asked to reflect on it, most agree that in some cases, some contact across a cutoff does not violate the basic right to cutoff.

Yet much of our cultural discourse about cutoffs functionally assumes the opposite, that any contact by the cut-off person is an act similar in kind—if not degree—to stalking, a violation of a right. This principle is succinctly summed up by an unnamed close friend of cutoff critic Jeff Reifman. Reifman achieved brief internet infamy for his writing about cutoff trauma and followed up his initial essay with commentary on readers' responses, including his friend's. In voicing their own objection to Reifman's emailing his ex, his friend asserts, "Writing at ALL after someone said NO is not Okay. If it is OK, where is the line?"[99] The view that any contact after cutoff is an unacceptable violation undergirds much of our discourse about cutoff, but it is by no means universally accepted or self-evident.

---

[97] Elliot Kukla, "It's Okay to Forgive, or Not: Grieving When You're Estranged from Your Family."

[98] Delia, private message to the author, February 27, 2020.

[99] qtd. in Reifman, "Shining Light on Internet Rage."

How I'll Characterize Stalking in This Book

A key premise of this book is that relationships are contextual, too complex to be describable as absolutes. By the same token, what constitutes stalking must be contextual too. Therefore, I won't attempt one uniform definition but will offer some general thoughts.

While legal definitions of stalking are important, it remains useful to have a broader concept of stalking to describe behavior that should be socially unacceptable, even if it is legal. That said, the word "stalking" implies criminality and threat; it's a serious word, on a par with "abuse," and it should be reserved for serious infractions. I'd argue that to be considered stalking, behavior should go beyond a modest degree of annoying, unwanted contact; it should describe a pattern that is likely to cause fear *or* significantly disrupt the recipient's life over a period of time. This is not to say that being annoying is good, simply that it should not be considered *stalking* (or abuse). In other words, we should recognize a difference between *pestering* and *stalking.*

In general, I would exclude from "stalking" short-term behaviors that express normal grief. For example, imagine Amy breaks up with Joe and tells him never to contact her again, and Joe spends the next week sending her a barrage of weepy texts before calming down and tapering off to no contact. I would generally say he is not stalking her; he is processing the shock and denial of an early stage of grief. We tread a dangerous line if we consider normative grief responses to be stalking. To do so is to pathologize or morally criminalize behaving as an ordinary human being, and when normal human behavior is considered morally criminal, we are all at risk of being labeled criminals. Such an attitude entrenches stigma and isolation. We have amply seen this with old stigmas against queer identities, having children outside of marriage, or interracial marriage. We do not need to stigmatize normal grief.

By that token, I would also generally exclude a small handful of attempts at outreach across a cutoff, whether it is a short-term blitz (as with hypothetical Joe above) or a smattering of attempts across several years (or both). Such actions often speak to a normal grieving process or an honest desire to communicate, which is not itself a bad thing; indeed, in many cases, it is a good thing. It also does not rise to a pattern of behavior that would negatively impact most people's daily lives over time. Again, this is not to say such actions are necessarily advisable, merely that they should not be labeled *stalking*, just as yelling at an acquaintance a handful of times across several years should not be labeled abuse.

In general, I would allow more leeway for contact across ghosting than explicit cutoff. Ghosting, by definition, occurs with no warning or stated reason. It may take some time for the ghosted person to even suspect they've been ghosted. In cases of ghosting, it is normal for the ghosted person to try to figure out what happened. It is not reasonable to ask everyone who has been ghosted to assume a) that it is intentional ghosting and not some other situation leading to a break in contact and b) that it amounts to an order to cease contact. One of my interviewees, Arlo, who is a licensed counselor, observes that expecting ghosting to communicate a clear message is particularly unfair to people on the autistic spectrum, many of whom struggle with interpreting even fairly standard social cues. For many autistic people, Arlo contends, "It is impossible they could reach those conclusions [i.e. that ghosting should be read as a cutoff] and understand what's happening."[100]

Finally, I'll repeat that it's all contextual. In some cases, even one attempt at contact might legitimately be considered stalking. If Joe threatened to kill Amy, for example, and later emailed her to say, "Hello," Amy may very reasonably be terrified, and the act might even rise to the legal definition of stalking or harassment. People who have suffered threats and violence may experience terror from an encounter that seems innocuous to an outsider. For example, some could be frightened if an ex approaches them in a store to ask how they're doing, even if that ex was never abusive. Ironically, even assessing whether a behavior should be considered stalking could require some communication about it, some signal, for example, to an ex-boyfriend, like, "Hey, man, that really scares her." There can be no absolute, perfect definition. In this book, however, I will reserve the term "stalking" for significant, repeated boundary violations, in keeping with the stigma of criminality and pathology associated with the term.

---

[100] Arlo in discussion with the author, December 17, 2021.

The Conflation of Breakup and Cutoff

Stalking is just one area where our concepts and language about relationships are hazy. It's commonly assumed that breaking off a relationship—any type of relationship—means cutoff, and cutoff means no communication. Hence, ending a close relationship means ending all communication, which can imply a moral requirement for the cutter (as well as the cuttee) not to reinitiate it. After all, one should be consistent with one's boundaries, goes the reasoning. Yet breakup, greatly reduced contact, and total prohibition of contact are all different things. Two people can stop being friends and still be on speaking terms. Two people can refuse to be on speaking terms but agree it's legitimate for one to phone the other to tell them a mutual friend just died. Nonetheless, the conflation of *breakup*, *generally not communicating*, and *zero tolerance for communication* permeates our current culture.

One example of this conflation can be found in Brenda H. Lee and Lucia F. O'Sullivan's (2014) study of post-relationship contact tracking among young adults for *The Canadian Journal of Human Sexuality*. It is a valuable study that sheds important light on breakups and communication, yet its methodology itself shines light on our cultural assumptions about post-breakup contact. To contextualize their research, Lee and O'Sullivan observe that "little research to date has addressed the prevalence of stalking-like behaviours, such as post-relationship contact and tracking, which do not meet criminal definitions [of stalking]."[101] They make a good point about the dearth of research. Yet in this sentence, they also rhetorically assert that *any* post-relationship contact with an ex-partner is a "stalking-like behaviour." Such a blanket statement was clearly not their intent, and, indeed, they note elsewhere that the study focuses on "*unwanted* pursuit behaviours."[102] But the slippage between *stalking-like* contact and *any* contact is significant and embedded in their study.

Lee and O'Sullivan's sample comprised respondents to an online survey, which asked about post-breakup contact. In a

---

[101] Brenda H. Lee, and Lucia F. O'Sullivan, "The Ex-Factor: Characteristics of Online and Offline Post-Relationship Contact and Tracking Among Canadian Emerging Adults," *The Canadian Journal of Human Sexuality*, 23, no. 2 (2014): 97, https://doi.org:10.3138/cjhs.2415.

[102] Lee and O'Sullivan, 97. (emphasis added).

gracious email correspondence with me, O'Sullivan stated that "from my understanding, we only got responses from those who did not want post-breakup contact...."[103] This, however, is a recollection from six years after the publication of the study. Lee, who was also very gracious in providing more specifics, confirmed that their questions did not explicitly distinguish between *breakup* (no longer dating) and a *cutoff* (refusal of contact).[104] While it is likely that their pool consisted of people who did not want contact with their ex, it is startling that a study published in a peer-reviewed scholarly journal *did not control for this factor* and apparently no peer reviewer found this relevant. The study *assumes* it is analyzing contact that is clearly unwanted—on the same spectrum as stalking—but does not *verify* this.

This leaves open possibilities like the following: let's say hypothetical Ron and Nick break up. Ron assumes this means no more contact is welcome but doesn't explicitly say this because (like Lee and O'Sullivan's study), he assumes it's implied. Nick, however, assumes they're back to being "just friends" and, as a friend, says "hi" to Ron on social media. Ron is incensed by this and records it as "unwanted pursuit" on the survey. According to the parameters of this study, Nick has engaged in a "stalking-like behavior," though, as far as he knows, he has merely said "hi" to a friend. To call this "stalking-like" is absurd and clearly not the intent of the study, but it's a possibility that the conflation of *breakup* and *cutoff* opens up.

Lee and O'Sullivan are by no means an outlier. The assumption that "breakup" implies "cutoff" pervades our culture. Indeed, miscommunication around this issue led to some anger in an exchange I had with an online friend, Lyn. A few years ago, I expressed to Lyn some consternation at Sophia's cutting me off.

---

[103] Lucia O'Sullivan, email message to author, 27 August 2020.

[104] Brenda H. Lee, email message to author, August 28, 2020. Lee wrote, "We did not ask about an explicit discussion between ex-partners to cut off contact. The prompt provided was as follows: 'when someone is having trouble letting go of an ex, they may do certain things to try to get their ex's attention, to get back at their ex, or to try to fix the relationship. Which of the following did you/this ex do after your breakup?' So there was (intentionally) a level of subjectivity in participants' own interpretations of their behaviours, as well as their interpretations of their ex's behaviours towards them."

(Lyn does not know Sophia.) Two years later, as I prepared to write this book, we revisited this conversation, in the course of which Lyn said this:

> If a person was really hurt by a relationship and decided to cut it off because they thought that that was the only way for them to stay healthy and take care of themselves, that doesn't make them a bad person. I don't think it's fair to expect people to stay in any kind of relationship if it's not good for them.[105]

For clarity, I never said that Sophia is a bad person; in fact, I'd said she is a good one.[106] That said, it's fair to say my tone suggested the opposite: the anger was surely there. What I find fascinating about this reply, however, is the way the meanings of statements slip. I had opened up a conversation about Sophia *cutting off contact* with me. Lyn replied with a statement about *leaving a relationship*. What, in fact, does it mean to "cut off a relationship"? Does it mean, for example, that two people are no longer *dating*, or does it mean they are no longer *speaking*? These are very different things. To my mind, Sophia ending our prior *relationship* means we are no longer *friends*, not that we are no longer speaking. The loss our friendship hurt me deeply, but I have never said to Sophia, Lyn, or anyone that her ending our friendship was a bad choice. I have, however, voiced this sentiment often (arguably unfairly) about her ending contact.

---

[105] Lyn, private message to author, August 30, 2020. Lyn had been incensed about what she perceived as my attitude for *two years*. In our first exchange, I recognized that she was angry and had misunderstood me, but I decided not to pursue it to avoid seeming defensive. Seeing that she was still angry two years later, with a great deal of anxiety, I did clarify my position. She thanked me and, as far as I can tell, her anger dissolved rapidly. I let two years of anger fester because our culture often views attempts to explain one's own perspective as making excuses. This is an example of why this book promotes communication as part of conflict resolution.

[106] My editor notes that calling people holistically "bad" or "good" argues against my thesis of nuance and context. I take her point, but I stand by my assertion that Sophia is good. This relates to my own ontology of "good/evil," which is outside the scope of this book.

What's the difference? Well, it's easy to imagine two people no longer socially spending time together or discussing anything beyond the superficial, yet still "friends" on social media or exchanging occasional messages: "Congratulations on the new job," and so on. It's easy to imagine them saying "hello" with a smile when they meet in the street. I myself am on these terms with at least two people with whom I did explicitly fall out as friends and with any number of people I once casually dated.

Lyn's defense of exiting "relationships" implies she thought I was objecting to Sophia's not staying my friend, that I thought she should stay trapped in that friendship to avoid hurting me. I did not mean this; I was only resisting the absolute cutoff. Lyn later confirmed some confusion over this.[107]

Our culture's conceptual slippage around cutoffs is immense. It's an obvious fact that many exes remain friends or acquaintances. Despite this, our discourse around breakups often assumes that *breakup* means *cutoff*, that ending a type of *relationship* means ending all *contact*. We, therefore, assume that cutoffs are implied even where they are not stated (or possibly intended). Thus, even if we don't know whether post-breakup contact is acceptable, we still define it as a violation of a cutoff and, thus, akin to stalking, even though can't agree on how to define stalking either. This slippage leads to odd formulations: Lee and O'Sullivan describe their study as engaging a "range of behaviours that manifest in stalking-like and cyberstalking-like cases, from common and benign forms of online tracking and monitoring behaviours (such as [social media] creeping') to more extreme cases of offline and online harassment."[108] This wording suggests that certain "stalking-like" behaviors are "benign." But if it's benign, how is it like stalking? Isn't something "like stalking," by definition, something akin to a serious violation and, thus, not benign?

Not every communication across a cutoff is damaging, dangerous, or suggestive of a failure to comprehend boundaries. Here's a simple example. A former caretaker for my kids asked me to write a testimonial for her on a job site. In my testimonial, which I intended to be glowing, I inadvertently included a statement she interpreted as impugning her professionalism. She

---

[107] Lyn, private message to author, August 31, 2020.

[108] Lee and O'Sullivan, 97. Company name omitted to avoid possible trademark infringement.

texted me in a rage, declaring that I had committed a vindictive act that would cost her work she needed to make a living. She swore she would never speak to me again, which certainly implies she didn't want me to contact her either. It didn't take me five minutes to transgress that wish. I wrote back that I had no idea the statement might be damaging and I would remove it from my testimonial right away, which I did. She, in turn, wrote back almost immediately with relief and understanding. Within twenty-four hours, we were on friendly terms again and have been ever since. In this case, transgressing her cutoff was clearly needed to address a miscommunication. But the principle can apply in more complex cases too.

The reality is that transgressing a cutoff is sometimes the best path to healing the wound that caused it. Four years after I cut Ryan off, he sent me a friend request on social media, one of the activities Lee and O'Sullivan classified as a "stalking-like."[109] When I saw the request attached to his name, I was angry, triggered, and in distress. After some rumination, I told him tersely that I was still too angry to reconnect and I did not wish to be social media friends but perhaps in another year or so my feelings would have settled enough to connect that way. He replied with civil acceptance and left me alone.

When he sent me that friend request, it saved our relationship. It catapulted me onto the path toward healing. See, I cut Ryan off because I felt like he didn't care about me. When he reached out to me to show he still thought about me, he proved to me that he did. It was exactly what I needed. If he had not transgressed my cutoff, my healing process would have been orders of magnitude longer and harder.

Our situation, of course, is contextual. What if I had done exactly the same with Sophia? No contact for four years and then attempting to friend her on social media? The result would be very different. Based on what I know of our situation, I believe that if I sent her a friend request, it would at best distress her and make her feel disrespected and misunderstood, not just in the moment but long term. At worst, it might feel threatening and be retraumatizing. Our context is different. Sophia didn't cut me off because she thought I didn't care. I suspect she cut me off, at least in part, because she didn't know how to deal with how much I *did.*

---

[109] Lee and O'Sullivan, 97.

The very same act from the very same motives can heal or harm. It can't be separated from context.

So how should our culture understand acts such as this? The friendship request, the amicable email or text that transgresses a cutoff, asking a mutual friend to ask the cutter how they're doing? Are these acts, indeed, "stalking-like"? That is, are they violations on the same spectrum as stalking but simply not as severe? Do they violate a fundamental right? Are they, in fact, stalking (at least if performed twice)? Or are they reasonable, innocent attempts at peacemaking? Are they a nuisance but minor enough that the sender is entitled to make them, assuming there is no restraining order? Are they vital to healing? Depending on the situation, they will function as all of these. What heals me harms Sophia. There can be no one-size-fits-all. Yet the concept of rights is predicated on one size fitting all.

The Ambiguity of "Rights"

All human persons have the same human rights.[110] All deserve the same protections. To a degree, this concept works well with cutoffs. We can agree that people have the right to cut off all contact with those who are a threat or make threats. We can agree certain acts legitimately trigger responses such as a sharp cease-and-desist message or a formal restraining order. Most would agree that these include but are not limited to threats, physically following people, violating private spaces, using surveillance tactics (on- or offline) to publicize people's private information to embarrass and expose them, and incessant contact of any kind, such as texting, phoning, emailing, etc. We can agree these acts violate the right to decide who we have in our lives.

However, this near consensus evaporates rapidly. What about friendly contact that is frequent but not incessant? What is the difference between "frequent" and "incessant"? What's the difference between "frequent" and "rare"? Is any contact across a cutoff ethically permissible, even "rare," even once? Does duration

---

[110] I'm specifying both "human" and "person" in the name of ethical precision. People in favor of abortion rights, for example, would generally not consider fetuses "persons" with human rights, though they are genetically human. Conversely, many cultures consider some other-than-humans to be persons, such as trees or deer, etc.

matter? For example, is it to be expected that a jilted ex will text a few times a day for a couple of weeks but for a couple of *months* is stalking? Are five texts within a week of a breakup more or less problematic than five texts in a week three years later? If ten years have gone by, is an attempt at contact a sign of healing or of obsession? Does impact matter? Should we consider an act to be peacemaking or stalking depending on its outcome? And if so, how can we translate that into an ethical standard when we often can't know the outcome of our actions before the fact, especially in highly fraught circumstances where there is no open communication?

The truth is we don't know. Our culture has no agreed upon standards. Depending on the circumstances and the person making the judgment, a given communication might be seen as permissible, healing, or violating. Or it might be a violation that was *good*, that *did* good, such as Ryan's reaching out to me. This formulation ought to concern us, as it has been used to justify many types of abuse and violation. Our culture does not have an answer. We do not know what the right to cutoff includes.

One reason we have trouble delineating the right to cutoff is that we use the word "rights" to mean different things. I am using it in the sense of Constitutional rights or natural rights, those unalienable Age of Enlightenment rights inherent in being human. But we routinely discuss "having rights" in more general ways too. We English speakers love our "rights," and we've embedded the language of "rights" into a casual usage with only a loose connection to the civic idea of rights. If we say, "I have a right to an explanation," we don't mean a person should be fined or jailed for not providing an explanation. We mean providing an explanation is the decent thing to do. If we say, "He had no right to say that to me," we don't mean his words were not protected by the United States' First Amendment. We mean his words were unfair.

There are, then, at least two main usages of "rights":[111]

---

[111] A third usage may be present in Sarah Schulman's *Conflict Is Not Abuse.* In discussing distortions that may arise in he-said, she-said narratives, Schulman states, "As a writer, I know that there is, after all, the right to be described accurately." This use seems broader than the legal right not to be libeled, but as an unalienable right, it's not enforceable. Many people don't know how to describe others accurately or even how to describe ourselves. Thus, it can't be put into practice as a right. Her use seems to carry more weight, however, than the idea that trying

1. Certain freedoms and protections we can never justly be deprived of, at least not without due process.
2. An expectation that we should generally be treated decently.

These are two very different things, but when we discuss cut-offs, they are almost invariably conflated. One of the most common conflations is in this formulation:

"I have a right to closure," says the cut-off person, desiring a final meeting or an explanation.

"No, you have no right to closure," replies a bystander.

This type of exchange could mean any of the following:

1. The cuttee believes they are literally owed closure (a natural right), and the bystander declares they do not have this natural right: they disagree but have an accurate communication.
2. The cuttee believes they should be treated with the compassion that a chance at closure demonstrates, and the bystander declares they should have no such expectation: they disagree but have an accurate communication.
3. The cuttee believes they should be treated with the compassion that a chance at closure demonstrates, and the bystander declares they do not have a natural right that requires this. This is a miscommunication. The bystander is not addressing what the cut-off person meant to say.

The last case is like Jane saying, "George shouldn't have called me names," and her friend replying, "No, it was fine because the First Amendment allows him to." There's a disconnect. The First Amendment of the US Constitution does allow it; that doesn't invalidate Jane's point. Should a cut-off person legitimately expect a chance at closure? We have difficulty even discussing this question, in part, because we often never get as far as actually asking it. We

to be accurate shows decency. Sarah Schulman, *Conflict Is Not Abuse*, (Vancouver, BC, Arsenal Pulp Press, 2016), 48.

get stuck on ambiguous discussion of "rights," and the underlying cultural question gets buried in semantics.

Should a cut-off person legitimately expect a chance at closure? What even is a chance at closure? I'd argue the answer, as with all of this, is it depends on context.

We Can't Talk—
And We Can't Talk about the Fact We Can't Talk

We can't agree on what the right to cutoff entails. We don't know. Yet we proceed as if we did. Our dominant cutoff discourse assumes this complex web is simple: we have a right to cut people off. This supports our safety and peace of mind, end of story.

This view is widely propagated with little commentary. One example is the meme "Things That Can Be True at the Same Time" by therapist Dr. Heidi Green.[112] It consists of a list of five tensions Green invites us to embrace to be more psychologically healthy. One statement is "You love someone *and* you know it's not healthy to keep them in your life." Undeniably, this can be true. But what does it actually mean to not "keep someone in your life"? Does it mean rarely seeing them, keeping communication superficial and tightly bounded? Does it mean cutting off all communication? Does it mean cutting off all communication without exception *for life*, even on a deathbed? If it means cutting someone off completely, it is useful, I think, to ask, "In what way is this loving?"

I posed this question to Carolyn, as she had stated that she loves her brother despite cutting him off. She paused, thought, and then said, "[The cutoff] gives him the opportunity by that void not to have something to fight against."[113] For her, that is a way of showing love. For Anna, cutting off Bright_Bird showed love by protecting her from possible persecution. For Cole, the emotions of love and goodwill exist across the cutoffs he had to make for his own peace of mind.[114] There are good answers to questions such as this, but in our social media-driven culture, where human

---

112 Heidi Green, "Things That Can Be True at the Same Time," Mind Journal, accessed May 9, 2021, themindsjournal.com/things-that-can-be-true-at-the-same-time/.

113 Carolyn.

114 Cole.

expression is regularly reduced to tweet-sized snippets, the questions themselves are rarely asked and the complexities often unrecognized.

But the context matters; each case is unique. In one instance, not keeping a loved one in our lives might mean eschewing frequent meetings and deep conversations. In another, it might, indeed, mean blocking all contact for life. These are radically different acts implying radically different situations. But I have found no such contextual discussion of the "Things That Can Be True..." meme. I first discovered it on a friend's social media feed, liked by several people, with no comments except variations of "good advice." I also found it on another social media site with some reblogs and no comments I've seen.[115] It is posted on the The-MindsJournal.com without comment.[116]

I contacted Green herself to ask if she cared to contextualize her intent. She did not reply. But it must be said I didn't try hard to reach her. I only attempted to contact her once, by direct message. She might have missed it; she might have meant to reply and forgotten. She might have been more responsive to another medium. I don't know. I was afraid to try again, afraid she would regard me a kook, a threat, because I raised questions about cut-offs. I didn't comment on my friend's feed either. I was afraid my friend would interpret me as undercutting people's right to support their own mental health.

The fact is, raising the contextual complexities of keeping people out of our lives is taboo. When I attempted this with Lyn, she interpreted me as denying people's right to choose to end relationships, something I would never do. This reading is common. To raise questions about cutoffs is read as denying the right to set boundaries. To raise questions about oneself being cut off is read as evidence one is a stalker or abuser.

This mental leap is starkly evident in the outcry against Reifman's essay in which he discusses the traumatic impact of being cut off by his ex-girlfriend, Emma (not her real name). The essay's tone is mature and reasonable, advocating communication as a

---

[115] Heidi Green, "Things That Can Be True at the Same Time," Quote Junkie, November 14, 2020, https://quote-junkie.tumblr.com/post/634815917821460480/things-that-can-be-true-at-the-same-time-your#notes

[116] Green, "Things That Can Be True at the Same Time," Mind Journal.

means of resolving conflict. For example, Reifman states, "When we don't tell people [we cut off] why we're angry at them, we're also robbing them of a chance to apologize and make amends. I would like nothing better than to understand how I've hurt or upset Emma and to apologize and make repairs."[117] This piece of compassionate common sense is typical of the essay. The response was a social media firestorm:

> "Abusers and stalkers probably are just really WOUNDED, ya know? It's so terrible."[118]
>
> "Glad he posted that cut-off culture thing under his real name, like a batsignal warning others to stay awaaaaaaaay."[119]
>
> "gross, creepy bullshit. Yuck."[120]
>
> "At no point in this article does he think of her feelings, at all. Textbook abuser."[121]

As to this last comment, in the sentences I quote above, Reifman explicitly says he would like to understand how he has hurt Emma and make amends. The contention that he doesn't think about her feelings is demonstrably false: he could not have written that sentence if he hadn't thought about her feelings to some degree. Nonetheless, on the basis of a demonstrable falsehood, the tweet labels him an obvious abuser. When this is the price of opening

---

[117] Reifman, "Shining Light on Relationship Cutoff." While Reifman was excoriated for stating such views, I find them similar to the sentiments expressed by marriage and family therapist Kelsey T. Chun: "[S]imply eliminating someone [by cutoff] rather than attempting direct communication (or therapy) about the issue denies you and the other person an opportunity to learn about yourselves." Kelsey T. Chun, "Is Eliminating 'Toxic' Relationships the Right Decision?" *Verily*, May 20, 2020, https://verilymag.com/2020/05/toxic-friendships-signs-of-a-toxic-friend-2020.

[118] Reifman, "Shining Light on Internet Rage."

[119] Reifman, "Shining Light on Internet Rage."

[120] Reifman, "Shining Light on Internet Rage."

[121] Reifman, "Shining Light on Internet Rage."

up a discussion about what cutoffs mean, it is no wonder our culture doesn't do it.

This is unfortunate, because when we do begin to talk about it, we can very quickly open up to nuances of human relationships. This came home to me when another social media friend posted, without comment, this aphorism on cutoffs by poet Kalen Dion: "Silently closing all avenues of communication may seem cold, but it's no worse than having a knock-down drag out fight with someone who knows exactly what they did and refuses to acknowledge it."[122] This statement implies a false dichotomy in which setting verbal boundaries (vs. ghosting) is not worth discussing as an option: useless fights and ghosting are presented as the only alternatives. I reached out to Dion to ask if he'd like to expand on his perspective, and he answered me promptly and helpfully. Specifically, I asked him about the duration of the cutoff he implicitly suggests. In this aphorism, was he referring to permanently severing contact, taking a break for month…? He replied,

> I think that decision is up to the individual. That is so very personal. And it's going to be based on their experience and what drives them to that point.
>
> I have an ex who hasn't spoken to me in a year. And then I have an ex who I will never speak to again. I have an ex who I am very good friends with. That's totally relative to the individual's experience. I'm also not a psychologist or a therapist. I kind of just call things how I see them. Either way... I don't think there's any way you can standardize that number.[123]

Within one brief communication, a decontextualized assertion becomes highly contextualized. How cutoffs should be handled depends on the situation, says Dion. There's no way to standardize it. He also somewhat disclaims his own authority: he is not

---

[122] Kalen Dion, "Silently Closing All Avenues of Communication...," GreatestTweets.com, July 20, 2021, https://www.greatesttweets.com/silently-closing-all-avenues-of-communication-may-seem-cold-but-its-no-worse-than-having-a-knock-down-drag-out-fight-with-someone-who-knows-exactly-what-they-did-and-refuses-to-acknowledge-it/wisdom/.

[123] Kalen Dion, email message to author, September 11, 2021. (ellipsis in original)

intending to provide absolute principles for all humanity. He is simply "call[ing] things how I see them." All this nuance is lost in a post presenting a sentence in a vacuum, with no comment, disconnected from specific, real situations. It is in such social media bites that much of our values around cutoffs form.

Our social discourse around cutoffs suffers from lack of context and lack of conversation. In advocating a relational ethics, I advocate for a contextual approach concerned with particularities of individuals and situations, for the benefit of all, an approach that respects but moves beyond only rights. Such an approach can help us when we need to cut others off but also when we are cut off. It is an approach that recognizes that while cutoffs are often necessary, they also often cause trauma. All people suffering trauma need support.

Part 2
The Destructiveness of Cutoff Culture

Chapter 4

Six Tenets of Cutoff Culture

That venerable mainstay of British science fiction, *Doctor Who*, uses the concept of a perception filter as one means of diverting attention from a person or place. A perception filter does not render something invisible. Rather, it affects the perceptions of the viewer. The eyes slip off the object. The mind ignores it. It falls to the side of recognition, like a crack in a floorboard we don't notice anymore.

There is a perception filter around cutoffs. They exist, we see them, but we don't see them. We often don't register them as a category distinct from breakups or drifting apart or other types of boundary setting. "Cutoff" is barely even a vocabulary term. The word is typically absent from psychology manuals. I have yet to find a research study that explicitly investigates it. Related concepts are studied, including abandonment, ostracism, estrangement, rejection, exclusion, breakups, ghosting, and (as a potential, unhealthy response) stalking—none of these is synonymous with cutoff. As I write this, our society's go-to reference source,

Wikipedia, offers twenty meanings for "cutoff"; relationship cutoff is not one of them.[124]

The unseen quality of cutoff is evident even in the impressive scholarly essay collection *Ostracism, Exclusion, and Rejection* (2017). Here, Zadro et al. divide styles of ostracism in *noisy silence* and *quiet silence.* Noisy silence advertises ostracism through acts like slamming doors or announcements like "I'm not speaking to them" when a person enters a room. Quiet silence ceases to acknowledge

---

[124] "Cutoff," *Wikipedia*, accessed August 3, 2022, https://en.wikipedia.org/wiki/Cutoff.

the ostracized person's existence.[125] Zadro et al. observe "[T]he most destructive form of quiet silence is *cutting off*—when the source deliberately and completely ignores the target, acting as if that person does not exist and wanting nothing more to do with them."[126] Cutoff, they tell us, is "the *most destructive* form of quiet silence," yet out of 289 pages on ostracism, this is the only place the book explicitly mentions it as an indexed term. In other words, this meticulously researched, scholarly work on issues directly related to cutoff simultaneously acknowledges it is a severe form of ostracism and almost fails to register it exists. This is indicative of our culture's perception filter around cutoff.

Given this filter, it is not surprising that there is little ethical discussion around cutoffs. Cutoff happens at the filter's edges, where open discussion to explore, develop, and critique practices is not permissible. In researching this book, I have studied a seemingly endless succession of blogs, tweets, posts, videos, and their comments, DMs, emails, and popular relationship and psychology articles (including many written and/or reviewed by professionals) that discuss cutoff.[127] The upshot is different people advocate different approaches. Some advocate ghosting people with no warning, though psychologists rarely do. Some advocate meeting in person to explain that you are cutting contact. Some advocate breakup cutoffs for a limited time, some forever. Many, including some psychologists, do not specify if they advocate cutoff for a limited time or forever, though these are radically different acts. Nonetheless, certain trends emerge around cutoff discourse, themes I'll loosely describe as the common practice of cutoff culture.

The general tenor of this practice is that cutoffs are healthy and should be validated as a good means of ending relationships and defining boundaries. Of course, variations exist. For example, cutting off a family member is often questioned in a way that other cutoffs aren't. The set of attitudes I identify as "cutoff culture" is

---

[125] Zadro et al., "Creating the Silence: Ostracism from the Perspective of the Source." 137.

[126] Zadro et al., "Creating the Silence: Ostracism from the Perspective of the Source." 137. Emphasis original.

[127] I'm excluding personal interviews from this list because they tend to produce responses that are more contextual and nuanced. There is nothing like real-time conversation for delving into the complexities of human experience.

just one set of attitudes toward cutoff, but it is one with a great deal of social power. In the left-leaning, culturally Western echo chambers I have experienced, it has the dominant social power.

These are the key tenets I have observed:

1. Cutoff ends a relationship and, thus, ends any ethical responsibility the cutter may have to the cut-off person beyond unalienable rights and duties.
2. Permanent cutoff is an effective, low-harm way to end relationships because it is sets and maintains clear boundaries, which reduces mixed signals and maximizes self-protection.
3. The cut-off person has a duty never to contact the cutter as long as the cutoff is in effect.
4. Those who *transgress* cutoffs should be ignored or rebuffed because they are disrespecting boundaries.
5. Those who *question* cutoffs should be reprimanded for disrespecting boundaries.
6. The cuttee should strive to immediately accept that the relationship is over and move on as quickly and totally as possible.

As general guidelines for conduct, every single one of these assertions is destructive to health and wellness in human relations. That does not mean these assertions always result in bad choices in context. In some cases, some of these instructions do describe the least destructive course of action. But these are usually extreme cases and should be treated as such.

What makes these assertions so destructive is that, collectively, they advocate ostracism, a systematic exclusion of the ostracized person, by either a group or one person. Indeed, they are premised on the notion that ostracizing someone doesn't really do much harm. This notion is incorrect. Ostracism is one of the most universally painful experiences a human being can suffer. Williams describes ostracism in terms of its effects on four basic human needs: the need for belonging, the need for control, the need for self-esteem, and the need for some meaning in existence.[128] He asserts, "I consider ostracism to be unique in its potential ability to pose a threat to all four needs. Ostracism serves to sever bonds,

[128] Williams, *Ostracism*, 245.

withdraw control, derogate, and render invisible and insignificant its targets."[129] The following chapters will explore how this common cutoff practice encourages harm to these four basic needs and how cutoff practices could be reimagined in ways that do less harm.

When a Harsh Practice Is the Lesser Evil

It remains true: sometimes cutoff is the lesser evil. To begin with, let's look at some cases where some of these common cutoff instructions clearly make sense. If someone is physically dangerous, it makes sense to take all measures necessary to sever all contact with them. If someone has repeatedly shown that they have little-to-no comprehension of boundaries, then the single clear boundary of no contact ever may be what they need to get the message. It may be the only way to make harassment or abuse cease. As to ethical responsibility, when you have to protect yourself from danger, abuse, harassment, or psychological breakdown, it absolutely makes sense to prioritize your own safety and wellness and deprioritize the welfare of the person hurting you. As Carolyn observed of cutting off her brother, "I still love my brother. I just love myself more."[130]

Intimate partner violence and familial abuse are examples of extreme circumstances where such practices make sense. My friend Valerie, one of the kindest and most forbearing people I know, found herself in a situation akin to this with her ex-husband and his new partner in the 1980s. In an acrimonious custody battle, Valerie's ex and his partner lied about her fitness as a parent and attempted to record her phone calls to use as evidence against her in court. The new partner even destroyed her property, including the sole copy of a novel manuscript she had worked on for years. To protect her children from this dysfunctionality, Valerie, who retained sole custody of the kids, cut off all contact with their father and his partner, going so far as to willingly sacrifice over a decade of child support payments rather than have any entanglement with them. Knowing Valerie as I do, I have no doubt that this course of action was prudent to protect the children's welfare. They all grew up to be high functioning and stable, and as adults,

---

[129] Williams, *Ostracism*, 245.

[130] Carolyn.

with their mother's blessing, all reconnected with their father to some degree prior to his death and all with a clear sense of the need to maintain careful boundaries with him.

Like many people who choose cutoff, Valerie suffered additional impacts as a marginalized person. In her case, her status as a queer person was used as evidence in custody proceedings to challenge her fitness as a parent. Marginalized people, in particular, may face multiple sources of trauma. Rabbi Kukla observes that such trauma often occurs within families of origin, and separation from that family—even up to absolute cutoff—may be necessary to the cutter's health and healing. At the same time, because family is considered a privileged category, they may be pressured to stay connected. Kukla notes,

> Homophobia, transphobia, ableism, racism, classism, and misogyny can play into family estrangement, compounding the silence around trauma, as well as the social pressure to reconnect with original family. Capitalism prioritizes the nuclear family for economic reasons, but many multiply [sic] marginalized people must find family in other ways, far from their family of origin.[131]

He raises an excellent point that intersectionally marginalized people may have a particular need to seek distance—even complete cutoff—from their families of origin, and a caring culture must validate that need. Part of the work of social justice is to listen attentively to marginalized voices in order to counteract the tendency of the dominant culture to silence, ignore, or attack them, either intentionally or through implicit biases. Each person must be the ultimate determiner of their own psychological needs.

Sometimes an absolute cutoff is a person's best choice, and not only in cases of systemic marginalization, abuse, or extreme dysfunctionality. Sometimes, regardless of the cuttee's culpability, this kind of severance is the only way the cutter knows to feel psychologically safe or be able to move forward and function. As Lyn puts it,

---

[131] Elliot Kukla, "It's Okay to Forgive, or Not: Grieving When You're Estranged from Your Family."

> Some people just don't have the capacity to attempt and fix something that's been broken and nothing we do can force them to develop that capacity.... I wanna be able to finish two party-sized pizzas all by myself and still have room for a bucket of fries but I just *can't*. Forcing myself will just make me throw up. I need to cut myself off from the food and distance myself from the restaurant.[132]

In such cases, absolute cutoff, rigorously guarded, may be the only thing the cutter can psychologically do.

These situations happen. But very many cutoffs happen in circumstances where less extreme boundaries could still meet the cuttee's needs. Permanent cutoff is commonly advised in romantic breakups, regardless of how well or how badly the partners behaved or how rapidly broken hearts heal. It is so common in friendships it scarcely registers in the public consciousness as an action. As Delia observes,

> IMO most people (if they're lucky) have a few others in their life where they would be devastated if that relationship irreparably fell apart—but no more than one or two individuals.... The thinking is that friendship definitionally doesn't rise to that level."[133]

Meg sums up this common perception well: "Friendships, in particular, are not bound by any commitment except 'this works for me.'"[134] I would argue that this is not actually a commitment at all: a commitment is a bond one person gives another.[135] In

---

132 Lyn, private message to author, October 6, 2017, (emphasis original).

133 Delia, private message to the author, February 27, 2020. Regarding the dismissal of friendship, Delia adds, "I don't agree with that on principle, and I do know other people besides you who have been profoundly hurt by terminated friendships, even (perhaps especially) young, volatile ones."

134 Meg, private message to the author, July 4, 2019.

135 My editor offers, "Friendships seem like they come and go based on growth of the individuals, and what is needed at the time. No long-haul agreements. As if we should be able to naturally let them go more easily [than family/partners]? I am not saying this strengthens the fabric of society, but maybe the come-and-go nature of them is functional." This

contrast, "this works for me" refers only to self-interest. According to this view, a friend may legitimately cut off a friend for any reason at all, serious or trivial. Such a cavalier reliance on cutoff is worlds away from Valerie's fears for the psychological security of her children or the extreme cases of family dysfunction Kukla explores.

Yet our culture commonly prescribes the same cutoff practice for addressing abuse and everyday quarrels, physical danger and hurt feelings, pathological manipulation and falling out of love. All these situations are often treated as remediable only by absolute severance. Sarah Schulman contends that while genuine violence and abuse are grave problems in our society, "*simultaneously*… a rhetoric of threat that confuses doing nothing, normative conflict, and resistance with actual abuse, has produced a wide practice of *overstating harm*. And this overstatement of harm is often expressed in 'shunning…'" [emphasis in original],[136] of which cutoff is an extreme form. This lack of proportion needs to change, because cutoff is a heavy hammer. We may treat cancer with chemotherapy, knowing that the chemo itself will do harm. But to treat a common cold with chemo is simply to make the patient sicker. Our current cutoff norms invite extensive and unnecessary psychological damage. They should be close to the last resort, not the first.

---

characterization accords with Delia's and Meg's (and our dominant culture's), and my response is it's true of some kinds of friendship. The word "friend" is slippery; it can mean someone we chat with at work, or it can mean a constant, emotionally intimate presence in our lives since preschool. Some friendships come and go as ephemera or are deep but temporary; some are lifelong lifelines: Kirk and Spock, Frodo and Sam, Achilles and Patroclus (who may have been lovers but were certainly *friends*). Yes, these examples are all male, which deserves its own essay.

136 Sarah Schulman, *Conflict Is Not Abuse* (Vancouver, BC: Arsenal Pulp Press, 2016), 21.

Chapter 5

Cutoff as Ethically Neutral

Tenet 1. Cutoff ends a relationship and, thus, ends any ethical responsibility the cutter may have in relation to the cutoff person beyond unalienable rights and duties.

When I was nine, I saw *Ben-Hur* for the first time. I remember my attention riveted by the scene in which Judah (Charlton Heston) and his childhood friend, Messala (Stephen Boyd), meet up after years apart: the love in their smiles and their eyes bright as they cross that wide hall to each other. A minute later, they are in the midst of a bitter fight, which ignites a lifelong enmity. My nine-year-old fangirl, friendship-bonding heart was shattered. I couldn't believe it. I spent the rest of the movie, right up to "There's enough of a man still left here for you to hate,"[137] hoping that they'd make amends. They don't.

I have always found the story of their lost friendship very painful. It is a profound instinct in me to reject the idea that enmity is final. It, therefore, surprises me how much I, even I, have failed to register the harm that cutoffs do. This speaks volumes about how normalized and trivialized cutoffs are in our society.

In the salad days of my friendship with Sophia, we worked together on a novel of hers (unpublished). She wrote it and I edited it, along with contributing substantial ideas to character backgrounds and setting. In this novel, the protagonist cuts off her father. She drops off the radar and ghosts him for about twenty-five years, and not because he was abusive or awful. On the contrary, the novel is very clear that the two characters love each other and, despite a fraught relationship, are both good,

[137] *Ben-Hur*, directed by William Wyler, performances by Charlton Heston and Jack Hawkins, Metro-Goldwyn-Mayer, 1959.

mature, decent people. The protagonist simply couldn't deal with the pain of her ambivalence about her dad. This ghosting culminates in her tracking him down and meeting with him once, after a quarter century of silence, when the father is very old and near death. They have a conversation about how proud he is of her and how well she's done for herself. Then she goes off. It's near the end of the book, and it's not clear if they'll ever try to meet again. This is not the main plot. It's a side note.

Sophia writes the human condition with excruciating nuance. And I loved this subplot. I remember praising their reunion scene for its sentiment and psychological precision. I did not see that what this character did to her father would likely cause him twenty-five years of agony. I did not see that his utter lack of condemnation when they meet again is the act of a saint. I just thought it was nice that protagonist had healed enough that she could speak to him again. As far as I can tell, that's what Sophia thought as well. All her psychological astuteness could not grasp the simple and obvious fact that she had made her deep-feeling, sensitive protagonist psychologically torture her own father for the span for a quarter century.

I don't think she grasped what she was doing when she cut me off either. I certainly didn't. I knew I was in agony, but I had no idea of the purgatory in store. I would be flabbergasted if Sophia understood it. I didn't understand what I was doing to Ryan when I cut him off either. For six or seven years, I didn't think about his pain at all. I genuinely believed that it was all about my pain. I have many failings, but I am not a basically callous person. Neither is Sophia. If anything, at least when I knew her, she was hyper-conscientious to the point of self-flagellation.

How could we have been so blind?[138]

I expect it was for the same reason that, for years, when I posted on my personal blog about the pain of being cut off, almost nobody replied. They sent condolences when my father died. They

---

[138] I am aware this language may be considered ableist, but I am also concerned about losing the richness of language to a rigid etiquette. My editor says this is not a hill I should die on, but I'm going to because it's relevant to my thesis. Having conflicting views is not the same as being enemies. Disagreement need not prevent us from also having productive agreements. Some will disapprove of my language choice. I hope they are able to so without discounting everything in this book, just as I am able to disagree with them while still respecting them.

sent condolences when my house burned down. But in response to my friend's abandonment, more painful than either of those events, they were silent. We are taught not to notice that cutoffs do harm. We are taught to regard them as carrying no ethical weight.

In his article, "How to Break Up Gracefully," life coach Mark Manson sums up this idea: "Once the relationship is severed, the other person's emotions are no longer your responsibility."[139] It's worth noting that this wording, like much popular relationship advice, implies a false dichotomy: another person's feelings are either your responsibility or they are not. All or nothing. We generally recognize (as Manson does) that someone else's emotions are never entirely our responsibility, regardless of whether we're in a serious relationship. We are less open to the idea that we have some responsibility for how we affect others' feelings, even if we are not in an ongoing, intimate relationship with them. In fact, many people bristle at such a suggestion. Our cultural values often suggest that disconnection is ethically neutral, even when it hurts others. As Zadro et al. note, "Studies of moral decision making repeatedly find that individuals see *omissions* that lead to harm to be more acceptable than *acts* that lead to harm."[140] Since ostracism is passive (simply refusing to engage), it falls into the category of an omission and is, thus, seen by many as more morally acceptable than other kinds of harm. Conversely, cutoff culture usually frames it as unethical to expect people to take steps to mitigate harm to those they cut off. This is regarded as imposing an unwarranted burden, often regardless of context.

Cord Jefferson illustrates this stance in his discussion of cutoff ethics in heterosexual romantic relationships. By his own account, his girlfriend, with whom he had happily discussed buying a house and having children, "turned her back on me without explanation… [and] ended a four-year relationship with just a two-minute phone call on New Year's Eve."[141] I do not know the full

---

[139] Mark Manson, "How to Break up with Someone," *Mark Manson: Life Advice That Doesn't Suck*, accessed April 27, 2021, https://markmanson.net/how-to-break-up-with-someone.

[140] Zadro et al., 132, (emphasis added).

[141] Cord Jefferson, "Men Aren't Entitled to Women's Time or Affection. But It's a Hard Lesson to Learn," *The Guardian*, July 18, 2014, https://www.theguardian.com/commentisfree/2014/jul/18/men-entitled-women-friendzone.

context, but based on what Jefferson shares, this sounds extraordinarily cruel. Yet Jefferson's point is that his girlfriend did nothing wrong. She owed him nothing. He underscores this thesis in the title of his essay: "Men Aren't Entitled to Women's Time or Affection." As a rule, I wholeheartedly agree. But if you ask me, "Does a person in a four-year relationship owe their partner more than an abrupt two-minute breakup on New Year's Eve?" Generally, I'd say yes. Yes, they do. Unless they are in a desperate situation, yes, they do. To be clear, I don't mean "owe" in the sense of an unalienable duty, regardless of context (see "desperation"), but in the sense of a responsibility inherent in basic decency. Yes, I think they do.

Jefferson describes intense attempts to try to reconcile with his girlfriend: "I called her a dozen times after our last tearful goodbye.... I emailed her a dozen more times after that.... I had flowers delivered."[142] In fact, he even planned a plane trip to "surprise" her with a reunion, a plan he wisely abandoned. He expresses regret for his fervent response, and it is not a response I would advocate. Yet his article implies that not only intense pursuit but any contact after any cutoff is uncategorically unethical. For example, Jefferson derides Reifman, who reports contacting his ex, whom he calls Emma, in only two emails after she cut him off.[143] Jefferson characterizes this as "continu[ing] for years to rehash a short relationship," suggesting that any contact is tantamount to severe intrusion. On the other hand, he implies any cutoff is ethically spotless, regardless of how abrupt or cruel it is. Of the girlfriend who cut off a four-year relationship with a two-minute phone call, he says, "She never owed me anything, and

---

142 Jefferson.

143 Reifman, "Shining Light on Relationship Cutoff." I suspect that many critiques of Reifman assume his communications with Emma prior to her explicitly cutting him off form a pattern of unwanted pursuit. However, he reports that, before she blocked his phone number, she was periodically participating in email communication. By his account, he did not know she wished to cut off contact. The act of contacting someone who has not refused contact cannot fairly be called violating a boundary. Yet this sense that a cuttee should infer someone wishes to cut them off is common. For example, it is a premise that underlies Lee and O'Sullivan's study of unwanted pursuit, which did not control for whether the pursuer knew contact was unwelcome.

what needed fixing back then wasn't her or us: it was me."[144] My point is not to pass judgment on Jefferson's girlfriend. She may have made the best choice. But even if she did, Jefferson's intense distress over her cutoff shows her actions harmed him. It seems strange to me to cast this harm not only as warranted (which it might have been) but as ethically *irrelevant.* Jefferson's show of personal responsibility is commendable, but the position that cutoff itself carries no ethical responsibility, regardless of context or consequence, enables harm by trivializing it.[145]

When I cut Ryan off, I didn't feel any ethical responsibility for any consequences of the cutoff either. I didn't put it that way to myself, but looking back on my sentiments, it's true. Being at the end of my emotional tether and, at that point in time, capable only of cussing him out or cutting him off, I decided that politely cutting him off would harm our relationship less, and I'm still inclined to think it was the less destructive choice. But the fact is I didn't view the cutoff as destructive at all; I viewed it as the noble way out. My hesitation to go to the extremity of cutoff came mostly from my own fear of losing a friend. My motives for not doing it sooner were largely selfish. As for Ryan, I just didn't think about his hurt. Shortly after I cut him off, a mutual friend told me that Ryan asked why I'd cut him off and with some show of anger. My only feeling about that was relief, because it told me Ryan cared, that's all. It wasn't that I wanted Ryan to be miserable; I just didn't see my actions as capable of doing worse than frustrating him, and being in considerable pain myself, I really didn't stop to think about it. It wasn't until years later I began to see the hurt.

In the statement he generously provided for this book, Ryan describes his view of this cutoff. "I know I felt blindsided," he says. "I knew we hadn't been writing as much as we had been, but I felt that was a natural progression as a result of time and distance."[146] Ryan didn't know why I cut him off. The only reasons

---

[144] Jefferson.

[145] My editor notes that cutting someone off is dehumanizing in that it tends to reduce the cuttee to just one thing: "He's a loser," for example. But, she notes, "Maybe there is something functional about that for the cutter. In order to be able to go through with it, they have to see things that black and white. Certainly, that is the way we talk about abusive relationships, which are the most difficult to leave." (editorial comment, October 3, 2023) I'm sure that's true for some cutters.

[146] Ryan, email message to the author, February 8, 2021.

he could think of seemed trivial. He says, "I wrote back trying to defend myself, and when I didn't get a reply I remember thinking something like 'well, if that's all it takes for her to cut me off then maybe it's not a friend worth having anyway.'"[147] I don't remember the email he refers to. I never blocked him, but I have no recollection of receiving an email in which he tried to defend himself, unless he's referring to a brief statement in which he said he thought I had misunderstood and I had a place of honor in his heart. I expect I didn't reply to that email because I'd already stated I needed to drop contact. But it's startling to me that he remembers with such a sense of betrayal something I don't clearly remember at all. If he is referring to that one brief statement, I remember I found it somewhat appeasing. It comforted me to think that I had, indeed, misunderstood and his care for me was deeper than I'd thought. That statement was probably the beginning of my healing, my lack of reply the start of his disillusion. I suspect these inverted emotional responses are common in cutoff, that the cutoff (at least initially) soothes the cutter at the same time it guts the cuttee. Sometimes the cutter needs that balm, harm to the cuttee notwithstanding. The harm remains real.

Ryan's hurt persisted a long time. Speaking of my first attempt to reconnect six years later, he says, "I think when you first reached out to me via [direct message] a few years back I definitely was just in a place where my knee-jerk response was 'why would I want to get back in touch with her?'"[148] While to my joy, he eventually relented, it's clear that my cutoff did genuine harm. It left him feeling baffled, betrayed, and trivialized. I'd argue that taking a course of action very likely to affect another person that way cannot reasonably be described as ethically neutral. It may be necessary, but I cannot call it weightless.

One of the things that makes me saddest about the impact of my cutoff on Ryan is that it left him feeling guilty for hurting *me*. I find it significant that in his statement for this book he wrote forty-two lines explaining, defending, and expressing regret for his own actions and only five lines on how I hurt *him*. Fourteen years after I cut him off, despite describing himself as a different person who's largely over it now, it's clear he still harbors pangs of conscience for what he perceives he did to receive that cutoff. And

---

[147] Ryan.

[148] Ryan.

when it comes to enumerating slights, he's not wrong; he has a pretty firm grasp on my reasoning at the time. But as I indicated in chapter 3, my disproportionate response to these actions derived largely from *me*, from my own insecurities and low self-esteem. Today, while I hold Ryan responsible for very little in our conflicts, it's clear he holds himself responsible for more. And while his sense of conscience speaks well of him, it illustrates the same ethical skew I find in Jefferson. When I cut Ryan off, our cultural assumptions (Ryan's and mine) automatically assigned the blame to him. I exonerated myself before the fact, while he carried years of guilt. I think the passage of time has moderated both our perspectives. I now see myself as mostly at fault, and he states he considers it all in the past. But there's no question in my mind: that initial skew left him bearing far too much burden.

My friend Casey's experience with cutoff, likewise, indicates the harm associated with this ethical skew. Casey's long-time best friend and former girlfriend, Ginsa, cut him off for several years due to emotional conflicts. (Both parties requested I not share details.) The cutoff was psychologically devastating for Casey. In the years that followed, I repeatedly witnessed him cry over it, ruminate on it, and express feelings of guilt, anger, confusion, and emotional helplessness. He worked with multiple therapists to process these feelings but with low-to-no relief. Throughout this time, Ginsa sometimes unblocked him or contacted him, only to block him again, sometimes after only a few messages. After about five years, she indicated an interest in being back in regular contact, though not emotionally intimate contact. Casey eagerly agreed. Even though they continued to have communication problems, he told me, "Just being back in contact was a huge weight off my shoulders."[149] For my part, I perceived a near instantaneous decrease in ongoing signs of trauma: the crying simply stopped; the rumination lessened.

Ginsa, however, requested they not have much discussion of the cutoff, something he felt a deep need to discuss. To date, she has acknowledged little responsibility or regret for hurting him. I don't know Ginsa as well as I know Casey, but I know her well enough to know she is a caring person: a devoted family member, great with kids, and in a successful, long-term partnership. I suspect she has not owned her role in Casey's pain because she is not

---

149 Casey in discussion with author, July 22, 2022.

fully aware that cutoff can cause (much) pain, just as I was not aware with Ryan. The logic model seems to be this: cutting someone off is ethically neutral, which means it's fine. But it is not fine to badly hurt someone. Therefore, cutoff must not badly hurt people. Therefore, Casey's pain must be insignificant next to Ginsa's. I don't know if this is Ginsa's reasoning, as she does not wish to talk about it. But it's a conjecture that fits with our cultural refusal of ethical responsibility to a person we cut off. I suspect this stance is implicated in years of suffering for Casey, which might have been greatly lessened if our cultural norms simply recognized that a cutoff would likely cause him significant pain.

Unfortunately, when our norms don't recognize this, we pass this lack of perception on to our kids, who then hurt other kids. My kids told me a story of one middle school student in their social circle whose friends blocked her on social media for reasons I suspect were fairly trivial. The next day, her friends, seeing her crying in the school hallway, asked a teacher, "What is she upset about?"

"She's upset," exclaimed the teacher, "because you blocked her!"[150]

These youngsters truly didn't understand that what they viewed as a small act of venting frustration caused their friend intense distress. Now, kids, by definition, are immature and still developing their sense of empathy. Yet I cannot help but note how closely their actions fit our cutoff norms. If someone has transgressed, the first recourse is to shut them out. The idea that cutoff can harm them often does not even register, yet the harm can be intense.

The Pain of Abandonment

It should, perhaps, be obvious that being permanently cut off by a loved one is a kind of abandonment, a painful experience that attacks our four core needs. It attacks our need to belong by separating us from a person or group we belonged to. It attacks our

[150] It's significant that what allowed these kids to see the harm they'd done was the face-to-face community made normative by our school system, which placed them in the same space with the person they'd ostracized. If they had been able to fully cut her off, just cease to interact with her, they might never have realized they'd done harm.

sense of control over our lives because there's nothing we can do about it. It attacks our self-esteem because it tells us we are not good enough to be around, a message that is deeply shaming. And it attacks our sense of meaning by removing a relationship we may have considered a core part of our lives.

The concept of abandonment is complicated. In our culture, some kinds are legal categories: parents can be prosecuted for abandoning minor children; health professionals can be sued for abandoning patients. That is not what this book is talking about. I am talking about emotional abandonment within interpersonal relationships, and I will use "abandonment" as a shorthand for that type of interpersonal situation.

To begin with, abandonment is hard to define—literally. Andrew Colman's *A Dictionary of Psychology* does not define it,[151] nor does *The Encyclopedia of Psychological Trauma.*[152] (Neither includes "cutoff" or "ostracism" either.) Ray Corsini's *The Dictionary of Psychology* defines an "abandonment reaction" as "A feeling of emotional deprivation, loss of support, and loneliness experienced by children deserted or neglected by one or both parents. Also experienced by adults who have lost a loved one on whom they have depended."[153] Clinical social worker and abandonment expert Susan Anderson, however, provides a more expansive characterization. Anderson calls abandonment "a cumulative wound containing all of the losses and disconnections stemming all the way back to childhood."[154] This impressionistic description is accompanied by examples ranging from "A woman being left by her husband of twenty years for another woman" to "A little boy wanting his mommy to pick him up from nursery school."[155] The top search for "define emotional abandonment" on one prominent search engine, produces a PsychCentral.com article

---

[151] Andrew M. Coleman, *A Dictionary of Psychology*, Fourth edition (Oxford: Oxford University Press, 2015).

[152] *The Encyclopedia of Psychological Trauma*, edited by Gilbert Reyes, Jon D. Elhai, and Julian D. Ford, (Hoboken, NJ: Wiley, 2008).

[153] Ray Corsini, *The Dictionary of Psychology*, (New York: Taylor and Francis Group, 2001), *ProQuest Ebook Central*, https://ebookcentral.proquest.com/lib/psu/detail.action?docID=4758773.

[154] Susan Anderson, "Q&A," *Healing Abandonment with Susan Anderson*, accessed April 18, 2024, https://www.abandonment.net/faqs-1.

[155] Anderson, "Q&A."

appealingly titled "What Is Emotional Abandonment?" But the article doesn't define it either; it talks about signs and symptoms and how it feels.[156] Yet this is the source *Wikipedia* cites for its definition. Though its editors appear to have made it up, *Wikipedia*'s definition is the best fit I have found for Anderson's rather poetic characterization: "Emotional abandonment is a subjective emotional state in which people feel undesired, left behind, insecure, or discarded."[157]

Why is it so hard to find a clear, agreed-on definition? One reason is that abandonment *is* hard to define. It's subjective and complicated. However, I would argue that this lack of basic discussion of terminology is also a sign of how much our culture dismisses abandonment harm. Emotional abandonment, like cutoffs, is not considered very important. In a society oriented around codified rights and duties, this absence of definition implies that abandonment doesn't exist as an ethical category.

Corsini's, Anderson's, and *Wikipedia*'s descriptions all imply this. In Anderson's poetic formulation, abandonment *is* the person abandoned: the wife, the little boy; it resides in the abandoned person. Similarly, Corsini's "abandonment *reaction*" among adults is "a feeling" the abandoned person has after they "have lost a loved one...." Linguistically, no one has abandoned them; they are the agent who has lost someone.[158] Wikipedia echoes this: "Emotional abandonment is a subjective emotional state...." It is, by definition, a feeling we have, not a thing that happened to us. It has no objective referent in the outside world. There is good reason for this. Different people will feel abandoned for a host of different reasons based on their own personalities and histories. One person might feel abandoned by a friend's distraction during a conversation. Another might be left by a longtime partner and scarcely feel abandoned at all. Because it is not possible to

---

[156] "What Is Emotional Abandonment?" PsychCentral.com, May 17, 2016, https://psychcentral.com/lib/what-is-emotional-abandonment#5.

[157] "Abandonment (emotional)," *Wikipedia*, accessed March 4, 2021, https://en.wikipedia.org/wiki/Abandonment_%28emotional%29.

[158] The whimsical part of me is reminded on Lady Bracknell's observation in Oscar Wilde's *The Importance of Being Earnest*: "To lose one parent, Mr. Worthing, may be regarded as a misfortune; to lose both looks like carelessness." Act 1, accessed May 9, 2024, https://www.gutenberg.org/files/844/844-h/844-h.htm.

concretely define what actions cause emotional abandonment, it makes sense to strip causes from the definition.

Yet the rhetorical elimination of an *abandoner* is significant. We feel abandoned, but no one has abandoned us. By implication, we feel hurt, but no one has hurt us. In this system, abandoning carries no ethical significance. There is no duty not to abandon. Therefore, within a rights-and-duties framework, there is nothing wrong with abandoning someone because only actions that violate rights or shirk duties can be wrong. Of course, few people hold this view in its extreme form. We've all commiserated with a friend over the so-and-so who ran out on them. We know abandonment does harm. Yet the constant cultural implication that it does not tends to erode this knowledge. It encourages us to forget.

There is, indeed, no duty not to abandon, and there shouldn't be. Sometimes we have to abandon someone. To use an obvious example, a person being physically abused by their partner is very sensible to leave them. The partner will probably feel abandoned. In some sense, she has abandoned them, but leaving is still a healthy thing to do. Yet the fact that abandoning someone can be right—indeed the fact that it is *a* right—does not mean it does no harm. It does not mean it is not traumatizing.

In her work on abandonment trauma, Anderson, a survivor of abandonment herself, identifies five stages of healing what she calls "the abandonment wound" and describes them as follows:

- Shattering: Knife in the Heart
- Withdrawal [as in "drug withdrawal"]: Acute Pain of the Open Wound
- Internalizing: Most Susceptible to Infection; Festering, Throbbing Pain
- Rage: Hot, Agitated, Nagging, and Pulling of Torn Flesh Trying to Mend
- Lifting: Scar Tissue Forms Over the Wound, Numbing the Area[159]

She depicts every stage as a physical injury. Even the final stage is not full healing but scarring, a numbness, a learning to live with

---

[159] Susan Anderson, *The Journey from Abandonment to Healing* (New York: Berkley Books, 2000), 219.

the wound's remains. Anderson notes that it is common for people "to experience their abandonment as a physical, even *mortal* wound"[160] [emphasis in original]. In an essay for the relationship website P.S. I Love You, Crystal Jackson describes being cut off by a friend as an amputation:

> I carried one loss [of the friend] with me for 10 long years, missing that person like a lost limb. This was a friend, not a lover, but it may be the strongest sense of loss I've ever experienced in my life. He managed to delete me entirely from his life as if I never existed at all.
>
> But I could never write him out of mine.
>
> Actually, he came to define mine, although he doesn't know it and may never realize it. That loss became something that defined me…
>
> Nothing had ever hurt like that, and I spent years grieving that loss.[161]

In a case study Anderson cites, a woman whose husband left her for someone else was so devastated that, for a protracted period, she was almost unable to eat. She says, "I would have preferred that he just stuck a knife in my heart. It would have been less painful, quicker, and saved me from nearly starving myself to death."[162] In fact, Anderson notes, many people liken being abandoned to death.[163] This is a powerful observation, and one I take up at greater length in Appendix B on surviving cutoff. Here, it is enough to say abandonment (re)ignites trauma, not just in a few overly sensitive people but as a typical human response. There is good reason for this.

Abandonment breaks your heart and blames you for it. If you weren't unworthy, goes the reasoning, you wouldn't be deserted, right? You must have done something to merit it, right? As Anderson puts it,

---

160 Anderson, 32.

161 Crystal Jackson, "You Deleted Me from Your Life. I Couldn't Write You out of Mine," P.S. I Love You. January 3, 2019, https://medium.com/p-s-i-love-you/you-deleted-me-from-your-life-i-couldnt-write-you-out-of-mine-bb1178896710.

162 Anderson, 33.

163 Anderson, 32.

> At the center of the emotional wound created when a loved one leaves is *shame*—the terrible shame of being thrown away. Shame is what drives you to keep silent about your feelings. *Loss* can be worked through, it can mitigated, it can be displaced, it can be projected, channeled, medicated, lessened. But the shame of abandonment evades almost all remedies.[164]

Shame is a profoundly social feeling, intimately connected with the fear being rejected by others. Shame researcher Brené Brown says, "I often refer to shame as the fear of disconnection—the fear of being perceived as flawed or unworthy of belonging."[165] Shame in the context of abandonment is intensified by a culture that, regardless of context, often exonerates the abandoner. Abandonment is a subjective state: it's all in your head, so if it hurts you, you must be crazy. If you're crazy, that's your problem, no one else's. The person responsible for the abandonment wound is, thus, the person who has been abandoned.

Anderson observes that many abandonment survivors experience symptoms of post-traumatic stress disorder (PTSD); in fact, she considers this phenomenon significant enough to identify it as a sub-category of PTSD, which she calls post-traumatic stress disorder of abandonment.[166] And yet, Anderson notes, abandonment is not commonly treated as trauma: "abandonment survivors experience many of the same symptoms as victims of other types of trauma.... The difference is that abandonment survivors are often not recognized as such."[167] In fact, PTSD of abandonment is not recognized as a diagnostic category.[168] Abandonment is a trauma often compounded by little social acknowledgment of the trauma.

---

164 Anderson, 134.

165 Brené Brown, *I Thought It Was Just Me (But It Isn't): Telling the Truth about Perfectionism, Inadequacy, and Power* (New York: Gotham Books, 2008), xxv.

166 Anderson, 39.

167 Anderson, 48–49.

168 Susan Anderson, "Borderline vs. Post-Traumatic Stress Disorder of Abandonment: Therapy Goals," Healing Abandonment, accessed June 27, 2024, https://www.abandonment.net/articles/bpd-vs-ptsd-of-abandonment.

It is a broken heart multiplied by shame multiplied by isolation. Abandonment in the context of cutoff is worse.

Within the context of serious emotional relationships, permanent cutoff is a particularly extreme form of abandoning. It is not just breaking up, not just a divorce, not just the removal of an intimate support: it is any or all of those things multiplied by a lifelong (or very long) refusal of the most basic human communication. It is a refusal to discuss what happened, a refusal of any future amicability, a refusal of any reconciliation, often even on the basic level of being able to say "hello" at a party. It is a reduction of a once loving relationship not to acquaintanceship or even to the state of being strangers but to enmity. Strangers can strike up a conversation. People prohibited from doing even that are, at least socially, enemies. The cutter may not *feel* enmity. They may have cut someone off because, for whatever reason, they had to, not because they hate the cuttee or wish them harm. Both Cole and Carolyn, for example, have expressed ongoing love for the people they cut off.[169] Nonetheless, when someone is shunned so totally that even the chitchat a cashier and customer might exchange is forbidden, the cutter's internal feelings do not alter the social reality. The relation is enmity. There is no other social category it can be. Cutoff abandonment is heartbreak multiplied by shame multiplied by isolation multiplied by a promise of lifelong enmity with someone you have loved. It is not a thing to inflict on someone lightly.

The Compounded Pain of Being Ghosted

The pain caused by cutoff is only exacerbated by ghosting, the practice of simply dropping out of contact with no communication about it. To be clear, this chapter focuses on practices our culture commonly endorses, and most experts do not endorse ghosting. While ghosting is common and many individuals defend it, most professional dating and psychological advice rightly

[169] I should clarify that Cole's conception of cutoff does not fit with "cutoff culture." It seems an older understanding of cutoff, where the cuttee is not prohibited from attempting contact; the cutter will simply not reply—or someday, maybe they will. All the boundaries feel more flexible.

repudiates it in cases where personal safety is not at risk. Psychologist Loren Soeiro sums up the common wisdom:

> [G]hosting is, by and large, not a great way to treat people you respect. It's passive-aggressive, it's self-protective at the expense of other people's feelings, and it's hard to stop: People who are ghosted become more likely to do the same to someone else.... [E]ven a brief explanation is much, much better than none at all.[170]

Hopefully, most of us already agree that ghosting is not a good practice. Nonetheless, I'll share one story of ghosting because it remains a common practice and fits the paradigm of the more controversial issue of ethical responsibility for cutoff in general.

Arlo and Kendra became friends in grad school, hanging out, studying together, and emotionally supporting each other for over two years, sometimes with frequent meetups, sometimes with gaps to accommodate their busy lives.[171] In the midst of this hectic life, Arlo didn't notice at first that Kendra had ceased to reply to his texts and voicemails. When they ran into each other a couple of times, it was cordial but never led to getting back in touch. Over several months, it dawned on him that she appeared to have ghosted him, and he didn't know why. There'd been no fight, no falling out.

The only thing he could think of was one seemingly small incident. Kendra had shared a story about her dating life, and Arlo had mentioned it to a mutual friend. While Kendra didn't ask him to keep her story in confidence, Arlo says in retrospect that was implied, and he should not have shared anything without her permission. A while later, a rumor got back to Kendra that Arlo had said something disapproving about her dating life. He had not done this. When Kendra confronted him about it, he explained the rumor was false, but it was true he'd shared some of her confidence. He apologized for this breach of trust, and she appeared

---

[170] Loren Soeiro, "7 Essential Psychological Truths about Ghosting," *Psychology Today*, February 25, 2019, https://www.psychologytoday.com/us/blog/i-hear-you/201902/7-essential-psychological-truths-about-ghosting.

[171] Arlo in discussion with the author, December 17, 2021. The following account is entirely taken from this interview.

to believe him and accept his apology. But shortly after that, she dropped out of contact. Was this incident the reason she ghosted him? Did the ghosting have anything to do with him or was it about issues in her own life? Was it even an intentional cutoff? Over ten years later, Arlo still doesn't know.

He did try to contact her a handful of times. Over ten years, he sent two or three texts and two or three voicemails. Her phone's voicemail message was generic, and he isn't certain if the number was still hers. Early on, he also tried once to catch up with her in person, waiting for her on her route to class. On that occasion, he asked her if they could talk. She said she had no time but would call him later, but never did. He never tried this tactic again, telling me he didn't want to be "stalkerish." He also asked a mutual friend to convey that he'd like to talk and apologize again, but this never resulted in contact.

When Arlo talked with me about his situation after more than ten years of silence from Kendra, he was in tears. "It drives me crazy when I think about it still," he said. "The uncertainty of it all just eats at me." This excruciating uncertainty exemplifies what Williams calls the *bewilderment* of ostracism.[172] "There's no one to talk to, so there's no resolution," said Arlo. "Because the only person capable of providing that for me isn't engaged." Of ghosting in general, Arlo says, "I think it's cruel." He notes that it provides no chance to adjust objectionable behavior, no chance to explain, by legal analogy, no "court." If Arlo hurt Kendra, he would like to atone, but as he observes, "It makes it hard to pursue that idea of atonement if I don't even know what I'm atoning for, or if it's even real."[173]

Arlo is speaking specifically of ghosting, which is a particularly damaging means of cutoff. However, many of his observations apply to cutoff overall. As Soeiro asserts, a clear cutoff message—even a short, sharp one—is vastly preferable to ghosting. Yet even a clear, polite message, even a few short messages over a few years, will rarely be sufficient explain why a close relationship ended in permanent ostracism: human relationships are simply too

---

[172] Williams, 21.

[173] My editor adds, "It seems quite possible she just didn't reply with anything because she didn't know what to say... and then that went on too long." (Editorial comment, October 20, 2023.) I agree, and that's one of the tragedies of cutoff culture.

complex, too constantly in flux. That makes closure, or even basic comprehension, elusive. Regardless of whether the cuttee has a right to closure (by the terminology of this book, the answer is no), that irremediable bewilderment is often intensely painful. Such pain is a natural cost of cutoff, and, yes, sometimes the need for cutoff is worth the price. But to say an action highly likely to cause long-term distress carries *no* ethical weight is a damaging principle. A healthy society does not ignore pain. Like an economic system that discounts ecological damage, our spreadsheet may balance, but the real costs keep piling up.

Chapter 6

Cutoff as a Responsible Way to End a Relationship

Tenet 2. Permanent cutoff is an effective, low-harm way to end relationships because it sets and maintains clear boundaries, which reduces mixed signals and maximizes self-protection.

Four years into writing this book, I felt squished pancake flat from reading endless articles on relationships that went wrong. Seeking a hook for this chapter and my research mojo all dried up, I reached out to couple of social networks and asked if anyone cared to share a story about a romantic breakup where they'd cut off their ex and felt better for it.

One friend quipped, "I think you've described all my breakups."

Fair enough.

Cutting off contact with an ex is very common and often comes as a relief. It won't surprise you to hear I'm going to argue that things are not quite so straightforward.

Prescribing Cutoff as a Breakup Best Practice

Most relationship experts advise a period of no contact after breaking up with someone, and that makes a great deal of sense. A period of no contact allows the addiction-like withdrawal symptoms to lessen, and it can spare both parties the pain of ill-advised words spoken in pain and anger. Many advise a no-contact period of a month to a year and note that exes sometimes do maintain or develop friendships in the future, once there has been a chance to heal. That's all perfectly reasonable.

It's also worth noting that romances come in all shapes and sizes. A romantic breakup might mean that two people who went on a few dates decided it didn't work, or it could mean two best friends are getting divorced after twenty years. In most cases, when a relationship has been superficial, the two parties are likely not to stay in contact or feel much drive to. One of them may protest at first: it's hard to be the dumpee. But after a few weeks or months, it will all be in the past. Delia said of cutoffs, "Most people on either end of the situation [cutter or cuttee] would say that a clear [sic] break is kinder, because then you can move on."[174] She may be right, but if two people ending a relationship prefer this, it is not much of a cutoff; it's just a mutual agreement, explicit or implicit, not to stay in touch.[175]

Yet much popular breakup advice does not distinguish between breakups in serious and superficial relationships. It does not distinguish between consensual and non-consensual silence. It tends to assume one size fits all. This assumption frames cutoff as so emotionally low impact that it doesn't really matter whether it is short-term, long-term, or forever; absolute (no contact ever tolerated) or impressionistic (just not inviting ongoing contact). But cutoff is often not low impact, and these distinctions are critical.

Human beings are social by nature, and being ostracized (including cutoff) threatens our core need to belong. In their review of over twenty years of research on the physiological consequences of social rejection, Ellie Shuo Jin and Robert A. Josephs observe that when we are socially rejected, the same areas of our brain are activated as when we are in physical pain.[176] The longer the rejection continues, the more extensive the consequences can be. Jin and Josephs note,

---

[174] Delia in discussion with author, February 27, 2020.

[175] I've dropped communication with and been dropped by a majority of the people I ever went on dates with. I don't consider myself cut off. They never ordered me to stay away; I never ordered them. We're not on hostile terms. This is vastly different from a cutoff. We could meet in the street and say hello. That's the difference.

[176] Ellie Shuo Jin, and Robert A. Josephs, "Acute and Chronic Physiological Consequences of Social Rejection," *Ostracism, Exclusion, and Rejection*, edited by Kipling D. Williams, and Steve A. Nida. (New York: Routledge, 2017), 82.

> Whereas immediate response to social exclusion includes negative mood, heightened physiological arousal and hostility, prolonged social exclusion and the resulting social isolation has been linked to chronic dysregulation of the HPA axis [hypothalamic pituitary adrenal axis, involved in fight-or-flight response], decreased immune function, and increased risk of a disarmingly wide variety of serious diseases.[177]

In other words, being excluded can put us in a state akin to long-term fight or flight, an acute stress response our bodies are not designed to sustain for long, including elevated cortisol, a stress hormone[178] and elevated testosterone, which is linked to aggression.[179] It may be intuitively obvious that it sucks to be excluded, but a significant body of research shows that it is also dangerous to our physical health, with potentially long-term physiological consequences.

Unfortunately, it is not uncommon for relationship advice to advocate extreme kinds of cutoff, regardless of context. Often advice articles do not specify if this cutoff should be temporary or permanent. For example, blogger Zoë Griggs writes, "Day of the split—contact purge. Block them everywhere: [list of social media names] and your phone, along with unfollows on [additional social media names]."[180] She also makes the sensible observation that you should not hack into your ex's online accounts—which, indeed, you shouldn't—and that's all she says about contact with the ex. She does not indicate that we should give any warning or explanation or sign of whether we ever intend to allow the person to contact us again.

This sentiment is echoed in greater depth by Elizabeth Svoboda in *Psychology Today*. Citing Florida State University psychology professor Roy Baumeister,[181] she states:

---

[177] Shuo Jin, and Josephs, 88.
[178] Shuo Jin, and Josephs, 82.
[179] Shuo Jin, and Josephs, 83.
[180] Zoë Griggs, "How to Handle a Breakup: 10 Do's and 5 Don'ts," ThoughtCatalog.com, September 23, 2014, https://thoughtcatalog.com/zoe-griggs/2014/09/how-to-handle-a-breakup-10-dos-and-5-donts/.
[181] Baumeister is an expert on ostracism. Elsewhere, his work shows that he understands its impacts, so I find it interesting that the quotes

> Do not try to cushion the blow by suggesting future friendly meetups. "Saying 'Let's be friends' might be a way for the rejecter to try to handle their own guilt, but it's not always good for the person being rejected." Baumeister observes. "Such a misguided attempt to spare a partner pain can leave him or her hopeful there might be a chance at future reconciliation, which can hinder the efforts of both parties to move on."[182]

It's true that meetups can stoke false hopes, yet this advice is problematic in its vagueness. Does not suggesting future friendly meetups mean the ex is, in fact, cut off—no contact? What if the ex suggests a friendly meetup? Presumably that same advice would apply: say no; don't try to be friends. But what does that actually mean? Not replying? Saying, "Don't contact me again"? Stay social media friends but refuse to hang out? If the two people aren't friends anymore, what are the parameters for contact? What is acceptable? This is a crucial question, but it is not addressed at all.

While this passage is unclear about whether it is advocating total no contact, the article later becomes explicit:

> In her neuroimaging studies, [relationship researcher] Helen Fisher found that the withdrawal-like reaction afflicting romantic rejectees diminished with time, indicating that they were well on their way to healing. But the recovery process is fragile, says Fisher, and last-ditch attempts to make contact or win back an ex can scuttle it. "If you suddenly get an email from the person, you can

---

shared in Svoboda's article don't seem to register breakup cutoff as having the impacts of ostracism.

182 Elizabeth Svoboda, "The Thoroughly Modern Guide to Breakups: How to End Affairs with Dignity and Minimal Distress," *Psychology Today*, January 1, 2011, reviewed on June 9, 2016, https://www.psychologytoday.com/us/articles/201101/the-thoroughly-modern-guide-breakups.

> get right into the craving for them again." To expedite moving on, she recommends abstaining from any kind of contact with the rejecter: "Throw out the cards and letters.[183] Don't call. And don't try to be friends."[184]

I previously noted that my friend Lyn conflated my anger at Sophia's *cutting me off* with anger at her *ending our friendship*. My second therapist did the same thing, assuming my central problem was that I wanted Sophia back as a friend. They aren't getting it from nowhere. Svoboda (and arguably her sources) performs the same conflation again. "Don't protest a partner's decision [to break up *romantically*]" is considered equivalent to "accept that the relationship [including *friendship*] has come to an unequivocal end" is considered equivalent to "abstain from any kind of contact." Yet these are three different things. A person can accept someone has broken up with them and stay friends (i.e. in some sort of relationship). Two people can cease to be friends and still have some sort of contact (e.g. at parties). No longer dating someone but being civil acquaintances is a radically different condition from no longer dating someone and blocking all contact for life. Yet this passage treats them as the same thing, or the difference as too trivial to discuss.

Again, this passage makes no explicit statement about whether the prescribed cutoff should be permanent, but "unequivocal end" implies it should be. The reason stated is to speed the alleviation of withdrawal symptoms that come from the end of a romance. As anyone who has suffered a broken heart knows, these symptoms hurt like hell. But they are generally temporary.[185] This passage seems to advocate a lifelong straitjacket to prevent us scratching a passing rash. Of course, that may not be the intent. I would be surprised if any of these experts objected to two exes saying "hi" if they bump into each other in a train station after twenty years. But how long *are* you supposed to cut someone off?

---

183 I have mixed feelings about the advice to throw things out. Since Sophia's cutoff, I have thrown out some documents pertaining to our relationship and kept others. I've felt regret and relief about both choices.

184 Svoboda.

185 When Sophia stopped being my friend, it broke my heart. That pain lasted about two years. As I write this, the pain of the *cutoff* is at nine years and counting—fading but still very present.

How absolutely? Should you shun them at a conference? Turn your head away in the street? When you are cut off, these details are critical. They are the difference between basic social inclusion and ostracism; between civility to an acquaintance and perceived harassment; between allowing time to heal and asserting lifelong enmity. Yet even professional psychological advice often does not register that these differences exist.

The purpose of the article professes to be minimizing the pain of breakups. Indeed, it is subtitled "How to End Affairs with Dignity and Minimal Distress." Svoboda further articulates this goal, saying, "The challenge of breaking up is to close the relationship definitively and honorably, without devaluing oneself or the person who previously met one's deepest needs."[186] It is ironic, then, that the article advocates the default use of cutoff, because cutoff is a form of ostracism and being ostracized is immensely devaluing. Being ostracized by someone whose deepest needs you used to meet is likely to be felt as an outrage.

This normalization of cutoff is common.[187] ReGain's article, "How to Get over Your Breakup" advises cutoff and opens with, "This may sound like a no-brainer."[188] Of course, we cut people off. Who wouldn't? Total disconnection from someone we've cared for: it's common sense! The article goes on to assert,

> To get over a breakup, you need to stop communicating with your ex—completely. Stop answering their phone

186 Svoboda.

187 It is so normalized to shun our exes that the Higher Ed Works training for Washington State employees advises trainees that, after a romantic breakup with a co-worker, "you should... Firmly refuse all invitations for dates or other personal interaction outside of work," to avoid difficult work situations. In effect, even the state advocates a soft form of breakup cutoff. It seems to me that advising employees on how to conduct their personal relationships in off-work hours when they are violating no law or policy is an overreach of state power. That this slipped by the training's editors speaks to the normalization of interpersonal disconnection. "Sexual Harassment," Higher Ed Works, accessed May 8, 2024, https://www.publicschoolworks.com/LMS/Student/lmsStudentView.php?di=423&dia=8rkm3&landing=transpage#.

188 "How to Get over Your Breakup," ReGain, Medically Reviewed by Audrey Kelly, LMFT, August 10, 2021, https://www.regain.us/advice/how-to/how-to-get-over-a-breakup/.

> calls and texts and stop reaching out to them in search of answers to what went wrong in your relationship. Staying in touch with an ex is dangerous because your emotions can take over, and you may find yourself wanting to get back together with the person. All relationships end for a reason, and talking to your ex will just make it harder to move on.[189]

In this formulation, not only is cutoff good practice, but not cutting off your ex is "dangerous" because it can make the breakup emotionally harder. Like *Psychology Today*, the article doesn't specify that the cutoff should be lifelong, but it doesn't suggest it shouldn't be. The typical conflation of ending a type a relationship (dating) with ending all relationality (friendship, acquaintanceship, kindness) suggests it's over: these two people should ideally never cross paths again.

Michelle Greene, a writer for the holistic health and wellness site Flowing Free, takes a gentler tone toward "cutting ties." Her conception is predominantly mental, severing emotionally negative energetic threads to allow the space for the positive. In many cases, she advocates this process within relationships that are likely to be ongoing. However, she notes the same process may be used for a permanent social cutoff as well. The article radiates calm and caring. In a rare move in breakup advice, Greene even acknowledges the grieving process of the other party: "Be aware that the person who has been cut [i.e. who you have cut an emotional tie to] may feel a sense of loss and try to reach out to you. If your wish is not to reconnect with this person, then allow adequate time for them to adjust."[190] I appreciate this acknowledgment that grief may be worth accommodation; it's a truly compassionate statement. That makes it all the more striking, therefore, how self-centered the article advises us to be.

As is common, Greene does little to differentiate between permanent cutoff and other types of cutting ties. To the extent she does differentiate, she offers this:

---

189 "How to Get over Your Breakup," ReGain.

190 Michelle Greene, "Cutting Ties: A Simple Technique for Getting Rid of Emotional Baggage," Flowing Free, accessed May 7, 2021, https://flowingfree.org/cutting-ties-a-simple-way-to-free-yourself-from-emotional-baggage/.

> Before cutting ties take a moment to acknowledge the relationship. If it is with a person you wish to remove from your life completely, think of how that relationship positively influenced your life, any lessons you may have learned, and what you are allowing into your life by cutting ties that connect you to that person.[191]

In other words, if you are about to start ostracizing someone for life, stop to appreciate how that person has profited you and how abandoning them may allow you to have better things. This may be a reasonable stance toward a milkshake. I drank it. It was nice. Then, I threw away the cup to keep my cup holder free.[192] It is a problematic stance toward a fellow human being. Again—because it bears repeating—cutoff is often necessary. If it is necessary to cut someone off and we can still find something good in having known them, that's good. Indeed, it may be a sign of astounding maturity. It can certainly be making the best of a tragic situation. The piece that's missing from Greene's article is the acknowledgment of the tragedy, the acknowledgment of the reality that cutting someone off is potentially far more damaging than other types of transformations in relationships, such as lessening contact or intimate sharing. This absence exemplifies our culture's failure to see the harm of cutoff. Greene is clearly writing from a place of compassion. She wants to help her readers; she doesn't advocate needlessly hurting anyone. Her article simply shows no awareness that cutoff can have the force of psychological assault, and that to focus only on the benefit you got from someone you're assaulting is neither compassionate nor peaceful.

---

[191] Greene.

[192] I say this may be a reasonable stance toward a milkshake, but actually there's nothing reasonable about the dominance of single-use, throwaway cups, which add to landfill, pollution, and our ecologically damaging culture. It's not a coincidence that the culture that routinely "throws away" people via cutoff is the same culture that routinely throws away literal trash. It is a culture caught in cycles of waste, devaluation, and disconnection from responsibility and reciprocity.

How Well Does Cutoff Work for Self-Protection?

Cutoff often harms the cuttee, and yet sometimes it's needed. Sometimes it keeps the cutter safe—physically and/or emotionally. But how reliable is that safety? Setting aside the cuttee's feelings, how well do cutoff boundaries protect the cutter? To what extent is cutoff, in fact, the clear path to self-protection that it's often framed as being?

Cutoff is about setting boundaries, but what exactly are "boundaries"? For all the emphasis popular psychology puts on maintaining good boundaries, psychology research uses the term surprisingly rarely. The most common usage I have seen is in the context of professional boundaries between practitioner and client, certainly not the most common usage on the internet. When I asked polyvagal psychologist Rebecca Bailey how she would define "boundaries," she paused in thought, then described them as "what we need to do to help our nervous system attain a place of regulation and safety."[193] In other words, boundaries are a way to protect our mental health by placing conditions on what behaviors we will accept from others.

My editor is adamant that we must distinguish between *boundaries* and *rules*. She observes,

> The way I understand boundaries (in the relational sense that you are using) is as rules of behavior for the person making the boundary. I can say, "If you speak to me in that condescending tone, I will end the conversation." They can still speak in a condescending tone, but it is up to me to DO the boundary action of ending the conversation. It is not saying, "You may not speak to me in a condescending tone." It doesn't set their behavior only my own.[194]

In this view, *rules* are essentially "you may (not)" statements and *boundaries* "I will (not)" statements. The difference is who is responsible for taking or refraining from action. This is a tidy and useful distinction—which I will not use in this book because our everyday culture doesn't use it. We say, "You need to respect my

---

[193] Rebecca Bailey in discussion with author, January 28, 2024.
[194] Editorial comment, October 25, 2023.

boundaries," not "You need to follow my rules, and if you don't, I will respond by enforcing this boundary." Corsini defines a "boundary" in a relationship as "A barrier... in which rules are established as to who may participate and who may not participate in certain activities,"[195] explicitly incorporating "rules" in the "boundary." In general, our culture favors the concept of boundaries as a shared responsibility: yours to set them, mine to heed them. When I asked Dr. Bailey who she thought was responsible for maintaining boundaries—the boundary setter, boundary respecter/violator, and/or bystanders—she said ideally everyone should be. She spoke of "the dance of the nervous systems," the social phenomenon of our different nervous systems interacting. In this dance, she said, "We all need to pay more attention." We should ideally all strive to be more aware of our impacts on others.[196]

PsychCentral, a popular and respected source for online psychological advice,[197] offers the following common-sense insight into the importance of setting boundaries:

> Setting boundaries is simply about communicating your needs for healthy interaction to someone else. It isn't always easy. Not everyone may like or understand your boundaries or your reasons for setting them. But if you don't set those boundaries, you certainly can't expect them to be followed.
>
> It often takes courage and strength to set boundaries, but when you do so, you can feel comfortable knowing your lines have been set. Your needs have been communicated. And if someone chooses to violate your boundaries after that, you would be within your rights to

---

[195] Ray Corsini, *The Dictionary of Psychology* (New York: Taylor & Francis Group, 2001), 124, ProQuest Ebook Central, https://ebookcentral.proquest.com/lib/psu/detail.action?docID=4758773.

[196] Bailey.

[197] PsychCentral was found to be a generally credible source for mental health information by John M. Grohol, Joseph Slimowicz, and Rebecca Granda, "The Quality of Mental Health Information Commonly Searched for on the Internet," *Cyberpsychology, Behavior and Social Networking*, 17, no. 4 (2014): 219.

> create further distance between yourself and that person.[198]

Cutting off all contact with someone and demanding no contact in return is a kind of boundary setting, and in some cases, it is necessary. Many people have difficulty respecting boundaries and, in some cases, any chink in the wall becomes an excuse for them to chisel away. A typical example is the experience my friend's teen daughter, Tilly, had with an ex-boyfriend, Clyde. In this case, Tilly attempted to stay on friendly terms after they broke up, but Clyde used her civility as an opening to regularly put her down or badger her to get back together. She refused his advances but continued to speak to him. After a few weeks, he began to stalk her in a traditional and unambiguous sense: staking out her house in his car, calling at odd hours and hanging up if anyone else answered the landline, and so on. Moderate boundaries had not worked: he interpreted every micron of tolerance as an invitation to demand her attention. Finally, Tilly's mother persuaded her that zero tolerance was the only solution. They would not speak to him on the phone. They would call the police if they saw his car.[199] Tilly would ignore him at school. After a few weeks of this total cutoff, he gave up and permanently stopped pursuing her. In this case, absolute cutoff was the language he understood, and once the family implemented it, he got the message fairly quickly. This is a reasonable use of absolute cutoff. And this part is important: it is in response to an extreme situation, a situation where someone has made it clear that more moderate boundaries will not work to maintain respectful and healthy social relations.

In this case, cutoff prompted a stalker to go away. In some cases, however, cutoff may actually exacerbate Unwanted Relationship Pursuit (URP) behaviors, behaviors commonly identified as stalking tactics. Far from making the cuttee safer, it may make them less safe. Cutoff is a form of ostracism. In her study of eight

---

[198] Leah Campbell, "Why Personal Boundaries Are Important and How to Set Them," PsychCentral, medically reviewed by Bethany Juby, June 8, 2021, https://psychcentral.com/lib/what-are-personal-boundaries-how-do-i-get-some#why-its-important.

[199] This option is culturally enabled by the fact that all people in this case are white and can generally expect the police to treat them with respect.

cases of unwanted relationship pursuit, Shelley Carolyn Taylor found, "For some of the cases, the feeling of being ostracized appeared to fuel more serious URP behaviors."[200] As previously noted, abandonment, of which cutoff is one example, is deeply tied to shame,[201] and shame, Taylor observes, "has been identified as a risk factor in aggressive behavior... and has been associated with stalking."[202] Intuitively this makes sense; at least, it makes a great deal of sense to me as person who has been cut off. As Williams notes, ostracism assaults our need to belong, our sense of control over our lives, our self-esteem, and our sense of being a meaningful, visible person in the world.[203] Unsurprisingly, these wounds can lead to such intense distress that self-regulation becomes difficult, potentially resulting in less self-controlled, more aggressive behavior.[204] Brené Brown shares, "Personally, I've learned that when I'm experiencing shame, I often act out in ways that are inconsistent with who I want to be. Again, we see the fight, flight, or freeze behaviors."[205] In some cases, cutoff may make the cutter less safe.

But wait, it gets even more complicated. Taylor's study also found the rejected parties "were more likely to slow down or abandon their relational pursuit goals after feeling shamed and betrayed. This supports previous findings that perceived hurtful behaviors could elicit feelings of shame... and that people tend to distance themselves, figuratively or literally, from the source of the pain."[206] This makes intuitive sense as well: it's natural to avoid pain. Here, we have another paradox: shame is associated with intensified pursuit and also with diminished pursuit. Do shaming acts, such as cutoff, serve to protect the cutter from unwanted pursuit or not?

You can already hear me saying, "It's contextual." I'll offer my own context as just one way out of this paradox. I felt shamed and betrayed by Sophia's cutoff. This sense of shame and betrayal did,

---

200 Taylor, 231.

201 Anderson, 134.

202 Taylor, 267.

203 Williams, 245.

204 C. Nathan DeWall, Brian Enjaian, and Sarah Beth Bell, "Only the Lonely: The Curious Case of Exclusion and Aggression," *Ostracism, Exclusion, and Rejection*, edited by Kipling D. Williams, and Steve A. Nida (New York: Routledge, 2017), 95–112. See especially pp. 100–05.

205 Brown, 29.

206 Taylor, 244.

in fact, produce both these effects in me. It intensified my perceived need to make contact with her, and it lessened my desire to pursue an active relationship with her. In the beginning, I just wanted my dear friend back. After a couple of years, however, I began to realize I did not want a friend I could not trust not to abandon me. Yet while my desire for an *ongoing relationship* faded, my desire for *contact* did not. In part, that's because I wanted my hurt to be acknowledged. In part, it's because I felt afraid of a potential enemy, someone who might—just might—call security if we bumped into each other at a conference because she might—just might—assume I'd orchestrated bumping into her to stalk her. Probably she wouldn't. But she might, and such fears plagued me. I wanted a peace treaty with her partly to feel treated like a human being and partly to assuage my fear by ending the hostility between us.

Such emotional dynamics are complicated—actually formally complex—and to complexify them further, rejected people may have undesirable responses not only to negative impressions but to positive impressions as well. This is why Baumeister advises against trying to be friends after a breakup, arguing it might actually be bad for the dumpee.[207] He's right: an offer of friendship can be misinterpreted as hope of rekindling relationship, and that can lead to more pain. More broadly, Taylor found that "contact events, whether direct or indirect, when benign or somewhat ambiguous, were likely to be interpreted as positive indicators of encouragement by the ex-partner."[208] In other words, any type of contact that wasn't explicitly negative was likely to be viewed as a sign that the romance could be rekindled. Thus, contact with an ex may, indeed, delay the rejected person's acceptance of the relationship's end, possibly protracting their hurt, as well as exacerbating unwanted pursuit behaviors.

Where does that leave us? Shame and ostracism may shorten the duration of unwanted pursuit, but they can also exacerbate the pursuit—and so can kindness. What's the answer? It's a theme of this book that there isn't just one answer: every situation involves unique people and circumstances that aren't fully predictable. That's the nature of formally complex situations. But in terms of general principles, it's important to distinguish between

[207] Svoboda.

[208] Taylor, 234.

permanent *cutoff* and short-term *no contact.* As previously noted, dating advice often advocates a comparatively brief period of no contact, such as a month, six months, or perhaps a year. In many cases, this kind of short-term break in contact might provide the best of both worlds: sending a clear message to the rejected person that the previous relationship is over while minimizing the shaming and ostracism of permanent or indefinite cutoff. This practice, indeed, may give both parties some breathing room and foster long-term healing.

It's also important to recognize that short-term cessation of contact is vastly different from permanent cutoff—and it's also very different from saying, "We can't be friends." Taking a break from contact has nothing to do with whether two people can be friends in two years, five years, ten years. In many cases, after a period of no contact, both parties will have moved on and decide not to stay in touch. And they will have decided this without permanent cutoff, meaning they can exchange words at a party or in the street without anxiety over boundary violations. In many cases, however, the two may wish to be friends or acquaintances. Yet when online breakup advice fails to explicitly account for time and healing, it gives the impression that cutoff should be permanent and friendship (or even acquaintanceship) is, by default, a doomed fantasy.

This prioritizes disconnection over human relationship, even in cases where short-term no contact would achieve the same purpose as permanent cutoff with far less negative impact. In many cases, the overuse of permanent cutoff can result in trauma for no positive benefit. Ironically, however, because cutoff is generally not recognized as damaging, our relationship experts often advocate it as a default way to reduce the harm of ending relationships, often without distinguishing between short-term and permanent cutoff. As a harm reduction technique, this may work but it may also backfire, especially when it imposes a strict injunction on the cuttee to never contact the cutter again.

Chapter 7

The Duty of No Contact

Tenet 3. The cut-off person has a duty never to contact the cutter as long as the cutoff is in effect.

The idea that the cut-off person must never contact the cutter is succinctly summed up by Reifman's friend, whom I previously quoted: "Writing at ALL after someone said NO is not Okay. If it is OK, where is the line?"[209] The ethics underlying this position is that contacting someone against their wishes is a violation of a boundary, and boundary violation is wrong. Further, this applies to any boundary violation, however small, because, if we allow any violation, there is no standard for "drawing the line" to protect against more serious violations.

In his generous email correspondence with me, Ferrett Steinmetz, another of Reifman's critics, offered a more complex take on the same basic principle: "It's pretty much my position [that there should be no attempt at contact], though there are nuances—like, if you're at the same con[vention], you're not obligated not to go or even to not be in the same room, but I wouldn't start a conversation. Basically, if they wanna talk to you, they'll let you know."[210] I hear this argument a lot: if the cutter wants to talk, they'll talk; if they don't talk to you, that means they don't want to. That conclusion sounds like common sense, but in many cases it's inaccurate. Zadro et al. observe,

> Ironically, despite the initial increased control that comes from ostracizing, real-world [vs. laboratory] sources [of

[209] qtd. in Reifman, "Shining Light on Internet Rage."

[210] Ferrett Steinmetz, email message to the author, June 28, 2022, 8:53 a.m.

> ostracism] often report losing control of the ostracism episode. As ostracizing the target becomes less effortful and more habitual, the source risks becoming unable to stop the ostracism episode even when he or she wishes to reconcile with the target. The habit of excluding the target, even after a few days, may become very difficult to break.[211]

It doesn't necessarily follow that continued silence means the cutter has no desire for contact. In fact, they may wish contact (or not mind it) but feel inhibited from initiating it, either by external pressures or self-inhibition. I feel this self-inhibition with a lot of friends even in situations less fraught than cutoff. We've drifted apart. We're probably still on good terms, but it just feels hard to take the step to reach out, so year after year, I don't, even though I miss them—and maybe they feel the same.

In our correspondence, I shared with Steinmetz that, while I respect his position, I do not fully agree with it. He replied graciously,

> And that's fine; I don't disagree that there are times [when contact may be warranted]—but I think that people on the whole are far too primed to try to ensure that THIS IS THE TIME, and as such if you give them a gentle "You should only do this if...." some significant subset will go "You should do this, got it."
>
> So on the whole, I default to a clear "no" until I hear a strong "yes."[212]

Steinmetz's perception accords with Taylor's findings that any contact tends to be interpreted as encouraging pursuit unless it is unambiguously negative.[213] He's not wrong that many people interpret civility as an invitation to pursue and that unwanted pursuit, even if not dangerous or frightening, can be very painful. In his critique of Reifman's essay, Steinmetz describes an unhealthy college dating relationship he had with a woman he calls "Allie." Sick

---

[211] Zadro et al., 138.

[212] Ferrett Steinmetz, email message to the author, June 28, 2022, 10:08 a.m.

[213] Taylor, 234.

of his clinging and demanding behavior, Allie broke up with him and cut him off. Steinmetz never attempted to transgress the cut-off and reports he has had no contact with her since. He notes that Allie can find him on social media if she wishes. He takes the fact that she hasn't as a sign she doesn't want to reconnect. Steinmetz has also cut off others. Of the people he has cut off, he says,

> It's not that I don't believe in the act of forgiveness, repentance, or growth. It's that for me, these people have shown me to be not worth the risk of having them around. They weren't perfectly toxic in the first place, or they never would have been my friends; there was something I liked about them, enough to give them multiple chances. They probably did at least one very good thing for every two bad things they did.
>
> Eventually, I realized that I didn't like continually wondering what hurtful thing they might do next. The damage of always cringing in preparation for the next blow is, in some ways, worse than the actual blow. And as such, letting them back into my life would mean cringing on some level… and I won't do that [ellipsis in original].
>
> They've burnt their time with me. I hope they can learn to make other people happy; I hold no malice. But they're not allowed back, no matter how many proclamations of change they make, no matter how many people vouch for them. It's not that I think they are bad, it's that I am no longer willing to find out.[214]

With Allie, he sees himself as one of those people who "burnt their time": "That's who I was for Allie. And that's why, no, I don't get in touch with her. She deserves a life free of cringing in expectation of the next blow."[215]

---

214 Ferrett Steinmetz, "She Broke up with Me, and Never Gave Me a Second Chance," *TheFerrett.com*, May 14, 2014, https://www.theferrett.com/2014/05/14/she-broke-up-with-me-and-never-gave-me-a-second-chance/.

215 Steinmetz, "She Broke up with Me, and Never Gave Me a Second Chance."

This is mature and considerate reasoning, and Steinmetz's personal decision not to contact Allie is valid. I also empathize with the idea that waiting for the next blow can be worse than the blow itself. I expect Sophia feels this way about me, and I feel something like this about theoretical contact from her. If I saw her name in my inbox today, the sight would trigger a fight-or-flight response, regardless of why she wrote or what she might say. Part of me is soothed by the fact it is extremely unlikely she will reach out to me.[216]

Yet cutoff is a double-edged sword. It can protect from psychological blows, but it can also cause them. Steinmetz himself says that twenty-five years after separating from Allie, "That wound still aches. It's an embarrassingly teenaged regret to reveal here, but yes—I'd feel better, on some levels, if we were friends, as it'd be proof that somehow I'd made up for my old tiger-level stupidity."[217] That absence of reconciliation continues to wound him after a quarter century. He says this in an essay that advocates *not* trying to reconcile. Still, the absence hurts. That's a powerful illustration of the damage of disconnection. In Steinmetz's case, it may, indeed, be the lesser evil. But it is not always the lesser evil.

The idea, voiced by Reifman's friend, that we must have zero contact or there is no way to "draw the line" is logically faulty. We could as easily say that no one should ever ask their partner to run a tiresome errand because, if they do, what's to stop abusive exploitation? What's to stop it is judgment, proportion, decency, thinking about relative impacts. The fact that ethical judgments may require nuance does not make them impossible to make. Even under the decreased self-regulation ostracism often elicits,[218] most people have some sense of proportion. Arlo knew that waiting for Kendra by her class could read as "stalkerish" and only did it once. Despite a lot of mental disarrangement, I've sent Sophia only one nasty communication in over nine years. My partner has

---

[216] Yet if Sophia did reach out in any peaceful way, as terrifying as it would be in the moment, it might also be the most healing gift of my life. Of course, she is the one who cut me off, so my role is equivalent to Steinmetz's, not Allie's. My point is that the initial cringing from the blow may sometimes be a small price to pay for an immense reward.

[217] Steinmetz, "She Broke up with Me, and Never Gave Me a Second Chance."

[218] Zadro et al., 130.

reached out politely to the best friend who cut him off on three occasions across thirty years. That's a lot of restraint.

In my experience, when invited to converse thoughtfully about these questions, most people readily accept that shades of gray exist. In my correspondence with Steinmetz, he acknowledges that zero contact rule should not be absolute, yet his 2014 essay implies it should be. Similarly, in my email exchange with Kalen Dion, he, too, expressed a view of cutoff quite open to subtleties, though the online quote that led me to contact him was written as an absolute. Unfortunately, our current cultural norms are not generated by thoughtful conversation but by decontextualized social media hot takes, echo chambers, and univocal communication, such an individual commentator's essay or video. We rarely get as far as the shades of gray.

In the online spheres we increasingly turn to for guidance, absolutes are our default. Consider this well-meaning and generally benign advice from PsychCentral.com: "No one has the right to tread on your boundaries. (But it's also good to keep in mind that you—likewise—don't have the right to tread on someone else's.)"[219] This statement is a good general practice, but as an absolute ethical mandate, it is problematic. Not all boundaries are healthy ones. In our current culture, which highly prizes boundaries (or claims to), we readily understand that some boundaries are too permissive. Someone may, for example, refuse to tolerate being *physically* hurt by a loved one but tolerate other unhealthy conduct, potentially enabling *emotional* abuse. Carolyn experienced this in her relationship with her brother. She put up with decades of financial and social exploitation and lies at great cost to her own wellness before finally cutting him off.[220] That's easy for us to understand.

It's harder for us to understand that boundaries can also be excessive. To take an extreme example, say someone sets a personal boundary that they will never exchange words with their spouse. This could be seen as a boundary: it defines a line the person put around what they will accept. Yet that expectation amounts to extreme ostracism, and it will very predictably produce immense distress in the partner. In his case studies of ostracism, Williams shares an account of a husband who refused to speak to

[219] Leah Campbell.

[220] Carolyn.

his wife for forty years. The wife expressed the impact like this: "I wish he would've beaten me instead of giving me the silent treatment, because at least it would have been a response.... The bottom line is that it's the meanest thing you can do to someone, especially because it doesn't allow you to fight back."[221] This boundary is abusive. Boundaries *can be* abusive. And what if this man's wife tread on his boundary by begging him to speak to her? To say she'd be the one in the wrong is absurd.

This example is, indeed, extreme, but the underlying point is important. Personal boundaries are complex. Generally, they must be respected. Yet not all of them are healthy. Yet again, even when a boundary is unhealthy, we should often still respect it because violating it would do even greater harm. I happen to think Sophia's cutoff boundary around me is unhealthy, but I also recognize that my violating it intensifies the harm that already exists between us. Likewise, Ryan's respect for my (unhealthy) cutoff boundary gave me space to heal, at the same time his minor transgression of it by friending me on social media sped my healing. And sometimes treading on a boundary is entirely reasonable. In the example above, of course we'd expect the wife to ask her husband to speak to her. She'd be trying to restore some semblance of humanity to their marriage. To say that she is committing an ethical wrong by doing so is to say, in essence, that it is wrong to speak up for relationship health, an assertion that is unhealthy. To put it another way, allowing all boundaries to stand unchallenged, regardless of context, can itself show poor boundaries.

Moreover, it is an uncomfortable but undeniable fact that sometimes transgressing boundaries heals. Reid fell out with his close friend Dina over his disapproval of her new romantic partner, whom he judged to be dishonest and manipulative. Reid explains,

> I didn't want Dina to get hurt or to watch her being mistreated, and my vocal opposition to these relationships ultimately led to her now-partner telling Dina to cut me off. She blocked my phone number and blocked me on social media, and it was quick and without warning. I was devastated and not prepared for the detrimental level of raw hurt that I experienced. I couldn't even have the

---

[221] Williams, 20.

> notice to change my behavior or the communication lines open to express myself. As the years went by, not a single moment passed where I wasn't rooted in guilt, regret and deep sadness. I didn't have another friend like her and I knew I probably wouldn't ever.[222]

Reid did not give up on his friendship with Dina, but continued to periodically attempt contact with her, though her ghosting of him clearly implied she did not wish it:

> Every July, on the anniversary of her leaving, I would send her an email with my phone number should she want to connect. This year I tried something different, telling myself that if it didn't work, I was going to officially give up. I made a fake [social media] profile and I sent her a small paragraph telling her that I missed her and that my lines of communication were still open. About a week later, she called my partner finally after three years and said she was hoping I still had a document I was keeping safe for her. I knew I had given it back but I tore up the house looking for it. By the end of that conversation he asked if she would like to talk to me. She said, "Yeah, real quick." I spoke with her and it was like nothing had changed. We picked right back up where we left off. I was so overjoyed to have our relationship back that I don't even care that she left me like that, I only cared that she was back. Whatever the reasons, I am still going to be there for her, and I hope we don't make the same mistake twice.[223]

Two realities stand out in Reid's account. First, he transgressed Dina's boundaries in a significant way, going so far as to create a fake account as a means of tricking her into receiving a message from him. Second, it worked. As she herself confirmed to him, once she received that communication, she quickly showed willingness to rekindle their friendship. His statement that he was still there for her moved her in a positive way.[224] Moreover,

---

[222] Reid, email message to the author, July 22, 2021.

[223] Reid.

[224] Reid.

Reid says he thinks it unlikely that Dina ever saw his other emails: over the period of their estrangement, she changed her email address and he didn't have access to her new address.[225] If he had not deceived her into viewing a message, the healing that message enabled might well have never reached her.

Deception is a contact strategy most of us would shun, even if we are sympathetic to certain minor boundary transgressions. I certainly do not advocate it, though in the interest of honesty, I will admit I have used deception once to make contact with someone; in my case, it deepened the injury. I regret it, and I would not use it again. Yet deceptive transgression of a cutoff saved Reid and Dina's friendship. That may make us uncomfortable, but it's the truth. What lesson should we take from this?

One lesson I take is that relationships are, indeed, contextual. Deception did not work for me; it did for Reid and Dina. It could terrorize some people. Others might consider it no big deal. This is an example of why we should be careful with absolute statements, such as "Boundaries should never be violated." If Reid had not violated Dina's boundaries, both of them would have lost a dear friend, possibly forever. That is a reality.

It's also worth noting that Dina's boundaries, in this case, could be considered unhealthy. She completely blocked out of her life a long-term, good friend on someone else's advice in the name of pursuing what proved an unsupportive romantic relationship: after their reconciliation, Dina disclosed to Reid that the girlfriend he disapproved of cheated on her repeatedly.[226] This does not mean Reid was right to badger her about the relationship. It may, however, mean that Dina was foolish to completely cut him off for it. The lesson I take from this ordinary example of humans being imperfect is that, roughly speaking, unhealthy boundaries may require some violation in order to restore some health. I don't say this lightly. I do not advocate ever violating boundaries lightly. At the same time, I balk at any absolute statement that says boundaries must always be respected, even at the expense of genuine attempts to restore health. To promote such an exacting rule is to perpetuate unnecessary human sorrow, and that we should not do.

---

225 Reid.

226 Reid.

The Duty to Cut Yourself Off

The absolute terms of our cultural norms require rigid obedience. With cutoff norms, this rigidity extends so far that even implied cutoff is often treated as ethical imperative mandating silence for life. With regard to ghosting, Arlo observes, "The cultural idea seems to be if someone isn't talking to you, you should understand that they don't want to talk to you, and *you* should initiate the cutoff."[227] Though Arlo is speaking of ghosting, the same principle applies to any cutoff without explicit parameters. If a person in the midst of an argument screams, "Get out of my life!" and doesn't seek out further contact, we should infer their angry scream literally means it would be an ethical wrong to say "hello" thirty years later. We are expected to default to assuming we're permanently cut off as a prophylactic measure against causing the cuttee possible future hurt.

Imposing this burden on ourselves is often cast as plain decency. In Steinmetz's account of Allie cutting him off, he doesn't say anything about her cutoff boundaries, merely that she "kicked my ass to the curb."[228] In our email correspondence, I asked him if she permanently cut him off. I'll quote his thoughtful reply at length:

> I honestly don't remember; it was over thirty years ago at this point, and it'd be hard to say what memory provides.
>
> That said… I've had old friends from college contact me to say "Hey, man, how's it going?" and… it would be highly unusual if she hadn't come across me. I've heard nothing; I assume, if anything, I'm a vaguely unpleasant memory, if I'm remembered at all.
>
> But the larger take that I will share is that contacting people like this is a burden, and you shouldn't be willing to subject people to burdens they haven't asked for. If I were to strike up a conversation with her, it would most likely be for me to get some sense of closure—but it would be on her to do the emotional labor to give or deny me that closure, and that's not fair. The reason she cut me

---

227 Arlo, in discussion with author, December 17, 2021.

228 Steinmetz, "She Broke up with Me, and Never Gave Me a Second Chance."

> off is because I had caused enough emotional damage that she felt the need to cut ties—and asking her to reevaluate that past damage, to bring up old pain to see whether forgiveness is still an option, to try to triangulate whether I'm still a potential danger to her or there's something to be salvaged...? [ellipsis original]
>
> No, if she really wanted that connection with me, she'd seek it out. Other old friends have gotten in touch with me, presumably out of fond memories; she has not, whether because of mere forgetfulness or active disdain, I do not know. But the potential is to do further harm, and considering I already dealt her a whammy, until I get clear and active consent the best choice is to go on the assumption that it's unwanted.
>
> You don't have to take every shot presented. In fact, ethically, often the best choice is not to. If your actions caused the bridge to be burnt, leave it to the people on the other side to start rebuilding it.[229]

I deeply appreciate the compassion and sense of responsibility that underlies Steinmetz's reasoning. The reasoning itself contains two somewhat distinct aspects. One is his reflections on his particular relationship with Allie. The other is a broader discussion of ethics around attempting to reconnect in general. Steinmetz is, of course, an expert on his relationship with Allie and best placed to make informed decisions about how to address it. The broader principle, though, I find dubious.

The core contention is this: "contacting people like this is a burden, and you shouldn't subject people to burdens they haven't asked for." This principle displays an admirable ethic of compassion and responsibility. It sounds great at first blush and, without doubt, describes the best guiding principle for many circumstances. But if we apply it as an absolute, you should not ever subject people to burdens they haven't asked for, that dictate will erode the human connection we need to be socially and psychologically healthy.

For the sake of argument, let's limit the people under discussion to reasonably self-sufficient adults. There are many situations where most would agree that burdening someone serves the

[229] Steinmetz, email message to the author, June 28, 2022, 10:08 a.m.

greater good. A hiker who sprains her ankle may ask another hiker for help, thereby preventing worse injury. A stranded traveler whose phone has died may ask to borrow a phone so they can call for a ride. A stressed single parent may ask their own stressed parents to babysit so that they can take a breather and come back a better parent. A friend might contact their chum's estranged ex to ask for a photo of the chum's recently deceased dog in order to surprise them with a loving dog memorial.[230] All these requests impose a burden. The person being asked to assist may not enjoy it. In some cases, they might resent it, but a good case can be made that the benefits outweigh the harm. The same can be true with cutoff. In cases like Reid and Dina's, one awkward communication could lead to years of peace and ease.

Moreover, this same injunction against imposing burdens could be used to invalidate the right to cutoff itself. Cutoff is, almost by definition, a burden the cuttee doesn't ask for. I didn't ask for the burden of never having a civil relationship with Sophia; what I asked for was her friendship. For that matter, Steinmetz didn't ask to be obligated to a silence that still made him ache after twenty-five years. By his own account, he'd feel relieved if Allie reached out amicably. Does that mean the people who cut us off must have been wrong because imposing burdens on others is, by definition, wrong? Of course not. It is a major premise of this book that cutoff is sometimes the best choice. Sometimes imposing some burden on others is simply the less destructive option.

It will be replied, however, that this doesn't apply to transgressing cutoff because there *is* a right to cutoff and no right to communication. Yes, the right to reject contact, in general, reasonably supersedes the wish for contact. That guideline preserves our privacy and safety. But to say that in all cases, disconnection imposes no relevant burden is simply untrue. Again and again, we see ostracism traumatize. Trauma is a relevant burden. It is reasonable to suggest that human beings should have some freedom to take moderate steps to alleviate burdens that are damaging their lives. In most cases that don't involve threat or abuse, saying hello on social media seems a moderate step. In contrast, a cultural stance that expects people to take on a self-harming, lifelong vow

[230] Yes, this is real example, and, yes, the estranged ex kindly provided a photo.

of self-silencing on the hunch that it might be what someone else wants is a gross imposition.

Yet I myself have succumbed to this expectation. One of Sophia's friends, Tammy, and I had a brief, tense online exchange about Sophia's cutoff, culminating in Tammy blocking me on social media. (I'll return to this exchange.) After she blocked me, I replied to her final email with a promise never to contact her again. Though it was clear she wished to break contact for the foreseeable future, she didn't tell me *never* to contact her again for life. I chose to impose that promise on myself. I almost immediately regretted it, and I still do. I straightjacketed myself into an endless promise to a near stranger to suppress my own ethical judgments on the guess it's what she'd want. I did it because I was worried she was afraid of me. I did it to assure her I was not a threat. I made a massive overcommitment that she never asked for: to treat myself as a danger to her for the rest of my life on the basis of a couple of awkward textual communications. I would argue this places an undue burden on both of us. It hurts me, and it has chained me to her psychologically in a way I can only imagine she would find deeply uncomfortable.[231]

My friend Derek has also chosen to cut himself off on the assumption it's what someone else wanted. Derek was neither obviously ghosted nor explicitly told to drop contact. In the end, he volunteered to drop contact for life, and the ensuing silence continues to cause him pain years later. In Derek's case, both parties were clearly doing their best to show compassion. Both worked to spare each other pain; the pain came all the same.

Nadine was a coworker with whom Derek explored a romantic relationship for about a week before she politely broke it off.[232] He accepted the breakup with equal courtesy. The following week, however, Nadine quit her job. A mutual friend at work confirmed that she had expressed discomfort about working with Derek, a discomfort possibly compounded by the fact that he held some

[231] It will be remarked that those chains are my own responsibility and within my own power to undo. That's true, and I am working on it. It would be much easier, however, just to be on distant, civil terms with her. I also suspect the impact of being on civil terms for her would be neutral to positive. There's no downside to it, merely a weird social expectation that it cannot be.

[232] Derek in discussion with the author, July 14, 2024.

supervisory authority over her. You have already spotted the problem, and Derek would agree.

Realizing that their relationship had placed her in a vulnerable position, Derek emailed Nadine and said, "It's obvious you're having problems with me, and if you don't contact me, I won't contact you. If you feel I acted inappropriately given our work relationship, I strongly recommend that you contact HR or our manager." She did not reply, and he never contacted her again. Yet he felt stricken that Nadine, a single mother, gave up a good job on account of their relationship.[233]

It was eight years after this incident that he first shared it with me. Derek is one of the most easy-going people I know. His usual manner is calm and conversational. But when he spoke about these events, he spoke with an agitation I had never seen in over twenty years of friendship, his words flowing fast, tone sharp and urgent.

During a pause, I said, "It sounds to me like you're still carrying guilt for this."

"Yes!" he said. "I feel very guilty—because I don't know what kind of hardship she may have had to suffer from leaving her job over me." Obviously, it would have been better not to date her, but that mistake having been made, "I don't know what else I could have done," he said. "I don't know what I could have done."

He has no idea where Nadine is now or how she's doing. These events may have left a lasting scar on her, or they may have slipped into her past long ago. But when he thinks of her, he is still in the same place, still stuck in the past, because he can't find any answers. He can't know the impact he had on her life or what she wanted him to do once the romance had ended. He doesn't know if she's okay, and that cuts him to the core.

This is the cost of silence. I know nothing about Nadine. It may be that withdrawal and silence was what she needed, and regardless of any cultural norms, it would be the best way for her to

---

[233] Derek tells me that Nadine could have transferred to a different branch with no loss of pay or status. To this day, he wonders if a little more communication about the issue (with HR, their manager, or other coworkers) might have assuaged her discomfort and supported her in retaining her job. She cut contact with her coworkers, however, so it's possible she never knew this option existed. (As to why she might be transferred instead of him, he had considerably more seniority and institutional knowledge about their branch.)

take care of herself. I do know that Derek promised her a lifetime of disconnection, a lifetime of no answers, that he volunteered to impede his own healing at least partly because that is our cultural norm, because he had been taught that common decency required it. Her lack of response fits that norm as well. It's a go-to system for ending an entanglement: say nothing. If our cultural norm were to talk through conflict, would she have talked? Would she have felt forced to talk even if it traumatized her? Or would they both have ended the situation with more emotional ease and better sense of closure? Would she have stayed in a good job with a healed relationship? I can't know the answer. What I do know is that, as the years go by, the silence continues to cause him pain.

In her discussion of our culture's overstatement of harm, Schulman contends, "Unfortunately, it is the distorted social norm to see the wish to repair [e.g. contact] as an assault..."[234] There is much truth to Schulman's observation, and as an ethical position, this "distorted norm" is unbalanced, placing huge responsibility on the cut-off party and none on the cutter—even in cases where no explicit cutoff has happened. Sometimes zero-tolerance cutoff is necessary, but its use as a default breeds unnecessary pain.

In addition to hurting the cut-off person, this overstatement of harm can bleed into other areas of our lives in surprising ways. Here's an example from my own life. Though its impacts are trivial, I think it reveals something about how cutoff trauma ripples out.

At eleven years old, my daughter went through a brief infatuation with shushing me. One time, she did it when I picked her up from her football practice.

I remarked, "The days are really getting shorter."

She said, "Shh. No talking."

And I felt so hamstrung by this order that I did not say a word (nor did she) on our five-minute drive home.

As we pulled into the driveway, she asked offhandedly if I could text her dad to pick up bagels.

I said, "Is talking allowed now?"

She said, with some show of puzzled awkwardness, "Allowed? Er. Um. Talking is always allowed."

I said, "But you told me not to say anything."

---

[234] Schulman, 43.

She said, "Well, that doesn't mean you have to listen. I don't control whether you talk."

I would argue that my daughter's behavior here is normal. She comprehends that people say all sorts of things in different moods in different moments and they don't all have to be taken seriously. Heaven help us if every word out of our mouths were taken seriously! My response, however, was a trauma response. It was a mild case of falling into fight, flight, freeze, or appease behaviors: I ended up stuck between freeze and appease. It was a response rooted in how I have been treated as cut-off person. It came from years of being castigated for the ethical crime of *ever* attempting contact after someone told me not to.

It strikes me that my daughter's statement, "I don't control whether you talk," is akin to Schulman's assertion, "I want to state here, for the record, that no one is obligated to obey a unidirectional order that has not been discussed. Negotiation is a human responsibility."[235] I love the spirit behind this statement, though I don't agree with it in an absolute sense. There are many unidirectional commands we should be ethically obligated to follow. Obvious examples would be refusal of sex or a restraining order, but even shy of such a mandate, we do have some obligation to respect people's boundaries around communication, even if part of that boundary is a refusal to talk about it. If we don't, it can intensify trauma. That said, it's all contextual. A great deal of the time, I'd agree with Schulman: the ethical dictate that any call for silence or severance must be obeyed without question is oppressive. It describes a radical power imbalance that gives silence domination over speech, regardless of circumstances, a kind of servitude inconsistent with free adults making independent choices. Reifman pushes back on this imbalance in his follow-up to his cutoff essay: "Certainly, I felt entitled to *ask* Emma for an explanation.... I do not think I have a *right* to an explanation from her..." [emphasis mine].[236] In this formulation, Emma is in charge of her own words, but so is Reifman, within reason, in charge of his. In my interaction with my daughter, after years of training as a cuttee, I relinquished my words. I instinctively accepted my subordination when I allowed her to silence me.

---

[235] Schulman, 45.

[236] Reifman, "Shining Light on Internet Rage."

I did it out of guilt for violating the rule that any contact after a "no" is not okay—or by extension, I had no right to speak when my daughter told me to be quiet. Now, obviously this last point doesn't logically follow, if only because I'm an adult and her parent: it's my job not to do what she says when she's unreasonable. But trauma response is not logical. At that point, I was so gun shy in the face of our culture's condemnation that it hampered my parenting of my child—because, of course, my thick silence, followed by odd harping on her throwaway words is not ideal parenting.

Boundaries, like everything else in human relations, are contextual. The only fairly invariable rule should be to do the least harm. In the messy soup of human life, however, it is not always clear where the least harm lies. When my friend Ryan violated my cutoff boundary by sending me a friend request, it healed my rage at him. But when I first violated Sophia's cutoff boundary by sending a short email saying I believed one day we could be friends again, my guess is it made things worse. We can't always guess right. We can't even rely on the Golden Rule. With four out of five of my messages, I treated Sophia as I would want to be treated, yet I suspect every single message did her harm. These realities illustrate why we cannot place an absolute rule around when violating cutoff is valid. The irony of cutting off communication is that it allows no way to know the context. Attempting communication may retraumatize, or it may be the only way to heal the trauma. We have to allow a space for that guesswork, and we cannot say a person is guilty of moral wrongdoing if they made an overture of peace and happened to guess wrong—and still less so if, like Ryan and Reid, they made an overture and guessed right.

Chapter 8

The Advice to Ignore or Rebuff Transgressors

Tenet 4. Those who *transgress* cutoffs should be ignored or rebuffed because they are disrespecting boundaries.

"A boundary crossed is a boundary crossed—end of story,"[237] says one of Reifman's critics. Any contact across a cutoff, by definition, crosses a boundary, and if all boundary crossing is impermissible, then any contact is "not Okay."[238] Because we don't want to encourage what is "not okay," it follows that cutters should reject all contact. As New Health Advisor puts it, "Take steps to shut down all lines of communication to ensure they [the cut-off person] don't affect you in any way."[239] Writing for Marriage.com, Rachael Pace advises that "the best course of cutting someone off without explanation is to completely ignore them. If you decide to cut him off completely from your life, make sure there is no turning back."[240] Like New Health Advisor, Pace specifies that this includes rejecting all communication: "Block them on all social media channels, and when someone tries to send you

---

237 Laura, comment on Reifman, "Shining Light on Relationship Cutoff."

238 qtd. in Reifman, "Shining Light on Internet Rage."

239 "Cutting People out of Your Life," New Health Advisor, accessed July 5, 2022, https://www.newhealthadvisor.org/Cutting-People-Out-of-Your-Life.html. New Health Advisor has a disclaimer that it should not substitute for professional advice.

240 Rachael Pace, "Cutting People Off: When It's the Right Time, and How to Do It," clinically approved by Silvana Mici, Coach, March 15, 2024, Marriage.com, https://www.marriage.com/advice/relationship/cutting-people-off/.

a message, don't open it."[241] Rejection of contact should be unremitting lest deviation send a signal that could intensify unwanted pursuit.

This guideline often extends not only to the cutter but to anyone involved in the cutoff situation, from friends and family to casual bystanders. The ideal is an impenetrable wall rebuffing all communication. There are understandable reasons for this. For one thing, in many cases, contact can stoke false hopes of reconciliation, as Taylor's findings suggest.[242] Likewise, Taylor found that friends and family can undermine a person's desire to break off a relationship by lobbying for them to reconcile with an ex:

> In the current study, over half of the cases [of rejected exes] reported being encouraged by their ex-partner's social network to continue the support-seeker's [i.e. rejected ex's] pursuit. Furthermore, the support-seekers attempted to persuade and use members of their ex-partner's social network as instruments in their URP [Unwanted Relational Pursuit] campaign. For the support-seeker, their ex-partner's friends and family encouragement was interpreted as condoning the URPs behaviors and persistence.[243]

However well-intentioned, a friend group's desire to facilitate a happy ending can exacerbate unwanted pursuit and possibly even be interpreted by the rejected person as condoning harassment or stalking behaviors.

Cutoff culture responds to this hazard by advising friends and family to facilitate cutoff instead. Continuous silence or rejection maintains a united front in support of a boundary setter. Refusing to communicate with someone whom a friend or family member has cut off is often considered a sign of loyalty. This view is on display in the family-friendly comedy series *Stuck in the Middle* (2016–2018), which recounts the daily lives of the Diaz family. One episode showcases the family rule, "Dead to Diaz," according to which the whole family agrees to cut off a person a family

---

[241] Pace.

[242] Taylor, 234.

[243] Taylor, 236. The term "support-seeker" refers to Taylor's case studies, people seeking emotional support on an online relationships forum.

member doesn't like, regardless of the reason. In the episode, the main character, Harley (Jenna Ortega), contemplates invoking this rule to shun a neighbor boy who is obnoxious to her.[244] Though the two eventually reconcile, the rule as stated could require the entire household to permanently ostracize their perfectly ordinary neighbor, explicitly treating another human being as "dead" solely because one of the family members doesn't like them. This brutal attitude is framed as a sign of family loyalty. Of course, the show is played for laughs; nonetheless, it dramatizes how our popular culture valorizes ostracism, not only as a person's right, but as a healthy and praiseworthy marker of group loyalty.

In some situations, the solid wall of rejection is, indeed, the best course of action. If you give some an inch, they will take a mile. Again, this depends on context. In some cases, having any contact may be physically dangerous or emotionally untenable. In some cases, a civil reply may, indeed, delay acceptance that the relationship is over and initially lead to more unwelcome contact—and, in some cases, it may also lead to faster and more complete healing in the end. In some cases, a judicious reply may even prevent escalation into stalking behaviors.[245] One-size-fits-all is a poor rule for human relationships. In his discussion of familial cutoff, every example Kukla gives involves cutting off an abuser, people like an unstable grandfather who brings a gun to his granddaughter's bat mitzvah.[246] But that grandfather is not Arlo waiting to catch his friend on the way to class or fictional Harley's sassy neighbor. It is important—indeed it is necessary to a compassionate ethic—to fit the response to the situation.

Though it sometimes is the lesser evil, the ethic of total rejection can easily cause significant harm. It assaults at least two of our four core human needs: *control* and *self-esteem*. It assaults control by leaving the cuttee with zero control within the cutoff situation. It assaults *self-esteem* by implying or actively engaging in derogation of the cuttee, in other words, by treating them as an unworthy human being. While total rejection is sometimes advisable, it should be utilized with caution.

---

244 "Stuck in a Nice Relationship," *Stuck in the Middle*, Episode 3.6, Disney, March 9, 2018.
245 Taylor, 231.
246 Kukla.

Loss of Control

Cutoff can feel like being trapped in a black box with no way out. Moreover, we often don't know how we got there. Williams describes a "pattern of bewilderment" from targets of ostracism.[247] He explains, "One of the peculiar features of ostracism is that… it is often not accompanied by an announcement of its onset or by explanations that justify its employment. This leaves the targets of ostracism wondering why it is happening to them."[248] Cutoff removes social relationships while providing no mechanism for reconciliation and not much for comprehension. The "bewilderment" this engenders can cause intense distress. Speaking of his own cutoff trauma, Reifman observes, "When there are emotional loose ends—unanswered questions, mistrust, betrayal, disbelief, bewilderment… it can be very difficult to heal."[249] When the cutter's social circle joins the initial cutter in cutting off contact, the only potential means for addressing the bewilderment can be blocked, leaving the cut-off person powerless to improve the social situation.

I don't know why Sophia permanently cut me off. I could list a lot of things I did that hurt her, but I do not understand why they merit lifelong ostracism: loss of friendship, withdrawal of trust, a temporary break from communication, yes; absolute lifelong ostracism, no. On a gut level, that does not make sense to me. Moreover, I cannot even be sure I'm aware of how much I hurt her. For example, I had a tendency to blow off suggestions she made about how to revise my writing. Did that badly wound her or was it trivial? Or did I do something I've forgotten, that I'm not even aware of doing? Across a cutoff, I can never know and, thus, I can never redress it. When any attempt at outreach is viewed as an unwarranted boundary violation, attempting to get information about the situation is construed as immoral; any action we could take to address the situation—not our feelings but the *external situation*—is impermissible.

The way out, of course, is to cease to want to contact. The hitch is that the refusal of a space for closure makes achieving that goal one of the hardest tasks we can set: to internally resolve a

---

[247] Williams, 21.

[248] Williams, 21.

[249] Reifman, "Shining the Light on Relationship Cutoff."

situation with no external resolution. Abandonment grief can be as intense as grieving the death of a loved one.[250] In my experience, it is more so. In that period of grief, of course, we want to reach out—to fix things, to make the pain go away. We naturally crave understanding. We want some degree of control over the parts of our lives that mean most to us, our relationships with people we have loved.

This loss of control is intensified when the cutter's social group joins the cutoff, refusing most or any contact with the cut-off person as a marker of regard for their loved one's boundaries. In some cases, such as physical danger or stalking, this is prudent. But as a general practice, regardless of the circumstances, it can needlessly compound trauma.

The Dehumanization of Silence

To be ignored—treated as nonexistent—is one of the most painful experiences we can suffer. To be yelled at is to be treated like a person who is there. To be ignored is to be treated like air, like void, like a forgotten ghost.

The second time I contacted Sophia was in January 2016, a year after my first brief email and fifteen months after the cutoff. My email said, "I miss you and I'd like to make peace." I began composing that email four months earlier. I agonized over every word; I attempted perfection. She did not reply. In other words, she followed supposed best practice.

If she had just said, "I can't be in contact and will never be able to," it would have hurt, but it would have hurt infinitely less than her silence. It would have answered my implicit question by saying, no, we can't reconcile. It would have provided some closure.[251] Even if she had just said, "fuck off," I would have known something about where I stood, had some idea of how to understand the situation. But more than that, it would have acknowledged I exist. *I have a voice.* As it is, I don't know if she ever

---

[250] Anderson, 121.

[251] Some might note that this is exactly what she told me when she cut me off, so why didn't that provide closure? Because time changes things. Because fifteen months placed me in a different place in my grieving process, and it is not absurd to think it might have changed her feelings toward me.

saw my email. I don't know if she blocked me, if she deleted it unread (as many advise). At the time, I felt thrown into the trash all over again. That feeling sparked the angry tirade I sent two weeks later. That tirade is my responsibility—and her silence sparked it. Both things can be true.

Silence and being silenced can be directly, intensely painful, but the harm of ignoring the cuttee goes beyond that immediate pain. It can also short circuit the psychologically healthy and essential process of reality testing.

The Need for Reality Testing

Sometimes a total ban on communication is needed. I would argue, however, that—where it's safe to do so—we should open doors in the wall of silence. While a third party's attempts to mediate reconciliation is often an overreach, simply talking to a cuttee about the cutoff can greatly facilitate psychological health and healing.

It is normal and healthy to seek perspective from third parties. When I cut Ryan off, one of his first moves was to ask a mutual friend what was going on with me. When Ginsa cut Casey off, he also asked a mutual friend for context on what was happening. These are examples of healthy reality testing.

Reality testing is a concept associated with Freudian psychoanalysis that describes how people differentiate their inner thoughts from external reality. A common example is the way we might interpret someone not returning our "good morning." We might imagine they're angry at us and trying to snub us when, in reality, they may not have heard us, may be distracted, may be in a bad mood for another reason, etc.[252] Psychotherapist Joshua Miles observes that reality testing is important to psychological health for several reasons:

- It allows us to distinguish between what is real and what isn't
- It allows us to judge situations appropriately

[252] Joshua Miles, "Learning to Think before You React," Well-Doing.org, August 30, 2017, https://welldoing.org/article/reality-testing-learning-think-before-react.

- It allows us to notice our own feelings and what they mean
- It gives us a basis of comparison
- It allows us to improve how we react to situations[253]

In psychoanalysis, reality testing may refer specifically to therapeutic techniques used to help clients distinguish between inner and outer realities. More broadly, however, being able to reasonably distinguish between our own thoughts and what's actually happening around us is a basic component of mental stability, whether we are in therapy or not. Miles cites two main approaches to reality testing: being objective and seeking external perspectives.[254] When we attempt to be objective, we consider multiple different interpretations of a situation. When we seek external perspectives, we directly solicit input from others, such as their perspectives or additional information about the situation.

One problem with our dominant cutoff practice is that it makes reality testing very difficult. This practice often advises both the cutter and their social circle to refuse to communicate with the cuttee about the cutoff. Ariane Resnick, for example, offers reasonable advice for shutting out stalkers: "Tell the people in your life whom you trust about being stalked, so that they can help you in any ways they can—including not engaging with the person who is doing the stalking."[255] Non-engagement is, indeed, often the best strategy for addressing true cases of stalking, cases that involve threat or harassment. However, as noted previously, we have no clear definition of stalking and sometimes classify anyone who transgresses a cutoff, even with a couple of text messages, as committing stalking behavior. Thus, a strict interpretation of this advice would be to simply avoid any engagement with anyone who resists a cutoff, and that's often the way such advice is interpreted.

If these guidelines are followed, however, the cuttee has no direct means to gather external information about the cutoff: why it happened, what feelings are associated with it, if anything has

---

253 Miles.

254 Miles.

255 Ariane Resnick, "What Is Stalking? How to Know If You're Being Stalked," Verywell Mind, June 28, 2021, https://www.verywellmind.com/what-is-stalking-5114376.

changed over time, etc. This leads to the bewildered feelings commonly associated with ostracism, the kind of years-long pain Arlo experiences over not knowing why his friend ghosted him. Even if the cutter gave some initial explanation, emotions around cutoffs are complex and can change, and the cuttee will almost inevitably be left confused and guessing about some issues.

Now, some means of reality testing remain. The cuttee can certainly attempt to be objective and look at the situation from multiple perspectives in their own mind. They can also seek external perspectives from people not connected to the cutoff, such as a therapist, their own friends, etc. However, these tools, while not useless, are far less effective for understanding the situation than actual information from people who know.

I have attempted a great deal of reality testing about Sophia, and after several years, I am still bewildered. I can try to have perspective on my own: I know she found our relationship hurtful. I believe certain aspects of her personality, regardless of me, make cutoff an attractive step. I know she has used it with others; she once told me that. I believe it's what she needed to do. But there is so much I cannot know: does she now feel comparatively healed? Does she still feel very raw, afraid? Does she look back on me fondly at all? Does she hate me? Does she actively fear I'll come after her? How badly did I wound her? Is it an unpleasantness receding into her past, or am I the person in her life who has wounded her psyche most severely? I've been asked if getting these answers would simply open up more questions and more hurt. Given the sense of stability I get from even the snippets I do know, I think my answer is no (perhaps more questions, not more hurt), though another person might have a different response.

I have also sought a great deal of feedback from people not connected to the cutoff, and some of it has been helpful. My therapist told me my long letter would probably devastate her: I think that was correct, and it was a good move in reining me back from sending it. My pastor noted that Sophia's three wildly different responses to my final email indicated she was conflicted.[256] That also sounds right and was a good piece of perspective to hear.

Yet people who don't know the person in question are necessarily hampered in their judgments about them, and certainly some

---

[256] Over about thirty-six hours, Sophia sent me three emails: the first was neutral in tone, the second kind, the third harsh.

feedback I've been given about Sophia has been wrong. My therapist, for example, once asserted that if Sophia were ever to leave her husband, I would probably be the one she turned to. I can't say for certain, but this sounds unlike Sophia. All I know of her suggests she'll never speak to me again. The same therapist thought it was a good idea to send my final 2017 email. She thought it would provide some closure for me and that Sophia would probably not reply. Sophia did reply—with condemnation. My steps toward closure were ripped apart. Delia thought just a few years might be enough for Sophia to be willing to accept some communication from me. Based on Sophia's own final message, this was wrong. As to what I should do, I have received responses ranging from heartfelt urging that I contact Sophia and demand a heart-to-heart to angry disapproval that I ever dreamed of contacting her at all. People outside the cutoff cannot know all the relevant context. Thus, a person cut off from the cutter's social network cannot know the emotional reality of the relationship, and that makes accurate reality testing impossible.

Of course, no doorway is foolproof. For one thing, social circles—and especially cutters themselves—may not give accurate feedback. A bystander may misunderstand the situation. For example, my own partner once thought Sophia had placed a restraining order on me; she never did. I inadvertently gave him this impression through the strict language I used to describe her no-contact demands. If the cutter themselves is willing to talk, it's likely their view of the relationship will be skewed by their own trauma and heightened emotions. In the case of Casey and Ginsa, for example, Ginsa long maintained all their relationship problems were Casey's fault. As a friend who witnessed their relationship, I can assert this was not so. Yet while people entangled with the situation may not give fully accurate feedback, it can still provide more insight than the guesses of uninvolved strangers.

Why does this matter? I know I can't contact Sophia, so what does it matter if I know how she feels? The most practical answer is that it matters because my understanding of what I did to Sophia affects my conduct with others. According to Miles, one problem arising from lack of reality testing is "We may decide to act differently due to how we perceive other people's reactions to us."[257] My better-judgment mind, at present, says I have probably taken

[257] Miles.

on too much guilt over Sophia, another hazard Miles notes from lack of reality testing.[258] As it stands, every time I vent about life to my partner, every time I raise my voice to my children, every time I send a terse email, I ruminate on the impacts of that negativity. Some of this is my INFJ personality.[259] A lot of it is my response to cutoff trauma. I cannot get my bearings about how I really am, what I am really responsible for, what degree of approximate flawlessness I should be striving for in my behaviors, in part, because emotionally, I do not know what happened with Sophia. I do not know what she thinks I did to her. I do not know how bad she thinks it is or why. Therefore, I don't fully understand how to avoid similar missteps. I am, therefore, recurrently afraid in interactions with other people.[260]

Arlo articulated something similar in his distress over being ghosted by Kendra. In his case, he framed his concerns in terms of a desire for atonement: "I don't actually know why there was a cutoff," he said to me. "If I hurt my good friend so badly she had to cut me off to protect herself, that's unconscionable."[261] But he doesn't know if this is the case—or if it is the case, he doesn't know what he did that hurt her so much. "I can't even apologize for it," he said, "if [what he might have done to hurt her] was more than I realized," adding, "It's so difficult to learn and change without feedback."[262] Apart from once asking a mutual friend to convey his apologies (which he is not sure ever happened), Arlo has refrained from asking their friend group for input. He explained that this particular friend group fell apart due to unrelated conflicts, and he is concerned it might cause discomfort to dredge up old issues. Effectively, he has no community to turn to for help in ascertaining what happened.

---

[258] Miles.

[259] INFJ (Introverted, Intuitive, Feeling, Judging) is one of the sixteen Myers-Briggs personality types. Among other things, it is marked by being sensitive to criticism and prone to shame. Sophia also self-identifies as an INFJ.

[260] I wrote this passage in 2021. As I reread it in 2023, I see my feelings have become less intense. I worry about these issues less. I wish to retain this passage, however, to illustrate the *process* of cutoff trauma. Permanent cutoff assumes the cut-off relationship can never change, yet human beings and our relations are continually in flux.

[261] Arlo.

[262] Arlo.

This sort of thing is exhausting, and speaking for myself, when I'm exhausted, I have less to give to others. Moreover, in some cases, my trauma-skewed responses backfire on other people. I have, for example, fallen into such profuse apologizing to my housemate over a small conflict that the apology itself clearly unsettled her. Now, the best available solution is just to stress about it less, and over the years that is happening. It's just happening far slower, more painfully, and more haphazardly than it would if I had some bearings for understanding the situation better. That is, in part, a consequence of lack of means for reality testing.

Rejection by Bystanders Amplifies Discomfort and Disconnection

One of the stranger and sadder outcomes of my cutoff with Sophia is the intense pain I formed around my relationship with her good friend, Tammy, a person I barely know. (I use the word "relationship" very broadly here to denote two beings that have some kind of relatedness.) I've met Tammy once. We had coffee in 2010, when Sophia and I were still friends, and it was very pleasant. We became social media friends, but other than my liking a couple of her posts, we had no more interaction until 2019, when I asked her for help with the cutoff.

By the time Sophia cut me off, Tammy was the only good friend of hers I knew at all. Not long after the cutoff, I asked my friend Derek how he'd feel if someone he barely knew contacted him asking for help because a mutual friend had cut them off.

"I'd find it very weird," he said. "Weird and uncomfortable."

On the strength of that outside perspective, as well as my own sense of caution, I pushed back the urge to contact Tammy. I went to therapy. I wrote Sophia five drafts of that long letter. I shared the letter with my therapists, Derek, my pastor, my mother, a couple of other trusted friends, and my partner. The response was almost universally that I should not send it. My second therapist put it best: "There's a lot of good stuff in here," she said, "but for someone who needs to withdraw, like Sophia, she could find it psychologically devastating." She didn't specify why, and I didn't ask, but the letter did lay out how badly the cutoff had hurt me. I wanted Sophia to know it hurt, but I never wanted to psychologically devastate her. I have on occasion had vengeful *fantasies* about it, but I have never truly *wanted* it. My therapist's statement alone has been a powerful deterrent to my impulses to reach out to her. I never sent the letter. Another door had been shut.

And so, five years after Sophia cut me off, I messaged Tammy. In my search for some kind of understanding, I felt left with no other recourse. I asked if she would meet with me to give her perspective on the cutoff so I could better understand, thus, and move toward forgiving Sophia. Or if she did not wish to do that, would she look at the letter I'd written and judge if any of it might ever be helpful for Sophia to know? I also said I hoped we could stay social media friends. She politely said no to my requests and stayed my friend on social media.

She may have made the best decision available to her, but I felt put back at square one on how to process my trauma. Some more time and thought brought me to this book. I realized I needed to share what I had experienced and learned about our culture along the way. It won't help my relationship with Sophia, but perhaps it can help others. In that mindset of social bridge building, I emailed Tammy one more time. I asked her if I could quote her refusal to engage with me as part of this book. As you might imagine, she forcefully said no and blocked me on social media. That, too, makes sense from the perspective of common cutoff practice. Yes, I can imagine how crazy I sounded asking if I could dissect her words in a book she likely assumed would be an act of revenge on her dear friend. Of course, she said no. Of course, she blocked me.

However, it leaves us—Tammy and me—in an awkward place. Because there cannot be communication between us, I have no way of understanding our relationship. It is possible I was an unsettling blip on her radar, who she rejected and blocked as best practice in boundary setting. It is also possible that she views me as a dangerous person who might turn to harassing her. It is possible that, in some background way, she feels she must defend herself against me for life. It is possible she recognizes that Sophia and I are both ordinary people who each contributed to dissolution of our relationship. It is possible she views me with compassion but feels her loyalty to Sophia incompatible with showing it. It is possible there is a mix of all these things. Because

I cannot talk to her or Sophia, I have no way of knowing. Thus, I don't know how to mentally orient myself toward Tammy.

It is tempting to imagine that she thinks of me kindly. That would make me more comfortable and help me feel more at peace. Yet I sense a danger in allowing that feeling, a concern that it might someday lead me to reach out to her again. What if, in a weak moment, I tried again, expecting compassion and received... what? A verbal lashing? More than that? Tammy works at an organization where I have professional ties. What if she told the staff that I'm harassing her and should be reported if seen? I might lose those professional contacts, be blackballed and shamed, my reputation permanently tarnished. It feels safer to assume the worst: that she fears me and, because people are dangerous when they are afraid, I, in return, must fear her.

And what if Tammy does view me as a threat? What if one half-hour, face-to-face conversation would permanently dispel that fear? I would like to give her that relief, but it can't happen.

Let me reiterate: this is someone I don't know. This is someone I had a nice coffee with over a decade ago and then exchanged a couple of short, mostly polite written communications with.

Several months before I first contacted Tammy, I went to the organization where she works in order to have an informational interview with a former colleague. We had a friendly, productive chat. And the entire time I was in the building I felt like an imposter. I kept waiting for my colleague to see through my disguise, to unmask the stalker, to realize I was a criminal and should be thrown out—all because I was in the building where Tammy worked, a building I had every right to be in, on business that had nothing to do with Tammy or Sophia. This feeling, of course, was not Tammy's fault; I hadn't even approached her yet. It certainly is not a situation Sophia ever wished on me. Yet this is one of the prices of a social system that prioritizes shunning over repair, this internalization of the belief that you must be dirty and guilty for wanting to talk about a problem.

The ultimate answer is clear: stop worrying about it, accept and let go. To stop worrying and let go is, indeed, the ultimate answer: to this, to death, to life, to everything—and perhaps the hardest task for any human being to accomplish.

Chapter 9

The Advice to Reprimand Those Who Question Cutoff

Tenet 5. Those who *question* cutoffs should be sharply reprimanded for disrespecting boundaries.

> "They are full of what's evil trying to hurt you!"[263]
>
> "These people are called narcissists and psychopaths."[264]
>
> "Stop feeding leeches… You're a good person. You got a good heart. They don't."[265]

This is a snippet of common social media comments about cut-off people. Social media comments are famously nasty, but these statements also align closely with more general attitudes about cuttees, recurring themes in advice blogs, popular articles on relationship, observations I've heard from friends. There's a wide belief that disdain is the only appropriate response to cut-off people. Three assumptions underly this position: (1) people are usually cut off because they did something to deserve it; (2)

---

[263] @shiamaxwell3482, comment on Tyler JTI. "Cut People off without Warning: Stop Constantly Explaining to Them What They're Doing Wrong," YouTube, 7 Sept. 2017, comment is c. 2023, www.youtube.com/watch?v=-IxQYvn2ivQ.

[264] @blondebombshellharris2447, comment on Tyler JTI. "Cut People off without Warning: Stop Constantly Explaining to Them What They're Doing Wrong," YouTube, 7 Sept. 2017, comment is c. 2020, www.youtube.com/watch?v=-IxQYvn2ivQ.

[265] Hassan Campbell, "You Have to Cut People off without a Warning," YouTube, August 11, 2019, https://www.youtube.com/watch?v=fmv7uiBMjsA.

therefore, if they question cutoff, they show poor awareness of their own misdeeds; (3) even if the cuttee has done nothing to deserve cutoff, it is still inherently bad to question cutoff because it shows disrespect for rights and boundaries. Thus, if someone questions cutoff, the only virtuous response is to shut them down with righteous condemnation. To do anything else is to tolerate entitlement, harassment, and violation of rights.

This position is problematic for two reasons: (1) It assumes there are no legitimate concerns about cutoff practice. Obviously, I am arguing that there are. (2) Responding with disdainful, often shaming critique can compound trauma because it acts as derogation, which Williams describes as one of the principal harms associated with ostracism.[266] *Derogation* means putting someone down, casting them as bad or unworthy. Being put down is always unpleasant, but when it becomes a pattern, it can be psychologically harmful and socially corrosive.

The Psychological Harm of Derogation

The social media skewering Reifman received for his critique of cutoff culture did not stop with social media. On his blog, Steinmetz dismissively describes Reifman as "a guy [who] had a four-month relationship with someone who (it's implied) is a decade younger than he is, and then was still stalkery heartbroken about it two and a half years later,"[267] a description full of *ad hominem* slaps. Yet Steinmetz derides himself even more harshly. When he describes his own ex cutting him off, his respect for her is evident, but the language he uses for himself is merciless: "I wasn't a good person back then," he says—not just that he was ill-behaved or toxic or even abusive, but *not a good person*, a bad human being.[268] "*I was the villain here*," he asserts in bold letters: the *villain*, a word that suggests the mustache-twirling bad guy, badness

---

[266] Williams, 245.

[267] Steinmetz, "She Broke up with Me, and Never Gave Me a Second Chance." Note the implication that it is suspicious for two consenting adults to date across a ten-year age difference, an idea that runs counter to the principle of sexual freedom among consenting adults yet has been a common dig at Reifman.

[268] Steinmetz, "She Broke up with Me, and Never Gave Me a Second Chance."

incarnate.[269] This language connotes inherent depravity. The Joker is a villain; Lex Luthor is a villain, so too, at least rhetorically, the mentally ill nineteen-year-old Steinmetz. I don't know the details of Steinmetz's situation, but based on the angsty teen he describes, my gut is sympathetic to his commenter, John, who tells him, "You're still writing about [the cutoff] and you're aware of how it shaped you because you're probably sensitive and care about what motivates your actions, and a lot of shallow people aren't. All this 'I was a bad person' stuff is ridiculous…."[270] But whether it's ridiculous in Steinmetz's case or not, it's typical of cutoff derogation.

Jefferson's critique of Reifman in *The Guardian* uses similar derogation. Of Reifman's essay, Jefferson states, "Though ostensibly the article sought to end the unheralded scourge of people refusing to talk with their ex-lovers, it mostly read like an entitled plea for attention…."[271] Leaving aside whether it reads like an entitled plea, the "unheralded scourge" is plainly sarcasm and not anything Reifman actually argues. In a word, it's a putdown. But like Steinmetz, Jefferson puts himself down too. Of his own flailing after his own girlfriend abruptly cut him off, he says that he "needed fixing" while she did not.[272] His pain was all his fault, none of it hers, and, by implication, the cutoff was all his fault too. He was the broken person harming the innocent.

Lyn uses a different metaphor. She describes her view of permanently cutting someone off as "throwing [the relationship] out with the rest of the garbage. It's gone, poof, no more. I've cut it out and thrown it away."[273] The thing thrown away here is the relationship, not the cut-off person. But when throwing away the relationship involves permanently ostracizing the person, it's hard not to read the person as part of the "garbage" thrown away: "gone, poof, no more," not a human being worth considering anymore, outside the cutter's circle of compassion forever.

---

269 Steinmetz, "She Broke up with Me, and Never Gave Me a Second Chance."

270 John, comment on Steinmetz, "She Broke up with Me, and Never Gave Me a Second Chance."

271 Cord Jefferson, "Men Aren't Entitled to Women's Time or Affection. But It's a Hard Lesson to Learn," *The Guardian*, July 18, 2014, http://www.theguardian.com/commentisfree/2014/jul/18/men-entitled-women-friendzone.

272 Jefferson.

273 Lyn, private message to the author, October 6, 2017.

Being Cut

Taken as isolated instances, many examples of derogation are not especially egregious. Some are venting on social media; some are sincerely meant to foster respect for boundaries and for survivors of abuse (some are both!). Lyn was just honestly answering my question about her cutoff experience.[274] But as a collective, the unremitting assumptions that cut-off people are self-entitled, villainous, broken garbage start to take on the force of a hammer on the brain. In 2018, I wrote a friends-locked blog post (now deleted) in which I shared the effect of this hammer on me. Here's a piece of it:

> Since my estrangement with [Sophia] began, I have been explicitly compared to a murderer, a stalker, and an abuser. I compared myself to rapists and serial killers, just to try to understand *why* she thinks this [cutting me off permanently] is okay....
>
> Do you know what this [derogation] has taught me...? It has taught me to identify with Harvey Weinstein. Seriously. Not with anything he did. I have no identification with that on any level at all, but with the weight of being damned in people's eyes forever. Trevor Noah told a joke about Weinstein that went something like if he woke up from cryogenic sleep in 1000 years, it would still be too soon. And all I could think was—my God, anyone deserves a chance at forgiveness after 1000 years...! I am so villain identified in my own head that almost every time I see some rat being made fun of on some comedy show, I cringe as if that rat were me—as if Trevor Noah had it in for me. As if I had... raped and molested countless people.[275]

---

[274] It may be evident that I find Lyn's view harsh, and at times my response is harsh too. Some years after the exchanges I've quoted, however, she noted that our cutoff experiences were very different. She cut off a coworker who had treated her horribly at work. I was cut off by a dear friend. These are, indeed, very different contexts, and it makes sense that we have different ideas about what cutoff means.

[275] I do not endorse derogatory language, and though Harvey Weinstein has much to answer for, my calling him a "rat" does not help with his answering for it. I include that language because it's what I wrote at the time. For legal clarity, the people Weinstein was accused/convicted of raping, assaulting, and/or harassing are not "countless." That was an

As is typical of my friends-locked posts on this topic, no one replied. (I emphasize this because this post is a fairly clear cry for help and persistent silence in response should not be the social norm.) However, my friend Anna read the post and referenced it in an email to me over two years later. This is her take on our society's common practices around cutoffs:

> I think on the whole, the common wisdom kind of means well, but often ends up doing more harm. I know the impossibility to reach out was one of the roots of your difficulty in finding your ground in the situation [with Sophia], not least because it was quite forcefully imposed on you and very much against every instinct. It's driven you to such bizarreness like likening yourself to H. Weinstein, ffs.[276]

It's hard to have friends, acquaintances, and online media persistently blame you for your own traumatization. It erodes self-esteem, stokes a sense of injustice. This is hard on everyone, but in a society that chastises men, in particular, for showing emotional vulnerability, it is hard on men in a particular way.

The Partial Red Herring of Male Entitlement

Cutoff culture responds to inequities in power and privilege. Arguably the principal inequity cutoff culture resists is the cultural construct that men are entitled to women's bodies and/or attention. While this construct takes many forms, an extreme example is the incel movement. "Incel," which stands for "involuntarily celibate," is a term of self-identification for a person who would like to have sex but cannot find a partner. The term was coined in the 1990s by a woman, Alana, who founded a mixed-gender online community to support people who had dating troubles.[277] Since

---

exaggeration for effect. I have also been unable to track down this clip by Noah, so it's possible my memory of his joke is not accurate.

[276] Anna, email message to the author, April 9, 2020.

[277] Zack Beauchamp, "Our Incel Problem: How a Support Group for the Dateless Became One of the Internet's Most Dangerous

that time, however, the incel culture has morphed into a male-only misogynistic movement that blames women for sexually alluring men, then refusing them. One poster on an incel forum expressed a common view:

> "Our whole lives we've had to endure the pain of being so physically repulsive to females that they'd never even consider giving us a chance. We are actually so genetically inferior that they HATE us. They need to suffer… Their hypocrisy is a crime [punishable by] torture for the rest of their slutty lives."[278]

In short, women who refuse to have sex with men deserve torture. Even if the poster intended the "torture" as hyperbole, the gross sense of entitlement to women's bodies is crystal clear.

Nor are such calls for violence confined to online ranting. In recent years, a number of mass shootings have been committed by men identifying as incels.[279] One of them, Elliot Rodger, killed six people in Isla Vista, California in 2014 before shooting himself. He left a 141-page manifesto describing his victimization by attractive women who did not want to sleep with him; he also became a figure of adulation for many incels.[280] The use of male entitlement to condone violence against women is terrifying, and we need to work swiftly toward a culture where it is aberrant, unacceptable, and, in rare cases when it happens, effectively addressed.

A rigorous validation of cutoff is one way of amplifying the power of marginalized people in the face of dangerous narratives of entitlement. Supporting the right to cutoff can help people escape abuse, harassment, and death. Let me reiterate: I support the right to cutoff. People should have the right to cut others off and,

---

Subcultures," *The Highlight by Vox*, April 23, 2019, https://www.vox.com/the-highlight/2019/4/16/18287446/incel-definition-reddit/.

[278] qtd. in Zack Beauchamp.

[279] Sam Louie, "The Incel Movement," *Psychology Today*, April 25, 2018, https://www.psychologytoday.com/us/blog/minority-report/201804/the-incel-movement.

[280] "Elliot Rodger: How Misogynist Killer Became 'Incel Hero,'" *BBC News*, April 25, 2018, https://www.bbc.com/news/world-us-canada-43892189.

in many cases, they must be fully supported in refusing any and all contact with the cuttee.

At the same time (both can exist at once), cutoff discourse tends to discuss non-familial cutoff as if it only occurs in the context of women protecting themselves from toxic male entitlement, as if a man asserting entitlement were the only possible thing that could trigger it. This is not the case, and the implication that it is forestalls a serious examination of cutoff culture.

A case in point is the media outcry against Reifman in the wake of his essay critiquing cutoff culture.[281] Virtually all of Reifman's critics approach his interactions with his ex from this perspective of male entitlement, though the criticisms range beyond Reifman's specific actions, with commentators such as Steinmetz and Jefferson courageously critiquing their own past actions too. This reduction of Reifman's argument to cry of male entitlement, however, derails discussion of his actual thesis: that cutoff without any means of closure does harm and, therefore, offering closure should be the norm.[282] In many critiques, his argument remains substantially undiscussed, short circuiting genuine discourse about cutoff.

Toxic masculinity is a huge problem in our society. Far too many men do feel entitled to women's bodies and attention. We see that in our rape culture and in our culture of intimate partner violence. We see it in the pervasive experiences of harassment women have shared in the #MeToo movement. It is no doubt almost universally true that if a man feels entitled to a woman's body and attention, he will feel entitled to communication with her too. Thus, there are certainly many entitled men who rail against being cut off. It does not follow that all men who rail against being cut off are toxically entitled. That contention is

---

[281] I struggled with how to phrase this, as Reifman himself has recanted his use of the term "cutoff culture." I toyed with using "relationship cutoff" or just "cutoff." But neither Reifman nor I am objecting to an individual person's choice to cut someone off. His essay and my thesis are both about culture, broader norms. I don't know what to call that other than "cutoff culture."

[282] I respect Reifman's essay, but I don't entirely agree with his thesis. Offering closure is wonderful, but I suspect most cutters are too angry and/or traumatized, at least at the time of the cutoff, to do so; thus, suggesting it should be a social norm is probably asking the impossible.

illogical. I mean that in a formal, ancient-Greek-logic way. Here's a good old-fashioned example of bad logic, an invalid syllogism:

> Some mammals are cats.
> Fido is a mammal.
> Therefore, Fido is a cat.

It doesn't follow, does it? Fido could be a dog—or a shrew, who knows? This is the exact same logical structure:

> Some men who object to cutoff feel toxically entitled to women.
> Jeff is a man who objects to cutoff.
> Therefore, Jeff feels toxically entitled to women.

It isn't logically valid here either.

Given that this book is written by a woman, I hope this is an obvious reality: even outside of family relationships, toxic masculinity is not the only reason to object to being cut off. I am not a man. I was not cut off by a lover. I did not ever want a sexual relationship with Sophia: I am on the asexual spectrum and oriented toward men. Even so, I was still ripped apart by a cutoff. Even so, I object to cutoff culture. Ryan was badly wounded by being cut off by me. We were not romantically involved. In fact, we had tried dating some years before, and he made it clear he was not attracted to me. He was, nonetheless, badly wounded by my cutoff. Arlo is still stricken by his friend cutting him off, though at the time of their friendship, he was in a happy, monogamous relationship with the woman he later married. Reid didn't want a romance with Dina. Reid is gay and has a long-term partner.

People object to cutoff for many reasons. They may object because they don't respect basic boundaries. Or they may respect boundaries and object to cutoff because it hurts them; it does damage. People may object because they want healing, for everyone involved. They may object because they want peace, for everyone.

The assumption that all men who object to cutoff feel toxic entitlement toward women is not only false; like many extreme positions, it has the insidious effect of supporting the attitudes it seeks to dismantle. In our society, men are encouraged to hide all emotions but anger. Sorrow can sometimes be acceptable, but as

Jonathan McIntosh of *Pop Culture Detective* observes, in TV and cinema, the window that allows men's tears is very narrow: they are allowed to cry briefly in response to obvious crisis, such as death; guilt over a failure to protect; or extreme physical pain.[283] An ex or ex-friend saying they don't want to speak to you certainly falls outside the acceptable window of masculine sorrow. Here's the rub. To dismantle toxic masculinity, men must be able to express vulnerability. But in cutoff culture, expressing vulnerability (trauma) means they are toxic men. The backlash is sharp and the command unmistakable: don't share your feelings, don't expect sympathy, don't admit to trauma. In fact, crawl back into exactly the emotional repression that generates toxic masculinity in the first place.

In his piece on cutoffs, Reifman notes that men, including himself, often lack the emotional support of intimate friendships. In his response, Harris O'Malley illustrates our cultural mixed messaging:

> [Y]eah, it sucks that men are socialized to be detached from their emotions and we're discouraged from having emotionally intimate platonic relationships.... If you [Reifman] don't have friends you can go to for support, well I feel bad for you, son, but that's *not [Emma's] problem.* That's *entirely on you.* You and you alone are responsible for your own healing.[284]

For starters, this passage is premised on a false dichotomy: either Reifman's lack of support is Emma's problem, or Reifman must be 100 percent responsible his own healing. Of course, his lack of support is not Emma's problem. *And* no human being should be held 100 percent responsible for their own healing. That's not how our social species works. On the one hand, O'Malley agrees that men should be able to share more feelings. On the other, he asserts that no one should expect emotional support from anyone.

---

[283] (Pop Culture Detective) Jonathan MacIntosh, "Boys Don't Cry (Except When They Do)," YouTube. July 1, 2021, https://www.youtube.com/watch?v=kGxW2toAvzc.

[284] Harris O'Malley, "'Cutoff Culture' and the Myth of Closure," *Paging Dr. Nerdlove*, May 19, 2014, https://www.doctornerdlove.com/cutoff-culture-and-the-myth-of-closure/.

These ideas are in conflict: we cannot have open expression of emotions in a social matrix in which we cannot expect some background level of support. Intimacy requires trust. Being able to express emotion requires trust. We cannot trust when we are at constant risk of being flayed anytime we share anything. By offering Reifman ridicule instead of serious engagement, by reducing his narrative to its worst possible interpretation, O'Malley orders Reifman to emotionally withdraw. He criticizes him for sharing his vulnerability, just as men have been socialized to expect. The end result is to reinforce the emotional stunting that drives masculine entitlement. One way to sort out such emotional tangles is to seek therapeutic help, but cutoff complicates this option too.

The Harm of Being Derogated by Professionals

It's a truism in our society that when we're struggling psychologically we should "get help." This is shorthand for seeing a therapist or joining a formal support group. Unfortunately, when it comes to cutoffs, professional help may be of limited use. To be clear, I absolutely encourage exploring such help. It has helped me somewhat and may prove beneficial to others. Yet the extent to which professional help often falls short in addressing cutoff trauma is a sign of how little cutoff is understood in our society. As I noted earlier, of the three therapists I saw about my cutoff, none of them recognized I was experiencing cutoff trauma. This is not uncommon. In her discussion of abandonment trauma, Anderson states,

> [I]t is hard for me to understand why [abandonment's] special type of grief has gone virtually unrecognized, unstudied, and untreated until now. Mental health professionals generally interpret the feelings of abandonment as a symptom of depression or anxiety. But abandonment grief is a syndrome all its own. It is the way in which your fear and anger are turned against yourself that gives abandonment grief its own particular character.[285]

[285] Anderson, 11.

It is not surprising that abandonment, of which cutoff is an extreme variety, often causes us to turn our fear and anger against ourselves when our culture also tends to blame us. This drive toward blame can extend even into professional support groups meant to help abandoned people.[286] Support groups are designed to offer a safe community for people grappling with a certain problem. In many cases, these problems are socially stigmatized: addictions or anger management, for example. It is generally understood that support groups will work to avoid further stigmatization. This is part of what makes them a safe space. Consider the non-judgmental language employed in descriptions of these support groups:

Support group for people living with Post-Traumatic Stress Disorder (PTSD):

> Peer support groups are a place where you can discuss day-to-day problems with other people who have been through trauma. Support groups have not been shown to reduce PTSD symptoms, but they can help you feel better in other ways. Because it can give you a sense of connection to other people, a peer support group could be a great addition to your treatment.[287]

Coaching for addiction recovery:

> Recovery Coaching helps individuals in recovery identify their own unique pathways to a joyful life. Recovery Coaches provide a framework for setting goals and looking at all areas of life that are important to the recovering person.[288]

---

[286] You may notice I am substituting "abandonment" for "cutoff" in this discussion of professional supports. As far as I have found, professional supports dedicated to cut-off people do not exist at all.

[287] "Peer Support Groups," U.S. Department of Veterans Affairs, accessed May 3, 2020, https://www.ptsd.va.gov/gethelp/peer_support.asp.

[288] "Recovery Coaching," Portland Recovery, accessed June 27, 2024, https://portlandrecovery.org/portland-center/recovery-coaching/.

Being Cut

Support group for people living with obsessive compulsive disorder (OCD):

> There is a sense of community that exists in a well-run support group. It can mean finding others who know how you feel or being seen as someone with a disorder rather than as the disorder itself.[289]

Now compare this text from the support group network for abandonment survivors, affiliated with Anderson's practice, which is prominent in abandonment recovery. It is important to note that the text below has since been revised, possibly in part as a response to my whining about it. I whined in a quite a testy email and received a very kind reply from Anderson. She now has a new website, and I recommend it as a resource for abandonment recovery.[290] It should also be noted that the Outer Child is a designation for the self-defeating part of us, and Anderson explicitly teaches that this is not our whole selves. Nevertheless, the older text (online until 2020) says a lot about our culture's attitudes toward abandonment. The bold is part of the original format.

> Of course, you [abandonment survivors] belong together—Abandonment leads to patterns of **self-sabotage** and vice versa.
>
> By getting involved in Outer Child / Abandonment support groups (and setting up *abando*holics[291] anonymous groups) you are helping each other heal your collective wounds which give rise to **self-defeat, love addiction, low self-esteem, chasing the emotionally unavailable, patterns of abandonment, heartache, problems in relationships, poor choices**, and more.

---

289 "Support Groups," International OCD Foundation, accessed May 3, 2020, https://iocdf.org/ocd-finding-help/supportgroups/.

290 Anderson's current website is www.abandonment.net, accessed August 18, 2022.

291 i.e. people serially attracted to others likely to abandon them.

> Outer Child groups gain their depth and dynamic from zeroing in on the issue of abandonment—the source of most **self-defeating patterns.**[292]

This is the only support group I have ever seen that berates the people it is supporting for causing their own trauma—and with the berating words in bold as the most crucial text! This statement, again, came from a premier professional resource on abandonment trauma. I applaud Anderson and her team for revising this text, but the fact that it was ever published speaks to how pervasively acceptable it is to disparage abandoned people.

Derogation obviously hurts the derogated person. Unfortunately, the hurt doesn't always stop there. The resulting intensification of trauma sometimes generates disordered feelings and poorly regulated behavior in cut-off people that impede peaceful relationships and respect for boundaries, exacerbating the very problems the cutoff was meant to solve.

Condemnation Can Hinder Letting Go

The goal of permanent cutoff is to sever a relationship, but sometimes unremitting rejection can perpetuate the connection by intensifying the cuttee's sense of bewilderment and injustice and their desire to remediate it. When she cut me off, Sophia was almost immaculate in following the standard rules. The one time she chose to disregard them was the one time I was almost able to accept her cutting me off.

When I wrote Sophia for the final time in 2017, I explicitly asked for a reply because being ignored is intensely painful for me. To her credit, Sophia did reply. Out of consideration for her boundaries, I had never explicitly asked her to reply before. The one time I did, she acceded to my request. That was a kindness, especially after the nasty letter I'd sent her the previous year. She replied with three messages, each varying in tone, suggesting uncertainty about how to handle the situation. Her first message did the minimum of what I asked for, verifying flatly that she still did not want contact. If she'd stopped there, I would have felt

---

[292] "Post or Find a Support Group Near You," OuterChild.net, accessed May 3, 2020, http://outerchild.net/post-or-find-group-near-you. (site discontinued)

tremendous closure. The message was clear and the communication kinder than the silence my therapist and I had expected. Her second message, sent a few hours later, was sensitive and caring. At the time, we were working at the same institution,[293] and she stated that she wished both of us to have a good experience at work. She stated that if we had to work together, she would be cordial, but otherwise, she wished no contact. In communicating with me and kindly, she did the opposite of what common cutoff practice advises as clear boundary setting.

I absolutely cannot overstate how healing that second message was! For the first time in two and a half years, I felt at peace. As soon as I read it, a vast weight evaporated. I emailed back a one-line acknowledgement and thanks for her reply. That evening, I wrote a locked entry in my blog (since deleted) in which I said that, because of that email, I felt 95 percent healed. Sophia still didn't want to reconnect, and that piece of reality testing itself answered a huge, lingering question: had time healed anything? Had thirty months led to any change in her feelings? The answer was no, but that was okay. Now I knew where I stood. I knew she wished me well and saw me as a decent human being, not a dangerous enemy. I knew I didn't have to be afraid of being asked to work with her. I could do what she wanted. I could let it go. This is what closure looks like. I did reflect that I might contact her some years in the future, just to ask again if anything had changed.[294] If the answer was no, that would be fine. For me, the situation was largely resolved.

About a day later, she sent her third message, in which she ordered me peremptorily to leave her alone forever. Given my angry letter of the year before, I set myself up for her reprimand. I understand—at least well enough—where it came from. The fact remains (both these things can be true), within the thirty seconds, that message undid all my healing. It erased all closure. It tore me open as fiercely as the first day she cut me off. It did this, not least,

---

293 I did not follow her there; I was working there before she was.

294 People ask me why I still want to talk. It's hard to explain in a few abstract words. Am I still pursuing our friendship? No. Imagine two old people who hurt each other badly in their youth running into each other in a retirement home, realizing suddenly that decades have passed, that things have changed, and sitting down for a coffee. Imagine them having a laugh with each other as it dawns on them the past is past. That's what I want.

by implying that I was, to use Steinmetz's formulation, the villain and she innocent, that my pain bore no relation to her actions—which is as absurd as saying her pain at my actions bore no relation to me. *But this is our recommended practice*, so much so that I would not be surprised if she was acting on her therapist's or friends' advice to set clear boundaries. Indeed, my friend Anna later confirmed she thought it read like a standard boundary-setting message.

That third message did accomplish one thing her second message did not: it terrified me into never contacting her since. However, I contacted Tammy instead, which ended up widening the circle of fear and disconnection. That third message also left Sophia and me in a state of cold war, each fearing any transgression. Her reprimand renewed my traumatization and my emotional investment in seeking closure. It locked the focus of my emotional life squarely back on her, precisely where she (and I) least wanted it to be.

Now, one could argue that's my fault, and not a sign of a poor cultural practice: after all, Sophia and I had already parted on cordial terms in 2014. I messed that up by pursuing her. That's true, but that narrative overlooks the nature of grief. Our initial messages were cordial, yes. I marshalled all my reserves to sound mature, and I suspect she did too. My psyche, however, was in wreckage. I simply did not have the power to say goodbye cold turkey then. Yet time does heal. While the polite cutoff of 2014 hit me like a sword through the heart, the polite cutoff of 2017 was a bandage on a wound I just wanted to stop oozing. The first was betrayal, the second was closure. That's because grief takes time, internalizing a new reality takes time. That's something our ethical systems need to account for.

One could also argue that, while Sophia's second message may have better concluded the situation, *she* couldn't know that. After all, I followed up my polite seeming acceptance of 2014 with my harangue of 2016. That's also true: Sophia couldn't know. My first response is that people who refuse to communicate should expect failures in communication. It goes without saying a handful of email lines can't explain complex mental states. That's a good argument for not relying on them and having real-time communication. It's a good argument for avoiding cutoff too when healthily possible.

My second response is that this is why we need a better cutoff practice. Though there is no one-size-fits-all, every culture needs norms we can default to unless there's a reason not to. Our current default is self-defensive nastiness, which easily backfires. It did with my nasty letter to Sophia. It did with Sophia's reprimand to me. It backfired, too, in the online attempts to mount a feminist critique of Reifman's cutoff essay.

Harsh Condemnation Can Hinder Problem-Solving and Allyship

In his essay, "Shining Light on Internet Rage," Reifman describes his attempt to open a dialogue with a social media user whom he describes as leading attacks on his critique of cutoff. Her own tweets used a sharp and angry tone:

> @reifman, just fyi, [your cutoff essay]… is a gross, entitled piece of writing. I feel sorry for anyone who's ever dated you. Get help.[295]

In addition, she described tweeting at him to her ten thousand followers as "a lil signal boost on that account," a boost that led to a week of online harassment.[296]

Reifman noted that this same person had co-founded a feminist workspace with explicit policies against harassment and had written about the need to reduce harassment on social media. He quotes a message he sent her in the hopes of opening up a more civil discussion:

> [T]he comment policy on your blog asks that commenters be "non-discriminatory, friendly, funny, or perspicacious" … I'm super open to a discussion about this as long as comments are civil and constructive. I would hope you would tweet as you wish others to publicly comment on your blog. [ellipsis original][297]

---

[295] qtd. in Reifman, "Shining Light on Internet Rage."

[296] qtd. in Reifman, "Shining Light on Internet Rage."

[297] Reifman, "Shining Light on Internet Rage."

She replied via tweet, "No, @reifman, I am not interested in talking with you, ever. I am interested in warning others about you. Do not contact me again."[298]

In his essay, Reifman observes that this response eliminated a possible chance for constructive discussion about cutoff:

> I was sincerely seeking dialogue—an opportunity she rejected. If activists expect everyone to understand their values and vocabulary yet are unwilling to engage in conversation, then how can someone respond? This is one of the side-effects that I wrote about in ["Shining Light on Relationship Cutoff"], when we cut people off, "we're also robbing them of a chance to apologize and make amends."[299]

Reifman is a self-described advocate of equity for women. In his published writings, email correspondence, and real-time communication, I find he consistently shows significant awareness of women's oppression and a desire to use his own privilege to support women's empowerment. Perhaps the harassment he received, in part, was intended to teach him to change his attitude toward cutoff. Unsurprisingly, it did not have this effect. If anything, it somewhat eroded his allyship with feminist causes:

> The weeklong harassment of me by self-identifying feminists made me suspicious of online feminism, a movement that I'd previously admired. It made me take a closer look and ask: what are the values of this community? It made me emotionally averse to reading material from them or engaging with them in any way.[300]

A course of action designed to support women's empowerment ended up reducing the enthusiasm of at least one ally of that work and preventing open dialogue about relationships and women's right to freedom from oppression.

The tweets by this particular critic of Reifman are far from the worst of internet trolling. Though they express anger, they often

---

[298] Reifman, "Shining Light on Internet Rage."

[299] Reifman, "Shining Light on Internet Rage."

[300] Reifman, "Shining Light on Internet Rage."

eschew profanity, make clear statements, and avoid name calling. They are not the online equivalent of screaming and stamping one's feet. Rather they represent a concerted practice, the same practice Sophia used in her final message to me: one that tells us to shut down so-called toxic people with reprimands. The goal is to set clear boundaries to make troublesome people shape up or go away. I think it is likely this critic did not view her tweets as harassment but as chastisement: an assertion of power in order to forestall an abuse of power by person with more social privilege, in this case, a woman "punching up" against a man. Much of our social discourse views this as the best way to assert power from a position of vulnerability. In this case, the critic's attacks likely did have the positive effect of emotionally validating many social media users who had been victims of abuse. I also think it is likely that her angry tone reflects harm the critic had suffered at the hands of other men. That anger is understandable. Voicing it is understandable and perhaps what she had to do. Unfortunately, these attacks also entrenched division among political allies without productive, transformative discourse. This does little or nothing to reduce abuse, which should surely be the ultimate goal.

Harsh Condemnation Can Exacerbate Dysfunction

I've mentioned that my blogosphere friend Delia once scolded me for a locked post in which I mentioned plans to contact Sophia. I deleted the text of that conversation, but looking at the timing, I must have written the original post just before or after my second post-cutoff email to Sophia. That email, the one that said, "I miss you and I'd like to make peace," I sent on January 25, 2016. I remember the date because it was precisely one year after my first email. I must have said something about that email—or planning to send a follow-up maybe; I don't remember. Delia chastised me for boundary violation and told me I'd better stop it.

I felt slapped by that comment, and to avoid further slapping, I deleted the offending posts and posted the following:

> I've deleted my last couple of entries, which means I also ended up deleting the very kind and helpful comments I got in response to them. I didn't delete them because of the comments, just because I didn't want the entries

> anymore. The comments were, indeed, very helpful, one and all, and it was for that outpouring of support, perspective, and thoughts that I posted in the first place. I really got it. I don't need those entries. Thank you.[301]

It's an interesting example of negativity bias—our human tendency to focus on negatives over positives—that I have zero recollection of those "very kind and helpful comments." Literally all I remember is Delia's scolding. In any case, "I got it." The message came through. I needed to stop talking about it, or I'd get slapped again. I couldn't go to my friends for help. I had to go through it alone. Two weeks later, I sent Sophia that ugly and nasty letter I will regret for the rest of my life.

So much for Delia's admonitions.

I was so buried in my trauma, however, that I didn't regret that letter at first. At first, I felt validated. It took me about a month to start to realize I'd made a mistake, about two months to fully regret it, and a year or two to realize just how egregious and how retraumatizing for her it probably was. The first turning point, however, the beginning of that regret, was one evening when I had dinner with Derek. He was listening to me rant about Sophia, and in the course of this rant, I mentioned that letter.

He said something to the effect of "That wasn't a good idea."

He said it with a smile and a gentleness of tone, in the course of a good hour sitting and listening to my woes. I think I asked him why. He probably said it would just push her further away. I don't remember the specifics, but I knew he had my well-being at heart. I trusted him, and I asked him to read another letter to Sophia—yes, I'd penned a follow-up. Its gist was something like promising to leave her alone if she'd have one conversation to talk things through. He said the letter was also a bad idea. He said, "What you want to accomplish—this letter will do the opposite." I didn't want to hear that; it made me angry, but it made sense, and he framed it in terms not of Sophia's boundaries but of my best interest. I never sent it.

Lest I sound like I'm making an invidious comparison between Delia and Derek, it's worth noting the crucial importance of the medium and the relationship. Delia sent me a short, written comment in response to a blog post. Derek had a three-hour

---

301 Arwen Spicer, deleted blog post, January 27, 2016.

dinner with me, face-to-face, listening to me weep about my life. Delia is a person I've never met but have had infrequent online interactions with for fifteen years. She is a person I profoundly admire, but Derek is a personal friend I've known face-to-face for decades. My relationship with Delia is thin, my relationship with Derek thick. Both had my best interest at heart—but with Delia I couldn't see that. I honestly never guessed it until we were discussing that incident for this book years later. With Derek it was obvious. The lesson from these two encounters is clear: depth in relationships matters. We need to know at least some people as full human beings, face to face. We need much more emphasis on those ties today, especially for the young who have grown up immersed in a soup of social media, exacerbated by years of pandemic-induced distancing.

That said, often online interaction is the social outlet we've got, so it's important to do it as well as we can. Our cultural norms told Delia my best interests would be served by a tough-love wake-up call. She meant well, but the dramatic misfire in the result illustrates a problem with this practice. The message I received was that I did not dare to reach out for support. Thus, I turned to handling my trauma all alone, and that is a deadly formulation. When we're traumatized, we don't think clearly. We lash out and hurt ourselves and others. To avoid this, we need support from our community. We need support, not to be driven out like King Lear into the storm. That way madness lies.

The hypothetical me who took Sophia's cutoff without one angry word…

The real me who sent four short, polite messages and one angry, invasive letter…

The hypothetical me who sent three or four angry, invasive messages totaling over ten thousand words…

These are all the same me.

They are the same person with the same hurt, thinking the same thoughts from the same perspective. The only difference between the me who never sent the angry letter and the me who did is that one day I chose to put a piece of paper in the mailbox without telling anyone or listening to the nagging in voice in my head whispering, "You know better." The only difference between the me who stopped with that letter and the me who sent thousands more browbeating words is that I decided to confide in a friend—that I had a friend to confide in, who kindly but firmly gave me an outside perspective. I decided, from then on, to lean on an outside perspective before taking any step to contact Sophia. These differences are microscopic. I do not want to live in a society in which the difference between perfection and moral criminality depends on such a tenuous roll of the dice.

If we are to transform that society, the crucial lesson is this: the difference between "paragon of virtue" and the "moral criminal" is no more or less than relationship. Alone, I made a mistake that clearly deepened Sophia's trauma. In relationship, I have pulled myself out of recommitting that error time after time, choice after choice, day after day, year after year. Just one dinner with a friend, one therapy session, one talk with my pastor—just a dozen or so communications with other human beings across several years—have not only spared me from possible prosecution for harassment but have spared Sophia from my profoundly compounding her trauma; my friends, my supports have protected her from that, not hers. Supporting *me* has protected her.

Chapter 10

The Advice to Begin by Accepting

Tenet 6. The cuttee should strive to immediately accept that the relationship is over and move on as quickly and totally as possible.

> People get to decide who they want in their lives. Most relationships end, one way or another....
>
> To feel "angry, hurt, heartbroken, betrayed, shaken, badly treated, resentful, etc." [at being cut off by a friend] seems disproportionate to me and, especially if it lasts for more than a couple of weeks, not rational.[302]

This statement is part of Meg's response to a question I posted on my blog in 2019 as part of processing my own cutoff trauma. I asked, "When someone abruptly (and somewhat nastily) cuts off all contact forever with someone they'd been close to, does the person cut off have *good reason* to feel angry, hurt, heartbroken, betrayed, shaken, badly treated, resentful, etc.?"[303] Meg's initial response was this:

> I don't think so, no. But I also don't think it matters. Feelings don't often respond to rational argument.... But if it is helpful to think yourself "unreasonably" upset, then I wouldn't argue with you.[304]

---

302 Meg, comment on Arwen Spicer, "A Question to You All about Values," *Dreamwidth* (blog), July 4, 2019, (post locked).
303 Arwen Spicer, "A Question to You All about Values."
304 Meg, comment on Arwen Spicer, "A Question to You All about Values."

No, it does not help me to see myself as "unreasonably upset." My emotional response to the trauma of cutoff is not unreasonable. That cutoff was traumatic, and trauma is, by definition, hard to process. Maté calls it "a psychic injury, lodged in our nervous system, mind, and body, lasting long past the originating incident(s), triggerable at any moment. It is a constellation of hardships, composed of the wound itself and the residual burdens that our woundedness imposes on our bodies and souls...."[305] Unreasonable is expecting this to resolve itself in a couple of weeks.

Meg's view, however, is a common one, undergirded by the cultural assumption that cutoff is not inherently traumatic, and, thus, accepting it should be fairly easy for "normal" people. For some, it is fairly easy. Cole has been cut off by both friends and family members and has taken it in stride as an understandable part of life.[306] Some are able to take this attitude toward the end of the relationships in general. Writing for the personal growth website The Overwhelmed Brain, Paul Colaianni states that he accepted the reality that his wife was never coming back only two days after she left him, though his full grieving process took longer.[307] These responses show admirable equanimity, but they are not typical. For many, cutoff abandonment is traumatic and the start of a long grieving process.

Psychiatrist Elisabeth Kübler-Ross famously outlined five stages of grief involved in facing terminal illness in her 1969 book *On Death and Dying*. The stages were denial, anger, bargaining, depression, and acceptance. To be sure, her framework should not be treated as gospel. It dealt specifically with dying, as opposed to other kinds of loss, and she didn't intend it as an exact science, later writing that her five stages were "never meant to help tuck messy emotions into neat packages."[308] Over the years, further research has found that grief can involve additional stages or complex meshes of feelings that can't be readily identified.[309]

---

[305] Maté, 20.

[306] Cole.

[307] Paul Colaianni, "Acceptance and Grieving the Breakup," The Overwhelmed Brain, accessed July 13, 2022, https://theoverwhelmedbrain.com/acceptance-grieving-breakup/.

[308] Elisabeth Kübler-Ross, qtd. in Lucy Burns, "Elisabeth Kübler-Ross: The Rise and Fall of the Five Stages of Grief," *BBC News*, July 2, 2020, https://www.bbc.com/news/stories-53267505.

[309] Burns.

Nonetheless, a common theme remains the fact that acceptance is a late or final stage.[310] It's generally where we end processing a loss, not where we start.

When people are faced with cutoff, however, we are often advised to *begin* by accepting. Reifman notes that when you've been cut off, "[Friends] want you to let go, move on, and definitely stop talking about it."[311] Svoboda, who advocates cutoff in breakups, is even more explicit: "The best thing a dumpee can do to speed emotional healing is to accept that the relationship has come to an unequivocal end."[312] But when we are confronted with the shock of suddenly being cut off from someone we love, it's normal to begin by feeling there must be some mistake, it can't be that bad, reconciliation must be possible—in a word "denial." Taylor observes, "Prior research has indicated that the 'abandoned' (those who did not initiate the breakup) were cognitively similar to individuals in intact relationships, both in the degree of mental devotion to the relationship and enmeshment of their ex-partner into the abandonee's own sense of self."[313] When a loved one suddenly cuts us off, it's nigh impossible we'll internalize it all at once. In the beginning, it's normal to feel like we are still in a relationship with them.

Williams states that ostracism assaults our core need for meaning in existence.[314] At first sight, it might not be clear why cutoff should affect our sense of life's meaning: in most cases, we still have our other relationships, activities, goals, job, etc. But our core love relationships define a key part of our lives. Losing even one of those leaves us scrabbling for balance. Like a death, cutoff permanently changes life. Accepting that takes time. When cultural expectations don't allow us this time, it places on us an unrealistic psychological expectation that frames us as irrational or immoral for having a normal grieving process.

---

[310] See for example, Sara Lindberg, "Understanding Therapy for Grief and How It Can Help," Healthline, March 22, 2021, https://www.healthline.com/health/mental-health/therapy-for-grief. Also "Grieving and Stages of Grief?" WebMD, August 20, 2023, https://www.webmd.com/balance/grieving-and-stages-of-grief.

[311] Reifman, "Shining Light on Relationship Cutoff."

[312] Svoboda.

[313] Taylor, 257.

[314] Williams, 245.

"You're Not Rational"

When I asked if there was good reason for a cut-off person to feel seriously aggrieved, Meg replied, no, that wasn't reasonable. In the same conversation, Lyn alluded to this trickiness of language. She responded, "I personally wouldn't use the exact words 'good reason' [to feel upset], but I certainly believe that any feelings of hurt or anger experienced by the person who's been cut off are valid. (I think my hesitance to use 'reason' is because feelings/emotions don't always follow reason/logic.)"[315] This caring and thoughtful response highlights the slippage between "good reason" and "reasonable." A "reason" is any explanation we present for doing something. "Reasonable," as Lyn observes, suggests "logical." The words sound similar, but the meanings are different: I might propose marriage because I've found the love of my life. That's a reason—probably a good reason—but it's not logical, at least not in the way we narrowly define logic as opposed to emotion. Thus, Lyn did not quite answer what I meant to ask. I meant, "Do these reasons make sense?" She answered, "These reasons are not logical," which is different from making sense, in the sense of showing normal thought processes. This might seem like mere semantics, but it speaks to our deep cultural assumption that reason and emotion are binary oppositions. If it is emotional, it is not reasonable, by definition.

This binary is deeply embedded in Western culture, which traditionally holds that if you act based on emotions, you are, by definition, not reasonable, irrational. This is a harmful perspective we ought to resist. The types of damage it does are manifold. For centuries, for example, the reason/emotion binary has been deployed to demean women, as well as other marginalized people. Within this binary, Man is reasonable and Woman emotional. Winnie Chang notes that historically,

> Persistent depictions of women's alleged inability to "transcend their bodily natures and sexual passions" fortified the belief in their essential irrationality and immorality (Pateman 1989, 4). They also defined women as animal-like, justifying their exclusion from the

[315] Lyn, comment on Arwen Spicer, "A Question to You All about Values."

> definition of the "liberal individual" as inherently rational beings with the capacity for civil participation (Pateman 1989).[316]

Because Woman is not reasonable, she is like an animal incapable of higher thought. It follows, of course, that such a person cannot be reasoned with but only controlled, like an animal tied up. Within the context of cutoff grief, it is interesting to note that research suggests women, on average, suffer it more keenly than men because our self-concept tends to be more grounded in social acceptance and we, thus, tend to ruminate on being socially excluded more than men do.[317] Unfortunately, this observation aligns with the stereotype of the irrational woman.

Consider this little syllogism:

> Intense grief over social exclusion is irrational;
> Women are more likely than men to experience intense grief over social exclusion;
> Therefore, women are more likely than men to become irrational over social exclusion.

The second premise is evidenced by some research. If we accept the first premise, then the whole statement is cogent—it's true. I do not accept the first premise. There's nothing irrational about grieving lost love; in fact, doing so suggests an understanding of love's value.

Nonetheless, such binary thinking remains common, and it has been a pillar not only of misogyny but also racism and other types of "othering." Chang cites Licia Carlson's (2014) observation that "reason, morality, and animality" have been three axes used to identify multiple groups of people as subhuman.[318] Chang further notes these oppressive discourses have especially brutal intersectional impacts on intersectionally marginalized groups, such

---

[316] Winnie Chang, "The Monstrous-Feminine in the Incel Imagination: Investigating the Representation of Women as 'Femoids' on /r/Braincels," *Feminist Media Studies*, 22, no. 2, 2020, p. 257, https://doi.org/10.1080/14680777.2020.1804976.

[317] Shuo Jin and Josephs, 83.

[318] Chang, 257.

as Black women.[319] At the same time, such narratives damage white male power holders as well, from Reifman, derided for daring to voice his pain, to the vivisectionist or Nazi scientist divorcing himself from compassion or conscience because such emotions interfere with his scientific objectivity. At its most extreme, the supremacy of reason has been used to justify torture.

Most people, of course, recognize that balance between rational thought and emotion is necessary to health and moral goodness. This is certainly true of my blogosphere friends. Yet even the subtle traces of this binary carry harm. Because my response to Sophia is emotional, they tell me, it cannot be reasonable. Because it is not reasonable, it is implicitly indefensible, because only reason can be reasonably defended. What's left is the language of emotional validity: "deciding how one should feel is a doomed endeavor," as Meg puts it,[320] and Lyn observes, "[A]ny feelings of hurt or anger experienced by the person who's been cut off are valid." Emotions simply exist. We cannot make them not exist, and so anything we feel is valid insofar as it is a real feeling. It is valid, but it is indefensible. It exists, but it does not make sense.[321] We have it, but to have it is irrational—and, thus, so are we. And being irrational connotes being mentally sick, incompetent, and possibly a threat.

Yet it is not irrational to be traumatized by abandonment and ostracism. That trauma makes perfect sense. We are social animals: to have our social relationships radically disrupted wounds on a deep, instinctive level. This is not inexplicable; it is an obvious consequence of having a human psyche. It is normal; it is how the human brain works. Emotion is an integral part of a reasonably functioning human being, and significant emotional wounds yield trauma. To expect anything else is not reasonable.

---

[319] Chang, 257–258.

[320] Meg, comment on Arwen Spicer "A Question to You All about Values."

[321] My editor notes that such thinking is decontextualized. I agree that a person's responses, in general, make sense when contextualized by their whole life experience. I would like to see more contextualizing in our culture.

When You Are Condemned for Normal, Loving Behavior

Grief can injure our sense of our life's meaning. So can cognitive dissonance, the sense that two views of reality are not comprehensibly aligning.

The failure to accept cutoff is often framed as an unacceptable boundary violation. Because it suggests a failure to fully *believe* someone's stated boundaries, it can be read as disrespectful, unhealthy, or even dangerous, even if our only *action* is to mention our disbelief to friends. But our friends' condemnation does not change the reality that we'll often start with not believing the cutoff is real. We can control when, how, or if we choose to transgress a cutoff, but we cannot fully control whether we believe it. We can't force ourselves to accept what we are not psychologically prepared to accept. That journey to acceptance is made more painful when we face recrimination for it not being instantaneous. Indeed, sometimes we face recrimination for feelings of loyalty to the cutter that would be considered a virtue in other contexts.

This book focuses on cutoffs in emotionally significant relationships. Such emotional significance can exist in a wide variety of contexts, but common examples are marriages, long-term romantic relationships, family, and close friendships. Most relationships of this kind involve commitment. At least, it is generally understood that they are supposed to.[322] Commitment is effectively a promise, whether explicit or tacit, to be there for the other person: to love them, to care for them, not to give up on them. When we are told that the relationship is over, and so thoroughly over that the cutter and cuttee can have no contact ever again, that gives the cuttee a difficult choice: we can keep our promise of committed love or break it.

If we keep it, it may be at best a promise in vain, leaving us, like Marley's Ghost, with a one-sided love we can never share with the person we wish to care for. At worst, it may become a kind of

---

[322] As noted previously, our society has mixed views toward commitment within friendships. Common sense dictates there is commitment among dear friends; otherwise, what's "dear" about the friendship? At the same time, inconsistently, we assume friendship isn't emotionally important. The "friend zone" is an insult. People who aren't lovers are "*just* friends."

psychological (if not literal) stalking, a mental obsession with a person who plainly wants us gone, the psychological antithesis of the boundaries the cutter presumably wants, at least if they are sincere in their desire to cut us off.

But if we break our promise, we commit one of our culture's cardinal crimes against committed love: to say (or show) we will be there for someone and then desert them. I want to be clear: breaking promises is sometimes appropriate. Divorce exists for good reason. Even priests can leave a priesthood if they must. Some promises are simply made in error, out of naivete or foolishness or the heat of the moment, and to remain straightjacketed to them is not healthy. All that said, to abandon a loving commitment is—and should be—serious. To do so carries overtones of betrayal, and the betrayal of a loved one is a heavy weight.

We are social creatures, and we rely on our commitments to each other to survive. To be committed means to be a support in troubled times. If someone is committed to us, we expect them to be there even when we are sick or unemployed or grieving a death. While none of these situations is a moral failing, they are all situations that typically generate unpleasant behavior. When we are sick, we are likely to be cranky and needy. When we are unemployed, we are likely to show stress, anxiety, and anger. When we are grieving, we are prone to tears, depression, and malaise. We expect that, within reason, someone emotionally committed to us will stand by us even so.

Yet, as soon as a loved one says, "I'll never speak to you again," cutoff culture advises that our commitment should be over. We should rapidly accept the relationship is null. As Reifman observes, "Our culture is very hostile to people in this situation [of being cut off]. We often judge those who don't move on right away."[323] We can *feel* whatever we feel, we're told, but if we *express* resistance to the cutoff, we are violating the other person's boundaries, and that means violating their rights. We are told it disrespects them to say, "I don't believe that"; "I know our love will find a way"; "Can we talk about this?"; "Why are you saying this?" They have refused their consent to contact, and we have not accepted it. For cutoff culture, that makes our words a violation.

Yet such words are characteristic of loving commitment. This is the same frame of mind that says, "This is just a fight, and we'll

[323] Reifman, "Shining Light on Relationship Cutoff."

get through it," or "I suspect you told me to get out because you had a migraine, and when I come back tomorrow, things will be better." We can no more expect someone to just shut off this love than we can expect someone not to grieve a loved one's death. True, the loved one is no longer there. It doesn't matter. The human psyche is not that agile. And it's a good thing too, because if it were, attached commitment would not exist. Without that commitment, we would likely not care for each other when we're sick or help each other through any trauma. As a species, we would probably not survive.

The first two messages I sent Sophia after she cut me off came out of pure loving commitment. At that time, I still had faith that our friendship was enduring. I thought someday we would get over the fight because that is what friends do. That is the nature of being committed to a person we love. However, our cultural practices around cutoff say those messages were a violation, the sort of thing Lee and O'Sullivan's study would characterize as a "stalking behavior," albeit possibly "benign." Arlo was similarly motivated when he waited to speak to Kendra on her way to class. He knew the move might look "stalkerish,"[324] but he was not stalking her; he was taking moderate action to try to understand what had happened to a dear friendship.

To be told that the normal actions of loving commitment are like stalking or abuse—are akin to a crime—is to be told something our whole being knows is a lie: it is immoral to try to heal a close relationship.

My editor told me a version of this. She called breaking (any) request for no contact "totally self-serving," i.e. not loving.[325] This the default response of cutoff culture. We subsequently got into a deep discussion over this issue. She devoted several extra hours of effort to this, beyond the hours I paid her for, and I'm profoundly grateful for her time and her thoughts. She shared this reflection:

> I've learned (the hard way) something that is often missed by the cuttee. We know when humans experience emotional pain, our fight, flight, or freeze [or appease]

[324] Arlo.

[325] Editorial comment, October 26, 2023. She later specified she was mainly referring to early in a cutoff: days or weeks, not months or years.

responses are activated. We all use a combination of these coping mechanisms to protect ourselves. We learned them in childhood. Cutoff can be seen as a freeze response.

If a person cuts a relationship off and asks for no contact, it can be because they are not emotionally able to continue engaging. They are frozen. Shut down. They truly need to get off the ride. They learned to do this before, and it worked; it helped them survive.

Cutoff itself—to sever close ties and isolate—can be a trauma response for people who learned this method of coping. When the brain shuts down to protect itself in the face of emotional pain, or freezes in this case, it is impossible for the cutter to participate in the conversation that the cuttee needs or desires. They just can't. This is so confounding to the cuttee. When the cutter says, "No. I am not going to engage with you," and the cuttee still pursues with "Can we talk this over? Why won't you talk this over?" that's when the cuttee is not acknowledging that this person (they love) needs no contact. They simply cannot talk it over. They are unable.

However well-meaning, an innocent appeal of "Can we talk?" to someone who just can't is, indeed, self-serving. The cuttee has pain, and they want to salve it with a conversation that confirms for them that the relationship mattered, that they matter. But seeking that from a cutter who is emotionally unable causes more pain for both, which isn't the outcome the cuttee wants.

When we ask someone to give something they cannot—and I mean they are truly unable—we don't see them for who they are, their own vulnerabilities.[326] We are just trying to get our own needs met. Who could fault that? It is painful to be cut out of someone's life.

I think we all make this mistake, asking for closure, believing we deserve it, but the source of pain will not

[326] This could also be said of many cuttees' trauma. Seeking contact can be "fight" or "appease" reaction. Though cutoff and contact are not equivalent acts, there is still a partial double standard in saying that the cutter deserves latitude to behave like a traumatized person but the cuttee deserves none.

heal us. Real closure has to come from within ourselves.[327] We decide we matter. We decide the relationship mattered without engaging them. I don't think it's about right and wrong. It's more about true love. When we truly love someone, we give them what they need. In some cases, that is our silence.

For myself, I know I've made this mistake of pursuit of a cutter. I did that because that is my own response to emotional pain. Pursue, entreat, get them to be nice to me again if I show myself as a true and loyal friend. That's how I learned to behave as a child when I was rejected or ignored. As an adult, when I pursued these conversations for closure, for peace in the world, it was self-serving. I didn't see that the person I loved needed the absence of me.

I also don't think it's a rarity that people who cut off and people who pursue have rich relationships when they are connected. They both desire deep connection. If you are a person who learned love and loyalty mean pursuit, you will find connections that require pursuing. If you are a person who shuts down and isolates but who also wants connection, you will find people who pursue and bring it to you.

Our pop culture valorizes cutting off toxic relationships, but the overpursuit of peace in the name of honoring the relationship and being loving is valorization

---

[327] "The source of pain will not heal us. Real closure has to come from within ourselves": I think this common formulation is problematic. It is true in an ultimate sense, in the sense that a person who experiences frequent microaggressions could develop enough inner peace not to be bothered by them, or a person who has been robbed could choose not to fret about it. This does not mean apologizing for a microaggression is irrelevant, nor that restoring someone's stolen property won't do them any good. Sometimes the source of pain won't help, and we have to heal ourselves without them. Often, however, the source of pain helps a lot. For example, a friend who ghosted me in high school friended me on social media. Briefly messaging with her dissolved twenty years of anger for me. Denying the reality that we can help each other heal can become an excuse for corrosive isolation and selfishness. I know this is not true of my editor, but it is the direction our culture is trending, and we should resist it.

> too. We are valorized for our love and commitment.[328] We want to see ourselves and be seen by others as having the moral high ground. We're all for love, a purpose higher than ourselves. But what we're ignoring is the real need of the other person for no contact.[329]

The dynamic my editor describes is common. A cutter can be overwhelmed and unable to deal with contact. The cuttee can also be overwhelmed and fail to register that their pursuit intensifies the cutter's trauma. I suspect this describes what happened with Sophia and me in the first couple years of her cutoff.

Yet though my editor's scenario is insightful, her argument contains a fallacy, one fundamental to cutoff culture. "This can happen" morphs into "This (always) happens." She says, "If a person cuts a relationship off and asks for no contact, it *can be* because they are not emotionally able to continue engaging. They *are* frozen" [emphasis mine]. The rest of the scenario no longer discusses what "can be" but what "is." This could just be a stylistic choice, except the argument is premised on this shift. Her condemnation of cutoff violation is based on the assumption that her scenario is not just possible but is the best paradigm for cutoff ethics. In other words, we should presume that cutoff violation is, by default, a self-serving act that harms the cutter and, thus, is not loving and should not be attempted.

I'd argue, however, that we should not assume all cutoff violation harms the cutter. Sometimes it does, but sometimes it limits harm. I agree that violating cutoff should be done with caution. I hold that, in many cases, the cuttee should wait and seek counsel from others before attempting contact; see Appendix B for a fuller discussion. Nonetheless, some contact from the cuttee is often crucial to preventing worse harm to both cuttee and cutter.

Cutoff Violation Sometimes Reduces Harm

Consider hypothetical couple Jules and Cleo, who are in a non-abusive relationship. (To make things simpler, let's assume

---

[328] I agree that we valorize pursuit, but I also think that this valorization is fading. Recent pop culture has rightly become increasingly critical of "stalkery" pursuit.

[329] Jennifer Brennock, email message to author, June 23, 2024.

they do not live together.) In the midst of a conflict, Jules tells Cleo it's over and demands Cleo never speak to them again. My editor's scenario could ensue, with Cleo badgering Jules to be nice to her and Jules retreating more and more into a traumatized "freeze" response. Yet many other dynamics could also be at play. Here are two of the most salient:

1. When angry, Jules shouts things they don't mean.
2. Jules is traumatized, but the trauma is based on a misunderstanding.

In both of these cases, harm to Jules and Cleo might be avoided if Cleo (the cuttee) reaches out.

Jules shouts things they don't mean.

In this case, Jules will probably reach out to Cleo after a while, but right after the fight, they may assume silence from Cleo means she is hurt and needs time away, so they may not contact her for a week or more. Let's say that, during this time, Cleo believes she's been permanently cut off by someone she loves, and Jules begins to believe Cleo's silence means she is virulently angry. By the time Jules contacts her, both have been needlessly miserable for days.

Or if Cleo texts the next day to ask if they can talk, Jules, who has now calmed down, can reply, "Okay," and they can begin relationship repair before the wound festers.

(This cutoff situation is very common, by the way, and probably rarely registers as cutoff because the cutoff ends quickly. In many cases, it ends quicker and with less pain because the cuttee doesn't keep silent.)

It's based on a misunderstanding.

Let's imagine that due to an unstable childhood Jules has trust issues. After seeing Cleo and a mutual friend in close conversation over a couple of weeks, they become convinced Cleo is cheating on them. With old trauma triggered, Jules texts her and the friend, demanding they never speak to Jules again. Let's say Cleo and the friend don't violate the cutoff, leaving both baffled and hurt by

Jules's outburst and Jules heartbroken over Cleo's perceived betrayal, too wounded to ever seek her out again.

Or the next day, Cleo stops by Jules's house, demanding to know what the heck has gotten into them.

Jules starts shouting about her cheating.

"Cheating!" she cries. "We were planning a surprise party for your birthday!"

Jules doesn't believe this at first, but other friends confirm it.

Jules apologizes.

Cleo is hurt and says they should go to couple's therapy to work on these trust issues, which they do, emerging as a healthier couple or, at least, as civil acquaintances with no deep scars from their relationship.

Taking steps to talk through problems is basic to conflict resolution. While communication across a cutoff can easily be taken too far, to categorically condemn it is tantamount to condemning a foundational architecture of relationship repair.

"Is It Self-Serving?" Is the Wrong Question

When my editor said that violating a cutoff is self-serving, I initially leaped down a rabbit hole of trying to show that it is not always wholly selfish. After a while, though, I realized that's not the point.

It occurred to me that both my editor and I had accepted an individualistic framing of relationships, a view that carves relationships up into individual people. Is Person A acting for themselves or for Person B? What slips through the sieve is the relationship itself, the space where A's and B's welfare is intertwined.

Jules cuts Cleo off. Cleo's amygdala fires up, and she violates Jules's cutoff with a flurry of pleading texts. Is her action self-serving? Sure. The amygdala puts us in survival mode, a self-serving mode. While there are exceptions, my editor is essentially right: most cutoff violations, at least early on, involve a lot of selfish flailing.[330] That selfishness can still be normal, loving behavior and can still sometimes lead to reduced harm. "Normal and loving" and "self-serving" are not mutually exclusive.

---

[330] Most cutters will also be flailing selfishly. I hope our culture can learn to show grace for both parties' trauma.

That is because relationality—sociality—is biologically baked into us. That doesn't mean individuals don't matter; it means relationships, as their own irreducible realities, matter a great deal. If an action helps resolve a conflict, generally all participants feel better, even if the actor's immediate motivation was mostly selfish.

Cutoff may be so intractable, in part, because it defies this tendency. In cutoff, the cutter's relief often comes at the expense of the cuttee. Conversely, contact may soothe the cuttee at the expense of the cutter. That is true, but it does not expunge the larger truth that solving relational conflict is important to human health, and solving it usually requires communication. Even in cutoff, this is often worth trying. And, yes, sometimes trying makes things worse. We need space for trial and error.

Human Relationships Require an Emergent Practice, Not a Best Practice

I have previously observed that human relationships are formally complex. In the terms of the Cynefin framework, that means navigating relationship problems falls into the realm of *emergent practice*, not *best practice*. In emergent practice, we must try things, learn, and correct course as needed. In interpersonal conflict, we must weigh up the pros and cons of our actions, assess possibilities, test them, and revise. A cuttee might guess that a couple of emails to find out what happened is worth distressing the cutter. Sometimes that guess will be wrong. Sometimes it will be right. Sometimes its effect will be ambiguous.

To morally condemn all cutoff violation is to impose a best practice where best practice is not appropriate. An interpersonal relationship is not a car engine. There is no manual for it. Each situation is different, and the participants have to try things to figure out what works. Humans are inherently communicative. Treating cutoff as a trump card that bans all communication will often do harm, especially when a cutoff is based on a miscommunication that this "best practice" prevents both parties from identifying.

To Be Condemned for Normal Relational Behavior

Minor cutoff violation is a normal behavior and often lessens relational harm, yet cuttees are routinely condemned for it, regardless of context, by friends, by blogs, by the silence or anger of the person who cut us off. We are condemned so persistently that we cease to know what to believe. Is loyalty wrong? Is commitment wrong? Is trust wrong? Is the belief that time heals wrong? The agony of this cognitive dissonance is difficult to overstate.

I considered Sophia one of my most precious friends. We had problems, but I could not imagine giving up on her. The day she cut me off, I replied with the words, "I will always love you, and I will always be there," and she replied back with a thank you. I meant what I said. Internalizing that our friendship was over was like forcing myself to believe the impossible. It was in the agony of that internalization that I sent her my one angry letter, in which I asserted, truthfully, that I finally knew we were no longer friends. But even beyond friendship, I kept my promise to be there for her. My 2017 email said it was all right if she never healed enough to speak to me again, that I would always be there if that changed. Given my previous nasty letter, her angry response was understandable. Yet it also made me realize I had to break my promise. I could not both love her (in the attached, interpersonal sense) and adhere to absolute silence for the rest of my life. Some can do this, but I could not. At best, I could keep my love to myself and ache for reconciliation in silence, and that would not be healthy for either me or her.

I forced myself to stop loving her. I forced myself to have a conviction that we could never be friends again or even civil acquaintances. I buried all my positive associations with her. Most advice to both cutters and cuttees says to treasure the memory of the good times. For the cuttee, however, treasuring fond memories of someone you never wanted to lose in the first place is a huge incentive to reconnect, which is forbidden. In many cases, saying "treasure those memories" invites either silent agony or cutoff transgression.

I replaced those memories with anger at first. I replaced them more lastingly with fear, lack of trust, with an expectation of being bitten that, to this day, serves as protection against any impulse to reach out. That fear protects me from her, and it protects her from me. It is my acquiescence to her explicit avowal that nothing between us will ever change. This is what I had to do to respect her boundaries, to believe her words.

It should be obvious that my mental process is not healthy. As I write this (in 2022), the anger flows out in my words, and I realize how deeply my mindset toward her is still primarily governed by fear and, yes, by anger, more than any good will, compassion, or forgiveness. There are shades of these better things, and they are growing, but they are far from being the driving impulse. This is what it means to kill love. It is a heavy, traumatic, almost impossible thing to ask, yet we ask it as if it were mere standard etiquette.

The way out of this catch-22, theoretically, may be obvious. If compassion is being attuned to what is best for the other person, then to love with compassion does not require strong attachment. It doesn't require speaking to a person or being in their company or getting anything back from them. I could love Sophia with compassion by leaving her alone. Then, arguably, that promise of love is neither abrogated nor invasive and can persist without doing either of us harm. Steinmetz seems to have achieved this state of mind. Given my own experiences, it amazes me that he can say he is a friend to his ex, Allie, even though she may regard him with hostility and will probably never speak to him again.[331] This shows immense maturity, and I admire him. I wonder, too, if one difference between us is that he is not afraid of Allie; he doesn't seem to be. I am afraid of Sophia,[332] which makes me feel powerless, and powerlessness stokes anger. Yet even Steinmetz achieved his equilibrium at the cost of the wound that "still aches" twenty-five years later.[333]

The benefits of selfless compassion are obvious, but as a default expectation of human beings, it overlooks how attached love works, both in our culture and in human nature. We don't generally love with pure compassion. If we did, we wouldn't need teachings like the Gospels or the Dharma to help us to do so. Indeed, to achieve that kind of compassion is so difficult that

---

[331] Steinmetz, "She Broke up with Me, and Never Gave Me a Second Chance."

[332] I don't I think she'll materially harm me. I mean I am non-rationally, emotionally afraid.

[333] Steinmetz, "She Broke up with Me, and Never Gave Me a Second Chance."

when people do we call them saints or bodhisattvas. On the contrary, our standard expectation of loving interpersonal relationships is that we will be deeply attached, that we will need each other and support each other, even in hard times, better or worse, in sickness and in health. When things are broken, we will mend them. Commitment says don't give up on someone. It says have faith that the relationship can heal. It instructs us to *act* to help it heal. If we respect the absolute boundary, we betray that faith. If we act on that faith, we violate the boundary. Either choice codes us as morally reprehensible. Of course, being forced into that bind is traumatic. To be told that your back-breaking attempts to do what is morally right make you reprehensible has the impact of gaslighting.

The Impact of Gaslighting

Gaslighting is generally defined a pattern of manipulative lies that makes someone doubt their own sanity. For example, Su tells Kyle she will home by 11:00, and she comes home at 11:00. Kyle, then, excoriates her for not coming home by 9:00 as she said she would. Su is pretty sure she didn't say 9:00, but Kyle's persistent indignation, especially if repeated over many incidents, begins to make her doubt her memory, her judgment, and even her sanity, giving Kyle increasing power to dictate what she considers reality.

Gaslighting has usually been defined as an *intentional* manipulation, a practice of lies and deception. *Merriam-Webster*[334] and *Psychology Today*[335] offer such definitions. However, in our popular culture, intentionality often slips out of the sense of the word. We might hear, for example, that someone is "gaslit" by people who express disbelief at an experience they mentioned, even if those people sincerely don't believe the person and intend no manipulation. *Wikipedia* reflects this sense, describing gaslighting as "making someone question their own reality,"[336] which could refer to intentional manipulation *or* unintentional harm. The term,

---

[334] "Gaslighting," *Merriam-Webster*, accessed August 15, 2022, https://www.merriam-webster.com/dictionary/gaslighting.
[335] "Gaslighting," *Psychology Today*, accessed August 15, 2022, https://www.psychologytoday.com/us/basics/gaslighting.
[336] "Gaslighting," *Wikipedia*, accessed August 15, 2022, https://en.wikipedia.org/wiki/Gaslighting.

however, is highly pejorative and suggests abuse; indeed, abuse is often included in the definition. As with words "abuse" and "stalking," I would argue for preserving the sense that true "gaslighting" is an intentionally manipulative violation.

By that definition, I have never encountered true gaslighting in the context of being cut off. No one involved in my cutoff situation has intentionally used deception to manipulate me. Nonetheless, suffering a profound trauma and being consistently assured it was (or should be) trivial can make you feel like you've gone insane. Over time and with many repetitions, this cognitive dissonance between what people tell you and what you feel to be true has the impact of gaslighting. An act need not be malicious or intentional to be destructive. The continual invalidation of the reality of someone's trauma is maddening: both infuriating and instilling doubt in our basic ability to parse reality.

Instead of such invalidation, consider this alternative approach to psychological trauma:

> Understanding and accepting the psychological state of an individual [suffering trauma] is paramount. There are many misconceptions of what it means for a traumatized individual to be in psychological crisis. These are times when an individual is in inordinate amounts of pain and incapable of self-comfort. If treated humanely and respectfully the individual is less likely to resort to self-harm. In these situations it is best to provide a supportive, caring environment and to communicate to the individual that no matter the circumstance, the individual will be taken seriously rather than being treated as delusional. It is vital for the assessor to understand that what is going on in the traumatized person's head is valid and real.[337]

In other words, in giving initial comfort to a traumatized person, *it doesn't matter* what caused the trauma. What matters is that the trauma exists, and trauma is serious and must be taken seriously. Anyone who has felt isolated by trauma will recognize the truth of this. Yet this basic piece of common sense is surprisingly underemphasized in our social discourse.

---

337 "Psychological Trauma," *Wikipedia*, accessed June 30, 2021, https://en.wikipedia.org/wiki/Psychological_trauma.

That passage I quoted is from *Wikipedia*, renowned for its lack of established authority. Actually, the crowdsourced encyclopedia is often well documented to authoritative sources. But in this case, it isn't; the article notes that the section needs additional verification. More authoritative texts on how to treat trauma often don't say anything like this. This piece of what seems to me kind common sense is, in fact, rather culturally marginal.

Observing that a traumatized person's perceptions should be validated is often not foregrounded in clinical articles, which more often open with discussing how the patients' thoughts and feelings are likely to be distorted and cause problems with functioning. For example, the American Psychological Association recommendation of Cognitive Behavioral Therapy (CBT) for trauma notes that CBT "focuses on the relationships among thoughts, feelings and behaviors; targets current problems and symptoms; and focuses on changing patterns of behaviors, thoughts and feelings that *lead to difficulties in functioning*" [emphasis mine].[338] Writing for Trauma and Acute Care, Priscilla Dass-Brailsford and Cimone M. Safilian emphasize "long-term adverse effects on *physical, social, emotional, or spiritual functioning*" [emphasis mine].[339] Rhetorically, the problem here is not the traumatic wound; it is the traumatized person. The thing to be addressed is not so much the person's experience of trauma as their problematic attitudes and behaviors arising from it.

Beyond the specific issue of cutoff, this emphasis on the maladaptation of the traumatized person and deemphasis on the emotional reality of what happened to them speaks to a profound cultural trivialization of the experience of suffering harm. It suggests that the only problem is the wrong-thinking of the wounded person, an attitude that is, at best, dismissive and, at worst, smacks of blaming the victim. My third therapist's default was to emphasize changing my attitude over listening to my feelings. In fact, I quoted her the *Wikipedia* passage above in the letter where I

---

[338] "PTSD Treatments," *American Psychological Association*, June 2020, https://www.apa.org/ptsd-guideline/treatments.

[339] Priscilla Dass-Brailsford, and Cimone M. Safilian, "Integrated Approaches to Treating Psychological Trauma and Substance Abuse in Women: An Update," *Trauma and Acute Care*, 2, no. 41, https://doi.org/10.21767/2476-2105.100041. https://www.primescholars.com/articles/integrated-approaches-to-treating-psychological-trauma-and-substance-abuse-in-women-an-update-107856.html

begged her to understand that I needed to talk about my trauma. She responded to that letter with compassion and a willingness to change our focus. In all honesty, though, I should not have had to write it. This is no criticism of her; it's a criticism of our dominant culture, which she was enacting to a T. She had been trained to address the symptoms while substantially ignoring the cause.

The message blares from all sides, from friends to therapists: you only feel wounded because you are messed up. That message, unfortunately, messes you up. It keeps telling you you're crazy until you wonder if it's true. Trivializing trauma intensifies it, and few sources of trauma are as trivialized as cutoff.

Is Cutoff Serious? A Mixed Message

Finally, it is worth noting that the advice to rapidly accept cutoff (tenet 6) and the order never to transgress it (tenet 3) can be at odds. That may sound counterintuitive. After all, both tenets argue for capitulating to cutoff, and both assume the relationship is over. Yet number 3, the absolute prohibition on contact, actually asks for a rigid relationship to *persist*, one defined by avoidance and non-closure. Perpetual avoidance and non-closure can be difficult to accept. This results in curious mixed messaging about cutoffs.

On the one hand, cutoff culture says it's about respecting consent (tenet 3): if a person withholds their consent to communicate with you, you are obligated to obey that prohibition every day without exception for the duration of the cutoff, even if that is the rest of your life. To fail to do this, cutoff culture suggests, is a grievous violation. On the other hand, it says, don't obsess. Why worry about the rest of your lives? Maybe the cutter's feelings will change, maybe not. Just let the future take care of itself, accept the present situation, and move on (tenet 6). There's a reading for these two messages that does, indeed, reconcile them. It is to assume the cutoff is forever, obey it, not dwell on it, but be open to the possibility that the cutter may change their mind. This is, incidentally, what the first therapist I saw about being cut off suggested I do.

This is logically possible. But it's almost unachievable for a person in the grips of trauma. When you care for someone—or just hate living with the constant background fear of having an enemy out there who might hurt you if you meet (emotionally, socially)—the drive to make peace can be incredibly strong. That's natural and makes sense. Reconciliation with people we care about is desirable, not having to be afraid of an enemy hurting us all the more so. That desire for peace, for safety, can create a strong compulsion to reach out, to attempt that email that says, "Can we make peace?" In the early days, it may be plain that such outreach would be rebuffed. But after five years, ten years, twenty years…? Things change, people tell us. They're right. Maybe that one email after ten years can mean the difference between lifelong peace and lifelong fear. Maybe the only reason the cutter themselves hasn't reached out is that they're afraid that contacting you would show poor boundaries; after all, our culture has told them it would. Or maybe they're afraid—for very good reason—that you'll verbally eviscerate them for hurting you if they try. So it rests on you to say that isn't so. You won't eviscerate them. You really want peace.

So you send the email. What if the cutter really meant what they said? What if they are furious that you violated their boundary? What if their response is a brutal harangue that tears all the wounds open again? What if they genuinely feel threatened (rationally or not) and broadcast to friends or professional contacts that you're a dangerous person? Then you're trolled on social media or lose your job because employing a harasser is a liability? These extremes aren't likely, but in our hyperconnected, hyperjudgmental world, they're possible, and this is the sort of calculation people living under the prohibition of a cutoff have to make. The only way to be reliably safe is to assume that we can do nothing to make peace, ever. We buy that safety with a lifetime of background fear.

We're told that when someone cuts us off, the relationship is over (tenets 1 and 2). Indeed, they cut us off *so that* it will be over. But it isn't over; it's a perpetual servitude to someone else's order to silence ourselves (tenet 3). The only way to escape that is (theoretically) within our control is to unilaterally learn to not worry about it (tenet 6). And that requires these psychological moves:

a. almost completely healing from a life-altering trauma, and
b. learning not to fear a real (if small) source of threat, while…
c. remembering to always reject the friendly impulse to reach out to mend fences.

It should be noted that (a) and (b) tend to act against (c). For many, if we are healed and not afraid, the most natural thing is the world is to reach out to mend fences, yet we must constantly fight that impulse off. Being healed enough to be comfortable with an ex-loved one's apparent lifelong hostility is a balancing act that requires vast psychological work and a high degree of maturity. For many, it will take a long time, if it is achievable at all. If we can't do it, the safest alternative is fear: believe that the cutter is willing to hurt you at any point in time for life—and that will keep you from trying to reach out, and you'll probably be safe. That requires taking a lifelong cutoff deadly seriously. Yet we're told that we're mentally sick if we do. That's not wrong. Living in fear over sending one text message is unhealthy, but it is also a stance cutoff culture virtually demands, at least for a long duration. None of this is conducive to rapid acceptance, and it deepens the injury to declare that it should be.

Chapter 11

Impacts Equivalent to Abuse

In 2020, when I showed my friend Anna the letter I never sent to Sophia, Anna reflected that "the whole text sounded disproportionately angry for something that's had five years to sit."[340] I've gotten versions of this response a lot. It assumes my trauma was a single wound, that no other trauma had happened since the initial cutoff conversation; it just "sat." But a permanent cutoff is not a moment; it's a lifetime. The cutoff is in force every minute of every day. I live under a threat of emotional harm if I even accidentally bump into Sophia—and probably so does she. We might be thrown into panic from just seeing each other's faces and burst into saying the wrong thing or say nothing in fiendish awkwardness, hearts hammering. I am on guard against her. Always. Like the relentless reality of climate change, this cutoff may not be a daily concern, but its shadow on my life has been continuous.

For me, this trauma has been compounded by lack of social support. Therapists miss what I'm trying to say. Online articles are often oblivious to cutoff damage, sometimes even calling it the kindest course of action! Scholarly research on cutoff? I've found zero. When I reached out to ostracism researcher Kipling D. Williams, he graciously sent me two studies on ghosting, but had nothing on cutoff per se. I've asked three people who knew Sophia if they could help me understand what happened: one ignored me, two said they couldn't help. From my own circle, I've gotten blank looks, confusion, scolding, and/or the assumption that it's all my fault. I have also received kind care that has mitigated a great deal of damage. But the relentless recurrence of negative feedback mounts up all the same. When a person seeks help and gets ignored or rebuffed, it retraumatizes. When the

---

340 Anna, email message to the author, April 9, 2020.

social system is designed to deny the reality of an injury, the very act of seeking healing pours poison in the wound.

Complex Post-Traumatic Stress Disorder (CPTSD) is a form of PTSD commonly experienced by survivors of abuse. It originates not in a single traumatic event but in immersion in traumatizing situations over months or years.[341] It is characterized by an inability to trust, emotional insecurity, imbalanced self-perception (a tendency toward disproportionate guilt or indignation, for example), and being preoccupied with the traumatic relationship.[342] Around 2019, I began to realize I had these symptoms of CPTSD. I expect I did not have a diagnosable case, but symptoms I had. I trusted almost no one. I was afraid to be my unguarded self with everyone but my mother. I was unwilling to make friends for fear they might one day cut me off. (To be honest, I still largely am.) I felt racked with either irrational guilt or fury. I ruminated obsessively on what happened with Sophia. When I tried to form a proportional image of myself, I felt at sea. I didn't know how to evaluate myself. Was I a victim? A monster?

This is not a response to a singular trauma. This is a response to ongoing retraumatization. I was so angry after five years because I had been living for five years in the psychological equivalent of an abusive situation. Ironically, one of the moves that helped me most was ceasing to seek help. At least then I ceased to be emotionally punched in the face for it.

But here's a crucial point: not one of the people involved was abusive, not Sophia, not her friends, not my friends, no one. The point is not that I was mentally assaulted by monsters. The point is this: when cultural norms practiced by decent people with good intent inflict psychological harm comparable to the effects of long-term abuse, those norms bloody well need to change.

There Can Be Impacts of Abuse without an Abuser

In current progressive equity discourse, we distinguish between *intent* and *impact.* To take an obvious example, let's say a

[341] Gary Gilles, "Understanding Complex Post-Traumatic Stress Disorder," Healthline, September 29, 2018, https://www.healthline.com/health/cptsd.

[342] Gilles.

white person on a college campus asks a Black professor if they're the janitor. The intent might be to make friendly conversation,[343] but the impact is to reinforce the idea that Black people can only do unskilled jobs and, by implication, that they aren't as intelligent as white people. Though intent does matter, it does not excuse impact. The person asking the question may have meant no harm, but harm was probably done. If the speaker realizes that or has it pointed out to them, they should apologize, own that harm, and make a committed effort not to repeat the same harmful act. People familiar with progressive equity discourse understand this distinction between intent and impact pretty well.

There is, however, a similar and equally important distinction that our society rarely talks about. As I'm not aware of existing terminology for it, I'll call it the distinction between *impact* and *culpability*. Sometimes our actions have predictable impacts, but sometimes the impact is out of proportion with the action. Equity discourse has established that a person can be culpable for harm their actions cause regardless of their intent. By the same token, sometimes the person is not culpable for the full extent of the harm triggered by their actions. Let's say Keith had an acrimonious divorce from his wife, Marlene, a respected painter. Let's say a few months later, a new acquaintance who doesn't know this history tells Keith that he adores Marlene's art. That statement may trigger intense pain in Keith, but it would be absurd to say his acquaintance is culpable for that pain. If Keith goes on to explain the divorce, kindness may dictate that the acquaintance say, "Oh, I'm sorry!" and resolve not to mention Marlene again. But that's compassion, not an admission of wrongdoing.

On a more serious level, my own cutoff trauma is evidence that people can suffer the impacts of abuse without an abuser. We must recognize this fact if we wish to heal our culture because failure to recognize it perpetuates a culture of condemnation and belittlement.

Here's another hypothetical example. Let's say Lee and Jenner are dating. Over the course of six months, Lee yells at Jenner a handful of times. Jenner feels that this yelling is tearing her apart, filling her with terror and assaulting her fundamental sense of self-

---

343 The identification of Black people with low-skilled jobs is a common example of implicit racism, even if the speaker does not consciously intend racist speech.

worth. These feelings are extreme and debilitating; they are equivalent to the impacts of abuse. If we accept the premise that only abuse can cause these impacts, then we are left with only two possibilities: 1) Lee is an abuser for yelling a few times; 2) Jenner is "crazy" and cannot or should not be feeling what she feels. Both of these choices require us to condemn or belittle a fellow human being. Either Lee is a toxic monster, or Jenner is a toxic weirdo. This, however, is a false dichotomy. It is entirely possible that Lee's infrequent yelling, though not good, comes nowhere near a reasonable standard for abuse, *and* Jenner's feelings are real and make total sense based on her own prior life experiences, personality, and so on. Jenner can suffer impacts equivalent to abuse without being abused. Both things can be true. If we accept this, we can engage more reasonably with two human beings who need help. Jenner needs support for addressing her trauma. Lee needs support to help her understand the impact of her yelling and to find less damaging means of self-expression. And if the two of them are incompatible and need to break up, both will need support during that grieving process.

The label of abuser is a vicious weapon. If it attaches publicly to someone's name, it can impact their career, reputation, and relationships for life. Our present society has a cavalier attitude to imposing that label, and that attitude must change. Schulman cites social worker Catherine Hodes, who has over two decades experience working with abused women.[344] Hodes observed many of her clients mistaking relationship conflict for abuse. Schulman writes,

> Hodes had boldly started to notice that clients were increasingly confused about what the word "Abuse" actually means. That it was overused. The paradox is, of course, that many women are unable to recognize that they are being abused, or cannot get acknowledgment of this reality from others. But at the very same time, Hodes found that some women were applying the term Abuse to situations that were really something else. Increasingly, she noticed that women who did not know how to

344 Schulman, 56.

> resolve a problem sometimes described that feeling with the word Abuse.[345]

Yet true abuse, Hodes argues, necessitates the abuser holding power over the abused. As she puts it, "Differentiating between *Power Struggle* and *Power Over*… is the difference between Conflict and Abuse."[346] Hodes's characterization provides a fairly clear definition of what constitutes abuse. If someone wields significantly unequal power over someone else—through violence, threats, financial leverage, laws, contracts, etc.—that person is in a position to be abusive. In general, if they don't, they aren't.

By this understanding, it becomes very clear that Sophia never abused me and I never abused Sophia. We never had significantly unequal power. Our relationship never involved violence, threats, or any financial entanglement. We never lived together; we never depended on each other for work or means to live. Materially, we were independent human beings. Thus, our conflicts were just that: conflicts. At any point in time, each of us had ample power to stay, to leave, or to make better choices. We both treated each other badly, but we didn't abuse each other. Yet both of us suffered the impacts of abuse. I have noted my own symptoms, and Sophia's 2012 remarks to me that my harsh words had required her to deconstruct and rebuild an entire identity certainly speak to trauma on the level of abuse. Both things are true: we suffered the impacts of abuse, and we were not abused.

Now, as usual, reality is a bit more complex. One implication of Hodes's definition of abuse is that mutual abuse is a myth.[347] It can't be mutual if it, by definition, requires the abuser to have more power. I'd argue that life is more nuanced than that. Imagine, for example, a married man and woman, where the man is physically stronger but the woman is the breadwinner. In this case, they each have a different kind of potential dominance (physical and financial). They could each leverage this power to significantly harm the other through violence, threats, and coercion. To say such uses of power couldn't be abusive runs the risk of downplaying egregious behavior.

---

345 Schulman, 57

346 Catherine Hodes. qtd. in Schulman, 58.

347 Schulman, 57.

That said, I'm less concerned with the specifics of a definition than the basic point that abuse is extreme. It's an extreme word that should be reserved for extreme cases. Most of the problems we deal with in our relationships are what Schulman and Hodes identify as conflicts, and that doesn't mean they aren't serious. Conflict can devastate our lives, as Sophia and I devastated each other. Yet it doesn't help to accuse people who have not done anything monstrous of monstrosity. To do so hinders reconciliation and healing. It even hinders accountability by presenting the perpetrator with a false choice between accepting the excessive title of abuser or protesting they have done next-to-nothing wrong.[348]

At the same time, we need to accept that the impacts of conflict are real, especially in an age when most of us are traumatized by something and, thus, can be triggered by very little. To say, as Sophia did, that a handful of angry emails from me required her to create an entirely new sense of her innermost identity is odd. In fairness, for me to feel my life eviscerated because one friend broke off contact with me is also odd. The intensity of the indignation I feel at Sophia's friend Tammy for shutting me out, even though she's a stranger to me, is odd. And frankly, the fact that Tammy apparently felt she needed to shun me instead of having one conversation also strikes me as odd.[349] My partner's high school best friend refusing to speak to him for thirty years and counting because of… he doesn't know: that's odd. Arlo's friend unexplainedly slipping from close camaraderie to intense avoidance is odd. All of these responses, I suspect, are trauma responses to some degree. It's a cliché, but it carries a lot of truth: "if it's hysterical, it's historical." In other words, past trauma can trigger intense negative responses even to small stimuli. All these

[348] Indeed, even when abuse has clearly occurred, it is not helpful to assume to abuser is an irredeemable monster. For an excellent discussion of this, see Kai Cheng Thom, "What to Do When You've Been Abusive: Annotated Edition," *Beyond Survival*, edited by Ejeris Dixon and Leah Lakshmi Piepzna-Samarasinha (Chico, CA: AK Press, 2020), 67–77.

[349] I say "apparently" because our contact has been so minimal I don't know how to interpret it.

responses have in common a disproportion, a backlash out of keeping with nature of the trigger.[350] That's how trauma works.

We live in a society increasingly in the grips of trauma, and this isn't about to change. Our global economic system is burying our world fast and willfully in an ecological apocalypse that the most powerful among us refuse to address. Virtually every person who will be alive twenty years from now will have experienced some kind of socioecological terror: fires, storms, floods, food shortage from crop failure or unjust distribution, unbearable heat, mass migration, more pandemics. This is already upon us, and it's going to get worse. If only for that reason, and there are many others, almost all of us can expect to live with significant trauma. We must build a culture designed to accommodate traumatized people. We must build a society sensitive to everyone's trauma, not just a sub-group labeled victims of abusers—or, for that matter, a subgroup seen as privileged people who matter[351]—but all human beings.

---

[350] Reverend Kosho Finch, the sensei of Henjyoji Shingon Buddhist temple, which I attend, told me that, in his experience, cutoffs were usually more about the cutter's needs than what the cuttee did. This seems to me a different way of observing that the response may be out of proportion to the trigger. Reverend Kosho Finch in discussion with the author, March 10, 2023.

[351] In progressive equity discourse, "privileged" tends to be construed as meaning white, cis, abled, middle-class people in the Global North, but it's worth remembering it can also mean the vast majority of all people in the Global North compared to the vast majority of all people in the Global South.

Part 3

An Alternative Approach to Interpersonal Conflict

Chapter 12

A Relational Approach to Cutoff

It was a lovely summer morning in Les Pascals patisserie in my hometown of Glen Ellen, California, and I was discussing this book with my mother. As I entered into the tangled web of cutoff rights and duties, she burst out laughing.

Incensed, I said, "You may laugh, but these issues are real. People really judge each other as abusive based on whether or not they send one email after a cutoff." (Admittedly, this statement represents an extreme end of public opinion, but I was venting.)

My mother, after taking a few moments to contain her mirth, remarked that she had never encountered the attitudes I described in over eighty years of life. Throughout her youth, her dating life, her formative friendships, nothing resembling our cutoff discourse existed. People fought, they broke up or made up, they fell out of contact, they screamed, "Never speak to me again!" But there was no assumption that such a statement was to be taken literally, that the receiver of that exclamation immediately had a sacred duty not to approach the sender for the rest of their lives—or even for the next year.

I don't want to indulge in nostalgic idealization of the 1950s. In many ways, our current social world is far healthier, and increased respect for boundaries is part of that health, especially for women and other marginalized groups. As a young woman in the '50s and '60s, my mother had to face sexist assumptions, social limitations, and hazards that I can't even imagine living with. At the same time, not every practice that is older is worse. As I listened to her talk, I was filled with envy for her ability to live her life blissfully unaware of our current obstacle course of lopsided boundary expectations that too often prize disconnection and pathologize attempts at peacemaking.

It is important to respect boundaries, but it is also important not to use the idol of boundaries to freeze ourselves into rigid molds with no space for being human. Humans are squishy, messy things. We need to be able to mess up and try again. We need to reclaim a little breathing room.

Rights and Duties Ethics vs. Relational Ethics

Imagine going to the store concerned with only rights and duties. We have a right to buy the things for sale. We have a duty to pay for them. We have a duty not to damage or displace unpurchased items or cause a disturbance. That's about all. In a system based purely on rights and duties, there would be no expectation of a "please" or "thank you," of a "Have a nice day," of a smile, of politeness. We could give those things or not as we chose. If we chose not to and our cold words or looks ruined someone's day, that would be ethically the same as smiling and warming it. But it is not the same. Hurting someone and helping someone are not the same. Hurting someone badly and hurting someone less are not the same. To behave as though they are is to invite a culture of cruelty, to invite exactly the social climate we increasingly live in, one steeped in nastiness. Too often, this is the way we approach cutoffs.

The common practice I've described around cutoffs is based on respecting boundaries and little else. It strongly upholds the idea that because cutoff is a right the cut-off person has a duty to respect that right by not attempting contact, presumably for life. There are virtually no other considerations. Any pain the cut-off person suffers does not matter. Reconciliation does not matter. Relationship closure does not matter. Forgiveness does not matter. Resolving ongoing fear and hostility does not matter. Clarifying miscommunication does not matter. Cutoff is, as Lyn once put it, "morally neutral": doing it carries zero ethical weight.[352] The cutter has only one ethical responsibility: to be consistent by never allowing communication. Unless they actually wish to rescind the cutoff, they should never respond to any communication from the

---

[352] Lyn, private message to the author, June 28, 2022. I recall Lyn introducing this concept a few years earlier but retained no record of it. When I asked her in 2022 if I'd characterized her view correctly, she said she thought so, though she did not remember the specifics.

cuttee unless it is to firmly warn them away. This is practice rooted in an ethical system that recognizes only rights and duties. Cutoff is a right. It is. This is true. There is, therefore, a duty not to violate that right. We could debate how far this right extends: does it prohibit all contact always? I'd argue it doesn't. But the right to be at least mostly left alone does exist; this is also true. Yet this is not all that matters.

It should not be controversial to say that being kind to people also matters. We all know this is true. It's why we teach our children to say "please" and "thank you." It's why we tell them, "Play nice." It's why we smile when introduced to a new colleague. We all know being decent people goes beyond just rights and duties. It involves the responsibility to treat each other with dignity. It involves a recognition that our actions affect each other, and, yes, these effects matter. Being decent involves relationality. There is no reason cutoffs should be any exception. To be clear, that does not mean that a person living with abuse should prioritize being nice to their abuser. Not at all.

A relational ethics is based on having awareness of the effects of our actions and taking responsibility for them. By responsibility, I mean that the effects of our actions should be weighed in the equation. They matter. They should not be considered "morally neutral." To illustrate what I mean by "weighing a factor," let's take a literal equation. Consider the expression:

$$x = 2y$$

Assume x and y are positive numbers (e.g. 1, 2, 3…). In this expression, x is greater than y. For example, if $y = 2$, $x = 4$. If x and y were ethical considerations, x would carry more weight. If I had to choose between x and y, I should choose x. Yet y still exists. It has weight; it's not zero. And if I have to weigh three y's against one x, y begins to tilt the scale.

Now, relationships are not math, which is why I won't plug in a real-life example to illustrate x and y. The point is that taking responsibility for our actions does not mean all considerations are equal. It does not mean we are ethically required to counteract every negative effect of everything we do. (Spoiler: that's not possible.) It means we do not dismiss the effects of our actions. It means we acknowledge they are not a zero. Of course, we're only human; we will always be unaware of many, perhaps most, of the ripples we cause. But to the best of our ability to imagine the ripples, we should think about them and strive to minimize their negatives.

A responsible, relational practice around cutoffs respects that cutoff is, indeed, a right, but it does not consider this right the only relevant factor. Such an ethics is nuanced and contextual. Its application will vary case by case, but its goal will always be to minimize the hurt, and not only the hurt of one person or two, but the total hurt, the harm in the world—to friends, family, bystanders, incidental interactions, all of it. Though this approach will vary by situation, the core principle of minimizing harm remains. To that end, instead of valuing only boundaries, it values both *boundaries* and *doorways*, the keeping out and the letting in. Boundaries are vital to mental health—and doorways are vital too.

Boundaries and Doorways

PsychCentral's definition of boundaries states, "Personal boundaries are simply the lines we draw for ourselves in terms of our level of comfort around others."[353] *Boundaries* are limitations we place on how we allow others to interact with us. They include such things as our need for physical space, our expectations around how people speak to us, our willingness to lend money, and much more, including, of course, what contact we allow and from whom. Boundaries are like walls we place around ourselves. *Doorways*, my own term, are ways we allow people to access us, the doors in the walls. In the vast majority of cases, both are necessary to healthy social functioning.

Of course, this is not always the case. Sometimes there can't be a doorway. Consider the extreme case of someone who might, in fact, kill you. It is entirely reasonable and healthy to cut them off, sever every tie, and do your best to disappear forever so that they can never, ever find you or bother anyone who knows you. A relational ethics is contextual. In some contexts, total cutoff is the only viable answer. Each person considering cutoff must be the ultimate judge of whether they are in such a case. Yet I'd argue those cases are comparatively few, likely thousands of cases, if not millions, fewer than our current practice. In most human relations, boundaries and doorways can work fairly well.

---

353 Leah Campbell.

Marriage and family therapist Kelsey T. Chun describes how to set clear boundaries with people who have been exploiting or disrespecting us:

> As a part of direct communication with the other person, you will need to be able to state the boundaries that you need respected—ones that have not been respected up until now. First, this requires you to know which boundary of yours is being crossed. Does your friend always bail on you? Does your sister only call when she needs something? Then, be able to set the boundary with her going forward, "Kate, don't make plans with me if you're going to cancel," or "Susie, you can't call if you're just going to ask me for help; you need to ask how I'm doing, too." It helps to be able to articulate how Kate makes you feel when she cancels your plans (unimportant, disrespected) or how Susie's one-sided phone calls make you feel (used).[354]

Note that both of Chun's examples state not only boundaries but doorways too—a path for maintaining the relationship. If Kate stops cancelling plans, the friendship can continue. If Susie starts to show an interest in her sister's well-being, their relationship will also stay intact. These are examples of fairly minor conflicts that can likely be addressed by simple, moderate boundaries. However, sometimes situations escalate. If Susie, for example, remains impervious to her sister's request, continuing to call only when she needs something, the sister may eventually feel so drained that she needs to set a stricter boundary with a narrower doorway.

I have a friend who gets along great with her daughter, but the daughter has a rockier relationship with her dad. As a young adult, exhausted by her father's failure to understand her need for emotional space, she decided to cut him off for two years. For two years, she told him, she would not respond to any contact and requested he attempt none; after that, she'd be open to reconnecting and seeing if things improved. In this case, the boundary is no

[354] Kelsey T. Chun, "Is Eliminating 'Toxic' Relationships the Right Decision?" *Verily*, May 20, 2020, https://verilymag.com/2020/05/toxic-friendships-signs-of-a-toxic-friend-2020.

contact for two years; the doorway is the limited timeframe. If her dad could respectfully wait out two years, they could try again. In fact, they did try again and were able to resume being on speaking terms. If her dad hadn't respected that boundary, however, the daughter could always have tightened it further, even up to permanent cutoff as a last resort.

Boundaries and doorways can exist around anything, but in the context of cutoff, the boundary is the refusal of communication, and the doorways are any ways that communication is allowed. These doorways can take many forms:

- *Time*: "We need to take two years totally apart. After that, I'm open to talking again and seeing where we are."
- *Medium*: "I don't want any digital, phone, or face-to-face contact, but you can write me by letter."
- *Method*: "If you want to contact me, email my friend Josie, briefly and politely, and let her know what you want. She'll let you know if I'm up for communicating or not."

These types of doorways may be combined into a precise path for communication, and such paths can be very restrictive. Here's an example of a precise, restrictive path:

> Don't contact me at all for one year. After that, if you still wish to get in touch, email Josie politely, briefly explaining what you want. She will reply to you on my behalf.

This example is rigid, sterile, and unfriendly, but it is a clear communication that sets clear boundaries, and it is infinitely less rigid than traditional absolute cutoff because it provides a means to get a message through without boundary violation. It allows the cuttee to communicate without resorting to harassment, stalking, deception, or any act that might (fairly or unfairly) be characterized as such. It provides a doorway. In many cases, providing such a means is critical to minimizing the negative consequences of cutoff.

Advantages of Doorways

A Doorway as a Low-Stakes Way to Empower not Only the Cuttee but the Cutter

Where doorways do not endanger the cutter's safety, they can provide a wealth of positive ramifications with little-to-no burden on the cutter. In the example above, note that Josie doesn't necessarily have to involve the cutter at all. The cutter could say ahead of time, "Josie, here's my stock reply to this person," and Josie could simply deliver it. Or, if Josie thinks something has radically changed that the cutter ought to know about, she might choose to tell the cutter. It may be a cliché, but imagine the cuttee is dying. A third party may be able to convey that to the cutter, giving the cutter the power to decide whether a deathbed communication might be mutually healing. If all communication is blocked, the cuttee may just die without the cutter even knowing. In this case, the cutter loses their freedom to choose whether to participate in a final meeting. A doorway empowers the cutter to make an informed choice.

A Doorway as a Means of Reality Testing

Just as a doorway can provide the cutter with potentially useful information, it can be a low-stakes way to let the cuttee do *reality testing* and, thus, have a healthier perspective on the cutoff. Within a social circle, a doorway need involve nothing more than straightforwardly answering a few questions. When my friend Heather stopped responding to my messages, for example, I asked a mutual friend about it. "Oh, she doesn't respond to mine either," was the reply. "She's just like that. She gets distracted and doesn't stay in touch." Though I miss Heather and I hope we can someday reconnect, that simple communication saved me years of hurt. Third parties can be a low-stress conduit for healing communication when other doors are closed.

For me, this was especially true when my friend, Olivia, ghosted me in 2006, after twenty years of friendship. For some time, she had shown a pattern of backing out on our social engagements without any advance notice. After a missed connection or two, I started taking the initiative to check in as a planned get-together approached, and she would regularly reply that she had to cancel. After several rounds of this, I wrote her a testy note, in which I called her out for irresponsible behavior and said she ought to act more mature. In response, she ghosted me for over a year. Over the next few years, she gradually crept back into contact, apologizing for the gap in contact and finally friending me on social media. As I write this, we are, blessedly, on amicable terms, though no longer close.

That experience with Olivia was like a tiny prelude to my experience with Sophia. It was not nearly so catastrophic, but at the time, it left me very angry. I did the natural thing: I asked Derek, who was our mutual friend, for his thoughts. He said she didn't speak to him anymore either. He also said he'd heard from another friend that she was struggling with depression.

That single piece of communication transformed the whole narrative for me. Suddenly, I understood her withdrawal from socializing not as a dismissal of me but as a symptom of psychological distress. Suddenly, I understood that my note had been a hammer blow on someone already knocked flat. Her silence was an attempt to protect herself from further blows. I felt guilty, but I also had a basis for putting that guilt in perspective. My note was insensitive but not egregious. Her response to it was excessive by the standards of healthy wholeness but understandable in someone grappling with depression. That small conversation with Derek transformed a narrative of blame and betrayal into one of human stumbling, on both our parts. To this day, it is the centerpiece in my ability to comes to terms with her actions—and with mine. It also served as a practical learning experience. Though I have certainly made mistakes since then, most notably with Sophia, that conversation made me much more compassionate toward other people's behavior. It helped me remember that I don't know what's going beneath the surface, and I should not make judgments as if I did.

A Doorway as a Means to Show Caring across a Cutoff

If we're fed up enough to cut someone off, we often don't mind if it hurts them, at least somewhat. I certainly felt this way about Ryan. However, sometimes people cut others off with zero desire to hurt them. Sometimes a dynamic just isn't working, and the cutter needs to separate themselves from someone they esteem and love. When you're cut off, however, it can be hard to feel that love. Our culture's failure to recognize the harm of cutoff can lead to harm even when the cutter truly wishes the cuttee well.

Cole has thought deeply about cutoff and generally feels at ease with it.[355] He has been cut off by family members in the past, and over a period of five transformative years, he found himself cutting off two family members and two close friends. Cole says of the people who cut him off that he doesn't fault them for it. He strongly supports people's right to choose who they have in their lives. He's made those choices, so have others: fair is fair. Of the cutoffs he has initiated, he says, "I did the right thing. It's okay."[356]

Talking to Cole, it's clear to me that he did do the right thing for him. It's notable that, though the relationships he ended all involved some conflict, none was abusive, and the two friendships, in particular, were emotionally intimate, multi-decade relationships that had mostly been positive and caring. Cole didn't cut these people off because of any gross dysfunction. Even so, emotionally he needed to. I've previously described Cole's decision to cut off his dear friend, Biva. In this case, he cut her off because she was not able to commit to the kind of primary emotional relationship he had come to feel he needed. Anything less was simply too painful to be part of. In the case of his other close friend and sometime romantic partner, Joelle, the trigger was her sharing some private details of their relationship with her current partner, which Cole felt as a betrayal. But though he acknowledges that this violation of trust upset him, he also says, "I don't hold anything against her.... I miss her. I care for her. I love her. She will always have that place in my heart, but I cannot for my own mental health return to a dialogue with her." It's liberating to him to realize he is no longer "her caretaker." Reflecting on that cutoff, he says, "Sometimes I think about this, and I amazed that I did this. I'm happy that I did this." Of the four cutoffs he's initiated, he says, "They amplify each other.... The impact has been powerful." He describes his feelings as "liberation, relief, self-care." Cole has thought about these relationships and his own psyche deeply. His manner shows a sense of great peace with his choices, as well as peace and love toward the people he has cut off.

---

[355] Cole, in discussion with author, August 17, 2022.

[356] All quotes from Cole.

It's also notable to me that, despite all his profound reflection on himself, his relationships, and the act of cutoff, Cole's sense of the nature of cutoff is impressionistic, imprecise. He has been through several experiences of cutoff that ended when the cuttee contacted the cutter and the two began amicably conversing again with no sense that the act of phoning or emailing violated cutoff boundaries. He seems to regard cutoff as more the cutter's choice not to respond to contact than an expectation that the cuttee cease contact.[357] He mentioned to me that Joelle has tried to contact him and he has not replied, but he expressed no sense of violation that she tried. When I asked him about cutoff boundaries, he said, "I can't remember it ever being stated directly [in any of his cutoff situations] that further contact is forbidden." Indeed, Cole characterized his relationships as "estranged," and he asked me explicitly what I saw as the difference between "estrangement" and "cutoff." I noted that there's no set definition of cutoff, but for the purposes of this book, *cutoff* is a subset of *estrangement* that implies ending all contact, while estrangement, broadly speaking, suggests being emotionally distant, withholding, and having (at most) infrequent contact. He readily understood this distinction, but it had not previously been part of his thought process.

One inference I draw from our conversation is that Cole may not have strongly recognized the particular impacts of cutoff as a complete blockage of communication. In particular, he may not have fully accounted for the bewilderment Williams identifies as a common effect of being ostracized.[358] In the case of Biva, the two friends had an in-depth conversation in which he explained that he couldn't be part of her life anymore and she stated she understood. In the case of Joelle, however, Cole simply stopped responding to her after she violated his trust: he ghosted her. These two are extremely different cutoff practices, but Cole described them in the same way. For him emotionally, they seemed

---

357 This view of cutoff (the cuttee is ethically allowed seek contact but the cutter needn't respond) seems to be more common among older people. Cole is Gen X, and I've heard this viewed echoed by Boomers and even older folks, like my mother. The sense that any contact by the cuttee is a violation seems relatively new, more common among Millennials, Gen Z, and some Gen Xers. Being old or new doesn't automatically make a practice good or bad, but this difference highlights how culturally specific our current "best practice" is.

358 Williams, 21.

to feel similar. Yet it strikes me that the impacts on Biva and Joelle may be very different. Biva is well-placed to understand why Cole is no longer in contact. Joelle seems not to be. I am not Joelle, but in her place, I would be wondering if the silence will be temporary or permanent, if I need to do something to make amends, if my old friend now hates me—and will hate me for life. Such a conjecture would be particularly unfortunate given that Cole states with obvious sincerity that he loves her, and he is not angry. But unless she has a very deep, intuitive sense of his psyche, she may not be well placed to know that. Moreover, because Cole himself doesn't experience much pain at being cut off, it's possible he may default to expecting that others won't either. Unfortunately, ostracism research shows the harm can be considerable.

Cole's case is one where, I suspect, a doorway might ameliorate harm while preserving Cole's core need to be out of contact with his cuttees. For example, if Joelle could ask a mutual friend what's up with him and get something like the explanation Cole gave me, it might put to rest many painful questions. If Cole gave the friend an explanation to share, the friend might be able to deliver it without Cole's being involved at all. Joelle might still miss him. She might still grieve, but she would have a way to know she is not hated or resented. She would have a way to know he still loves her and wishes her well.

A Doorway as a Low-Stakes Way to Allow for Things to Change

A doorway involves boundary setting, and many will remark that we often cut people off precisely because they show no respect for boundaries. In such cases, they won't pay attention to a stated doorway. Indeed, they might respond with added indignation to the clear implication that they are not welcome. That's all true. In some cases, total silence or no doorway can be the best and safest solution.

In many cases, however, people with little regard for boundaries will violate any cutoff, whether it involves silence (ghosting), a stated doorway, or explicitly no doorway. If there's not much to lose, I say consider providing a doorway: there might be much to gain. For example, let's say the doorway is to contact the friend, Josie, and the cuttee doesn't honor this, texting the cutter directly instead. As long as they don't honor the doorway, it's perfectly reasonable and probably advisable not to reply, to block phone numbers, etc. But what if one day they do honor it: they contact Josie in exactly the way permitted? In many cases, nothing is lost by replying as the doorway promises. In fact, that act can help habituate the cuttee to respect boundaries by showing that such respect will be rewarded. Sometimes, the cuttee may mature over time and learn to respect boundaries, and that little doorway might be the passage to a moment of peacemaking that will soothe years of pain.

Yes, people can grow. People can change. Here's a gripe about the movie, *Frozen*. That movie is one of my favorite kids' animated film, but it's wrong when it parrots the old adage that people don't change.[359] Of course, when the movie sings about not trying to change people, it's gesturing at the myth that an abusive man will reform out of love for the right woman, that she can "fix" him. That's a dangerous myth and needs to be debunked. While such a trajectory may not be impossible (the world has eight billion people with eight billion stories), it is certainly rare. But the *Frozen* song "Fixer Upper" doesn't offer that adage provisionally. It offers it as a totalizing truth, a truth amply contradicted by the movie itself, which is all about the profound psychological change in snow queen Elsa, and to a lesser extent, her sister, Anna. I wouldn't nitpick one line in a kids' movie when the intended context is clear, except that the song reflects something about the society that created it.

We often put forward this adage as a totalizing truth: people don't change. If someone does something bad, you'd better give up on them because they're bad and they always will be: cut them, cancel them; they're garbage people. You're a fool to believe they can change, we say.

Yet people do change. Most of us change throughout our lives, even those of us who struggle with great psychological hardships. Complex Post-Traumatic Stress Disorder (CPTSD) is

[359] "Fixer Upper," *Frozen*, directed by Chris Buck and Jennifer Lee (2013; Walt Disney Pictures and Walt Disney Animation Studios). I may be unfair to this song, which has the good message that people can make bad choices under stress and love helps us be our best selves. I still reject the truism that people don't change. Our basic personality types may not (or rarely), but most of us can and do change profoundly.

characterized by fundamental lack of trust and balance in interactions with other human beings, attitudes that can lead to self-sabotage in relationships. A person struggling with CPTSD, for example, may show inordinate suspicion of a trustworthy partner, thus driving the partner away.[360] Psychotherapy generally improves functioning,[361] yet even without therapeutic intervention, people living with CPTSD tend to become somewhat more balanced and confident as time goes on. Though they often still have relationship problems, the severity of those problems diminishes over time. In his analysis of complex post-traumatic disorders, Andreas Laddis observes that, even without therapeutic help, "The statistical data from the natural course of complex posttraumatic disorders are that with age subjects learn to control their negative emotions, act them out less, and doubt their [negative] beliefs about relationships that generate the emotions."[362] Human beings naturally grow. Life teaches us.

As a community college instructor, I often see the path of change in full flower with my non-traditional students. Some of the most insightful, high-functioning people I have ever taught are recovering addicts or people who went to prison for crimes they themselves now deplore. They're people who found treatment for once crippling mental illness. They're parents who once lost custody of their children but now provide a stable home to their grandchildren. Of course, not everyone changes profoundly. Many remain stuck in destructive patterns. But many do get unstuck. If there is a possibility for healing in a relationship—if that can be held as just a tiny doorway without additional damage—the rewards for everyone involved may prove incredibly rich, as rich as peace and love, or simply replacing fear with relief.

---

[360] Andreas Laddis, "Lessons from the Natural Course of Complex Posttraumatic Disorders," *Journal of Aggression, Maltreatment and Trauma*, vol. 20 (2011): 426–44.

[361] Laddis, 431.

[362] Laddis, 433. Laddis finds that with and without psychotherapy, healthy interpersonal and professional relationships often remain elusive for people with CPTSD. My point is not to trivialize the barriers to healing but to affirm that a degree of change toward healing is both attainable and normal.

A Doorway as a Safeguard against Escalation of Pursuit

In some cases, not providing a doorway could enable escalation of the trauma on both sides. As Taylor's study notes, ostracism can intensify unwanted pursuit behaviors.[363] The commonsense cause-and-effect is clear. While cutoff trauma generally may be greater on the cuttee's side, cutoff can exacerbate trauma for the cutter as well. One example is the nasty letter I sent Sophia. Based on what I know of her, I suspect that letter badly retraumatized her. I am ashamed of that letter; sending it is my responsibility. At the same time—both these things can exist at once—this is a reality: if she had not blocked all communication, I would not have sent it. I sent it because she blocked communication. If she had provided *any* doorway, even a stark, domineering one, I would have used that doorway, and instead of an unexpected splat of unhinged venting, she could have received, for example, a short, polite communication buffered by a third party. It would have hurt her less. How could it not? That letter was the attack of a cornered animal, and, in many cases (not all), the best way to avoid attacks like that is to give the animal a way to escape: a doorway.

Doorways can be pretty narrow. The example above with Josie running interference reads as angry and strict. Though it's not as extreme as total cutoff, it's still a rigid boundary, one we might expect to be set by a frightened, exhausted individual who needs assurance that the person distressing them will not bother them in any unexpected way. It's a laying down the law by someone who needs a high degree of control in order to feel safe. I'm not too far off feeling this way about Sophia. In the hypothetical case that I could contact her to state my own boundaries, I would be more polite, but I would, indeed, say that if she ever wished to contact me, the initial communication should be brief, polite, and channeled through a third party. In return, I would promise a polite response. I would make this doorway narrow because, as of the time I write this passage (in 2021), I am still often afraid and easily triggered by just thinking about her. I need some buffer from her

[363] Taylor, 231.

in order to feel safe.[364] She certainly needs this from me. But not all doorways need be this narrow.

Choosing the Highest Level of Connection That Is Healthy for the Cutter

A good guideline for boundary setting is to favor as much open, positive connection as is consistent with maintaining healthy boundaries. In other words, by all means, let's set all the boundaries we need in order to be safe and healthy. We should, however, think twice about setting boundaries our safety and health *don't* need. Prioritizing connection over disconnection, where it's consistent with our health, makes sense, simply because we are more content when we're connected. We're a social species; we evolved to live in groups. As young kids, we literally can't survive alone, and even as adults we suffer without connection. Conversely, feeling connected helps us feel healthy and calm.

Neuropsychologist Dr. Rick Hanson puts it this way:

> When you experience connection, your attaching to others system goes green, into its responsive mode [i.e. its calming, non-stressed mode]. You can build up both your capacity to *be* connected and your sense of *feeling* connected by regularly taking in a sense of *feeling cared about*, *feeling valued*, *compassion and kindness*, *self-compassion*, *compassionate assertiveness*, *feeling like a good person*, and *love*.[365]

It may seem obvious, but it bears saying that almost all of these senses require *being in relationship*. Self-compassion we could theoretically feel outside relationships with others. Being a good person, however, implies doing good for others; feeling cared about or valued implies others feeling something for us. Compassion and kindness, in general, are stances toward others. Assertiveness exists in relation to others, and love, of course, implies sharing love with others. Now, certainly we can have connection with some while blocking out others—and sometimes

---

[364] As of 2024, while the idea of hearing from her is still scary, I no longer feel a need for that narrow a doorway. We change.

[365] Rick Hanson, *Hardwiring Happiness: The New Brain Science of Contentment, Calm, and Confidence*, (New York: Harmony Books, 2013), 204.

we must. But in general, the more connection we can healthily embrace and less blocking we have to do, the more connected and less stressed we will feel. I should clarify that when I say more connection is better, I do not mean we should cram our lives with more interaction and commitment than we can manage. I mean "connection" here as an openness to interaction with others, an ability to be present with people in the moment, to reach back (in safe circumstances) if someone reaches out.

I also want to underscore that connection is consistent with having boundaries. Hanson's *compassionate assertiveness* points to how connection and boundaries mesh. In a state of compassionate assertiveness, says Hanson,

> You maintain your boundaries and say what you need to say and if need be say it again. You can communicate with dignity and gravity without getting sucked into pointless quarreling. You are loving, while not waiving your rights or getting exploited. Each time you register the combination of compassion and assertiveness, it deepens your capacity to be direct, revealed, and free with others. And as you feel stronger, more independent and autonomous, you'll feel even more comfortable in the depths of your intimacy.[366]

Healthy boundaries along with compassion form a positive feedback loop that helps us be simultaneously more independent and more intimately connected.

In the context of cutoff, compassionate assertiveness means the communication boundaries should generally be as open as health and safety make reasonable. I suspect that Sophia believes she must cut me off for life to feel safe. I'm sad about that, but it seems likely to me. There was a time I had to cut Ryan off; I couldn't have responsibly and civilly handled any more communication with him. Yet today, Ryan and I are social media friends and occasionally email because we can: it doesn't damage us. There are no explicit boundaries around when and how we exchange messages, except one that he set: he does not wish to talk in real time about what happened between us, and having contributed his help to this book, he does not wish to talk about it

[366] Hanson, 216.

anymore at all. That's a boundary to keep him safe, and it's a moderate one that does not preclude his sending me links to amusing pop culture references by direct message or my replying.

While Ryan has expressed a wish not to discuss our past, and I want to honor it, he has not phrased this in terms of an absolute order. There's no requirement that I never mention the breakdown of our friendship again. I will certainly tell him when this book is in print, even though it discusses that breakdown, which he would rather put behind him. He contributed to this book and deserves to know. Such flexibility allows for exceptional circumstances—like the publication of a book, or, say, discovering a new piece of information that sheds light on an old misunderstanding, or reaching out to communicate about the death a mutual friend. Life is rich in context and, where feasible, boundaries that express wishes or requests rather than commands allow for a safe space without rejecting occasional, atypical communications that might be uncomfortable but enable a greater good.

We all want to feel at ease. Boundaries can help us feel at ease, but so can doorways. Indeed, there's a tradeoff here. The more rigid the boundary, the more control it gives—though this can backfire, as I've noted, by making retaliation, such as stalking behavior, more likely. Nonetheless, in many cases, this control can be necessary to feeling at ease. On the other hand, the more rigid a boundary, the more effort it can take to respect, creating less ease in the person shut out. For example, agreeing to generally avoid discussing the past is much easier than being constrained never to mention it under any circumstances. Where feasible, moderate boundaries can allow more ease in the relationship, and ease allows faster, truer healing.

This moderate boundary setting is even possible in relationships with a high degree of estrangement. Cora has had a difficult relationship with one of her two sisters, Vera, for decades.[367] For a time, while the sisters shared a house, Cora explains, she bore the brunt of the emotional work to smooth out conflicts within the extended family while caring for her own daughter and special needs son. One day, her other sister said to her, "You look so depressed." Cora realized, that after six years, it was time to move into separate houses. Looking back on life with Vera, she says, "I

[367] Cora, in discussion with author, January 14, 2022. All quotes from Cora.

can't say ours was ever a loving relationship, and I know I made some big mistakes in the time we lived together." At the same time, she says, "I sort of blame my sister," especially for a failure to take action on evidence that Vera's ex had sexually abused their daughter, Cora's niece. Likely linked to this trauma, her niece struggled with mental health issues as she grew into adulthood, and Cora was often left trying to offer support, particularly after Vera relocated far away. Meanwhile, Vera's phone calls focused on her own relationship problems and money problems. "In hindsight," Cora reflects, "my sister was always needing to be rescued."

Eventually, the family slipped into obvious estrangement. When their mother passed away, Vera stated she did not have money for travel to the funeral and the rest of the family did not pay for her to attend. The niece, whose behavior at the time was erratic, was barred from speaking at the funeral. There were hurt feelings and accusations, and contact became sporadic and dwindled out, much to Cora's relief. "I don't have to deal with that drama anymore," she said to me, "And sometimes I think I should feel bad about that." She paused a moment in thought and added, "I honestly don't feel that bad about it."

Cora presented this story to me as a cutoff. But it was never a hard cutoff in the sense of demanding no contact. When I asked her if she was willing to speak to Vera again, she said, "If she called today, I'd talk to her, but I don't feel the need." I would call this an estrangement that is not a cutoff because, actually, no one is cut off. Though the sisters have drifted into silence, a phone call would not necessarily be refused.

It may be significant that Cora comes from a generation that grew up before the existence of our current cutoff culture. The hard boundary of cutoff, the "never speak to me again," may simply not have been a large part of her formative cultural experience. Yet the boundaries the family has developed work pretty well for Cora. She doesn't have to "deal with the drama"; she's largely free from the stress of her sister's and niece's needs. Still a doorway remains open. If Vera were ever in life-threatening trouble, or if her mental state ever took a healthier turn, nothing would be blocking her from reaching out. The cost of this openness might be a stint on the phone listening to Vera's troubles. The reward is the ability of the family to be present in real need or to have the chance, however remote, of future growth and reconciliation.

Support for People with Cutoff Trauma

Not everyone who experiences cutoff, even within a close relationship, experiences lasting trauma, but many of us do. Understanding that trauma is a likely consequence of cutoff, we should adopt cultural practices that support trauma recovery.

As part of their transformative justice work, Staci K. Haines et al. cite six factors that survivors of sexual abuse have stated they need:

- Tell their own stories about their own experiences, with a context of trust and safety.
- Experience validation that the harm they experienced was and is real.
- Observe that the person who… abused them feels remorse and is accountable for their actions.
- Receive support that counteracts isolation and self-blame.
- Have choice and input into the resolution of the harm they experienced.
- Be accepted and encouraged, not shamed and blamed, for coming forward by their families, peers, and communities.[368]

This list is identical to what I have needed to heal from cutoff trauma. I do not like to say this. Sexual abuse is an egregious violation different from cutoff in both degree and kind. For one thing, cutoff does not physically harm someone or violate bodily autonomy. For another, cutting someone off is not inherently abusive. Many will find it trivializing and triggering to compare sexual abuse trauma to cutoff trauma. Nevertheless, this list is identical to what I have desperately longed for.[369] That's ugly, but it's true.

---

[368] Staci K. Haines, Raquel Laviña, Chris Lymbertos, RJ Maccani, and Nathan Shara, "Excerpts from *Ending Child Sexual Abuse: A Transformative Justice Handbook*" in *Beyond Survival*, edited by Ejeris Dixon and Leah Lakshmi Piepzna-Samarasinha (Chico, CA: AK Press, 2020), 112.

[369] My editor "wonder[s] if cutoff for a survivor of sexual abuse has exponential impacts": an excellent question that deserves study. Editorial comment, October 31, 2023.

I suspect that this list, while compiled in the context of sexual abuse, sheds light on the nature of trauma recovery broadly, and paying attention to that can help us build a culture of healing for everyone.

I find it significant that every single one of these avenues of healing has regularly been closed to me. When I have voiced my own story or sought support, I have often been shamed and blamed, which makes trust and safety hard to find. Few have validated that the harm to me is real—or, to be more accurate, acknowledged the degree of the harm. I have never observed any sign of remorse or accountability from Sophia: the cutoff itself makes such accountability impossible because it would require communication with me. I have no choice or input into a resolution to the harm. I can—and do—work on my own psyche, but I am explicitly prohibited from every action that could lead to some sort of resolution with Sophia. On the contrary, I am told not only that I am not owed resolution, but that it is morally wrong to expect one and it is a sign of toxicity to resent this situation.

I've previously noted that my friend Anna was surprised I still seemed so angry about being cut off five years later. In light of Haines et al.'s research, it should not be surprising. Our dominant practice toward people traumatized by cutoff is to deny every single thing survivors of relationship trauma may need to facilitate healing. No wonder I responded like a person living under abuse. The good news is that Haines et al. chart a clear path for what to do differently.

To what extent can we follow that path while respecting the right to cutoff? Haines et al. provide six factors that assist in recovering from sexual abuse. If we translate this into the context of cutoff trauma and the cuttee's emotional healing, two of these points may require the cutter's involvement and four do not. The two that may require the cutter's involvement are:

A. Seeing that the cutter feels remorse and is accountable for their actions.
B. Having choice and input into the resolution of the harm the cuttee experienced.

The four that do not require the cutter are:

C. Telling the cuttee's own stories about their own experiences, with a context of trust and safety.
D. Experiencing validation that the harm they experienced was and is real.
E. Receiving support that counteracts isolation and self-blame.
F. Being accepted and encouraged, not shamed and blamed, for coming forward by their families, peers, and communities.

Let's start with the two acts that might require the cutter. They might not be things the cutter wants to do, and often for good reason. For the cutter to express remorse and accountability minimally necessitates two things: (1) a suspension of the cutoff in order to send the message and (2) an actual sense of remorse and accountability. Both are often impossible, and that's one of the things that makes cutoff so devastatingly painful: almost by definition it closes one of the central avenues to healing. If the cutter does not regret the cutoff and/or is not willing or able to suspend it, there's nothing to be done. This need cannot be met.

Similarly, if the cuttee's preferred means of resolving the harm they've suffered involves communicating with the cutter—as it often does—this may be unattainable. Sometimes the cutter won't, can't, and/or shouldn't communicate. Even if our ethics were to allow slight transgressions of the cutoff—a text message or two over the years—the cuttee still has a fundamental duty to respect the right to cutoff. In many cases, they cannot have any input on resolving the broken relationship.

That said, if there is not an iron reason that the cutoff must be total, it is worth considering that just one statement of accountability from the cutter may profoundly help with healing. It need not admit culpability; it need not express regret. It could come via an email, quoted by a third party, for example, "I heard that you got really hurt by me cutting you off. I do need to cut contact, but I'm truly sorry it has hurt you so much." To reduce the risk of miscommunication and mixed messaging, it may be advisable to ask the third party to refrain from commenting themselves—and to choose someone who can refrain.

In some cases, the cutter may, indeed, come to feel remorse, as I do for my failure to recognize the harm I did to Ryan. In such cases, where it's safe, it may be advisable to express this. If a cutter truly feels they did something wrong—either the cutoff as a whole or some piece of how they handled it—expressing regret for this is decent, responsible, and, even if difficult in the moment, may be healing for both cuttee and cutter.

Even if no input from the cutter is available, there are still four kinds of support (I've labeled them C, D, E, and F) that bystanders can give to help heal cutoff trauma. These supports boil down to one overarching stance: that cutoff trauma is real and must be treated seriously. As bystanders, if we begin with the premise that the trauma is real and say so explicitly and repeatedly, we have already achieved support D, validating that harm occurred.

The other three points (C, E, and F), however, all imply that the cuttee (as the victim of a relational trauma) is not at fault. Here, cutoff is categorically different from sexual assault. The victim of sexual assault is *never* at fault. It doesn't matter what they did, what they said, what they wore, where they were, or what their relationship to their assailant was: no one is at fault but the assailant. There is an iron-clad duty not to commit sexual assault. On the other hand, in many cutoffs the cuttee is partly at fault. In many cases, they did commit harm that incited the cutoff. In some cases, such as physical threat or assault, it's reasonable to say the cuttee is entirely at fault. Without denying culpability the cuttee may have, how can we help support them?

As to being able to share one's own stories, while this implies a sympathetic ear, it does not require the cuttee to be innocent. Indeed, they could be 100 percent at fault and still have experiences they need to share in a safe space, but it can be tricky to listen to this. As Brené Brown notes in the context of talking about shame, "It's not easy to ask someone to listen, and it's not easy to be one of the listeners."[370] In some cases, we might not be the right listener, particularly if the cuttee is not safe to be around, or if the cuttee's past actions trigger us, if they evoke harm we, too, have received—or perhaps committed. In some cases, a therapist, clergy, a social worker, or support group may be the best available listener. But such listeners are a poor proxy for a full community. It is not enough to have a therapist to unload to. Human beings also need friends, allies, good neighbors. We cannot be that person for everyone all the time, but if someone comes to us seeking a listening ear and we can reasonably provide it, I think we should.

---

[370] Brown, 153.

How can we encourage coming forward and counter excessive self-blame in contexts where the cuttee may, indeed, bear some blame? For one thing, we can look at each situation contextually and encourage accountability without senseless self-flagellation. Some cuttees have committed heinous acts; some have done literally nothing objectionable. As friends and community members, we can act as a sounding board, as reality testers, to encourage reasonable accountability. My second therapist did this when I confessed to her, with great shame, the nasty letter I wrote to Sophia in 2016. "So you messed up," she said. "So what? So does everybody sometime." While it wasn't enough to counteract other negative messaging and my own deep sense of guilt, those words rained on me in shower of relief. My friend Derek filled the same role when he told me gently I shouldn't have sent that letter. His sense of my culpability was clear, but his manner was kind and his emphasis on my healing, not my punishment. When we can offer this kind of proportionality, when we can simply commit to listening without showing anger, we allow people to share their situation in a context that provides support and perspective. In short, it will go a long way just to be kind to folks, just to refuse the voice that whispers that virtue always demands righteous condemnation. It doesn't.

In recent years, when I ask my students what's one change they would like to see in the world, more and more often they say, "I'd like people to be kinder." That is not always easy in today's angry, fractious world, but when we can, let's try to be kinder, even to cut-off people. Ostracism hurts, and if there's anything we can safely do to lessen how much we have to ostracize someone, even the smallest doorway can be a means to healing. If we are a bystander to cutoff, let's be kind too. If we safely can, we can validate that cutoff pain is real and provide a space for cut-off people to talk about it without condemnation. We can treat cut-off people as people. That simple act can be one piece of rehumanizing our broader culture. Kindness spreads kindness.

Chapter 13
A Relational Approach to Forgiveness

Almost by definition, cutoff is a conflict. If two people mutually wish to drop contact, it isn't really a cutoff—or it's a cutoff in name only—because there is no *need* to cut the other person off. Both parties can voluntarily depart. Conversely, virtually any cutoff that requires, or feels like it requires, some reinforcement of the cutoff boundary is a conflict, a power struggle between a person who wants silence and a person who wants communication.

Conflicts hurt and often scar, and when we hurt each other, we can build anger, resentment, and grudges. The antithesis of those feelings is forgiveness, a coming out on the other side of anger and condemnation. Thus, our view of cutoff is entwined with our view of forgiveness, and to reconceptualize cutoff, we must explore forgiveness too.

To begin with some cultural context, in Western cultures, our concepts of forgiveness are deeply informed by Christianity, in which forgiveness is a core value. Though I have never been Christian, my cultural background is. I am deeply rooted in Christian cultural understandings of forgiveness and am partial to that view. Within a Christian frame of reference, forgiveness often implies reconciliation within a relationship. This is certainly the view that feels most natural to me.

Rabbi Kukla, however, notes that Judaism has a different viewpoint on coming to terms with conflict:

> Reconciliation is originally a Christian word and concept. I believe that our American cultural celebration of reconciliation, regardless of family circumstance, is due to the primacy of Christianity. Other cultures engage other approaches toward wholeness.
>
> My own tradition, Judaism, holds the concept of *teshuva* (return) at the end of life, which can include reconnection between people, but also implies a profound return to the self, and justice in the world. Coming to wholeness and peace can mean many things, and eventually you will need to define it for yourself.[371]

Different cultures have different approaches to the social and emotional healing of conflict. Though I favor certain principles, I want to recognize that different cultures, like different individuals, may find many different paths. As Kukla observes, ultimately, we must each find our own solution.

As a general principle, though, I want to begin by asserting that forgiveness cannot be forced. If it is not freely given, I, for one, do not consider it forgiveness, merely a coerced sham of reconciliation. I question any creed that says, "You have to forgive them," as an article of virtue. It is not fair to make our virtue dependent on doing something we may not be able to do. Forgiveness is a beautiful thing, and based on my own experience, I think it is, indeed, necessary to living fully at peace with oneself and others. But sometimes the hurt simply runs too deep for forgiveness to be available at a given point in time. It's also worth noting, as Kukla does, that intersectionally marginalized people may be under especially strong social pressure to reconnect with those who harm them.[372] Especially in such cases, pressure to forgive can result in bullying (and in some cases endangering) people who already live under oppression.

At the same time, considerable scientific evidence supports the importance of forgiveness to psychological and physiological wellness. Peggy A. Hannon et al. (2012) observe that a number of studies, including their own, associate granting forgiveness with

---

[371] Kukla.

[372] Kukla.

positive physiological functioning.[373] In the less studied area of receiving forgiveness, Hannon et al. also found a positive correlation between conciliatory behavior from victims and reduced blood pressure in perpetrators.[374] L. L. Toussaint et al. (2016) found that forgiveness correlated with reduced stress, which, in turn, correlated with improved mental health symptoms, though not physical health symptoms.[375] They speculate that the lack of perceived improvement in physical health may be related to the short duration of their study (five weeks).[376] Conversely, in a 1997 study, the George H. Gallup International Institute found that not feeling forgiven by family members was a prominent concern for people at the end of life.[377] Along similar lines, Marjorie Baker (2005) offers a case study of the positive psychological effect on one man of being able to reconcile with his estranged daughter at the end of his life.[378]

Forgiveness heals; that's pretty clear. It heals the forgiver and, depending on how it is delivered, can heal the forgiven. In this book, I trumpet my belief in contextual specificity, but the healing power of forgiveness is evident across many contexts. While advocating forgiveness can, indeed, slip into disingenuous demands that we overlook harm, it is also based on well-evidenced practices that promote healing and health.

It's curious, however, that despite the well-evidenced positive impacts of forgiveness, our society has no clear consensus as to

---

[373] Peggy A. Hannon, Eli J. Finkel, Madoka Kumashiro, and Caryl E. Rusbult, "The Soothing Effects of Forgiveness on Victims' and Perpetrators' Blood Pressure," *Personal Relationships*, 19 (2012): 285. https://doi.org/10.1111/j.1475-6811.2011.01356.x.

[374] Hannon et al.

[375] L. L. Toussaint, G. S. Shields, G. M. Slavich, "Forgiveness, Stress, and Health: a 5-Week Dynamic Parallel Process Study," *Annals of Behavioral Medicine*, 50, no. 5 (2016): 732–33, https://doi.org/10.1007/s12160-016-9796-6. Full text available at https://www.ncbi.nlm.nih.gov/pmc/articles/PMC5055412/

[376] Toussaint, Shields, Slavich.

[377] Marjorie Baker, "Facilitating Forgiveness and Peaceful Closure: The Therapeutic Value of Psychosocial Intervention in End-of-Life Care," *Journal of Social Work in End-of-Life & Palliative Care*, 1, no. 4 (2005): 93, https://doi.org/10.1300/J457v01n04_06.

[378] Baker.

what forgiveness actually is. Forgiveness researcher Everett L. Worthington, Jr. (2004) writes,

> I've come to believe that how we define forgiveness usually depends on context. In cases where we hope to forgive a person with whom we do not want a continuing relationship, we usually define forgiveness as reducing or eliminating resentment and motivations toward revenge. My colleagues Michael McCullough, Kenneth Rachal, and I have defined forgiveness in close relationships to include more than merely getting rid of the negative. The forgiving person becomes less motivated to retaliate against someone who offended him or her and less motivated to remain estranged from that person. Instead, he or she becomes more motivated by feelings of goodwill, despite the offender's hurtful actions. In a close relationship, we hope, forgiveness will not only move us past negative emotions, but move us toward a net positive feeling. It doesn't mean forgetting or pardoning an offense.[379]

Even within the same cultural frame, what constitutes forgiveness can depend on the type of relationship involved. For people not in ongoing contact (including cutoffs), it can mean simply ceasing to feel negatively, while for people in ongoing close relationship, it is more likely to conclude active goodwill. In my own reading and conversations, I have found that perspectives on forgiveness range across a vast continuum, from considering it a social action with no bearing on internal feeling to an internal feeling with no bearing on social action.

Take for example, the situation of Jace, a young man who has experienced emotional abuse at the hands of his father. In conversation with me, Jace noted that his family repeatedly pressures him to forgive his father, but he says, "I don't want to forgive my dad because every time I do, he uses it as permission to come back into my life and mess things up again."[380] Forgiveness, in this

---

[379] Everett L. Worthington, Jr., "The New Science of Forgiveness," *Greater Good Magazine*, September 1, 2004, https://greatergood.berkeley.edu/article/item/the_new_science_of_forgiveness.
[380] Jace, in discussion with author, October 7, 2020.

model, is purely a social contract, an agreement that boundaries have been reset to the terms that existed before the transgression. To Jace's dad, this seems to signify that he doesn't need to change because anything he does can be forgiven without his showing accountability. Jace's feelings don't really enter into it; what matters to his family is the social move of allowing his father back into his life. Jace comes from an Asian cultural background that emphasizes a child's responsibility to their parents. As Delia remarks, "Western society… expects us to get rid of the bad spouse or bad parent; I'm Chinese, and it's unacceptable in Chinese society to cut off one's parents—although that is changing."[381] Culture always informs our relational concepts.

On the other end of the cultural spectrum, we have the concept that forgiveness is purely internal. Michelle Pegues, a coach specializing in women's life after divorce, describes forgiveness this way:

> The act of forgiveness is not for the other person, it is for you, and only you, because you deserve it. You deserve to be free. It is not your job to release them and make them feel better about themselves. They are responsible for doing their own work and fixing their own issues. By forgiving, you are freeing yourself, allowing yourself to detach from the negative feelings of anger, resentment, shame, or guilt that are bringing your energy levels down and holding you back, and ultimately keeping you from finding peace.[382]

Pegues makes it explicit that forgiveness, in this model, carries no necessary social dimension. It implies no external change in the standing of the relationship. It is purely a feeling on the part of the forgiver. This is a distinctly Western view of forgiveness, rooted in individualism, the idea that each person's own wellbeing takes priority over community or relational wellbeing. It's the antithesis

---

[381] Delia, private message to the author, February 27, 2020.

[382] Michelle Pegues, "Forgiveness Part 1: Myths of Forgiveness," *MichellePegues.com*, July 7, 2021, https://michellepegues.com/blog/forgiveness-part-1-the-myths-of-forgiveness.

of the strongly collectivist view of Jace's family, which prioritizes relational duties at the expense of individuals' feelings. These views mark two extremes on a continuum, and they are far from the only ways to understand forgiveness.

Certainly, in some cases each of these polar opposite views can describe the best approach. For example, in many cases, the path of least resistance may be to accept someone socially and keep lingering resentments to ourselves. Particularly if the transgressions are relatively minor and the person not an intimate acquaintance, I find this often works well enough in my life. It allows for civil social functioning without deepening the discomfort by dredging up old problems. Similarly, in some situations purely internal forgiveness is the only viable option. One example would be if the transgressor has died. In this case, there's no possibility of expressing forgiveness directly to that person; however, as Pegues notes, we can ease our own suffering by embracing forgiveness in our hearts. The same holds true in cases where it is inadvisable to have contact with the transgressor, for example, if that person is a threat or has repeatedly shown an inability to comprehend boundary setting. Steinmetz sums up this perspective well when he says, "It's not that I don't believe in the act of forgiveness, repentance, or growth. It's that for me, these people [he has cut off] have shown me to be not worth the risk of having them around."[383] Here, what prevents active reconciliation is not ongoing resentment but a need for psychological safety.

As a generalization, however, I would argue that forgiveness is best understood as a combination of internal release and social reconciliation. Within my Western frame of reference, I would not call what Jace describes "forgiveness," though I recognize that a different frame of reference might legitimately do so. I would call it something more like toleration, a ceasefire perhaps, or agreement to take on a social duty. Listening to Jace, I hear the flame of indignation in his voice. Whether or not he has officially forgiven his father for the latest act of harm, the situation in his heart is not settled. That, at best, is a provisional and potentially quite painful forgiveness. Pegues, I think, is right in this: forgiveness should not cause us pain; it should give us peace.

---

[383] Steinmetz, "She Broke up with Me, and Never Gave Me a Second Chance."

At the same time, purely internal forgiveness leaves the relationship broken. Sometimes this is the only realistic option, but if it is not, I would advocate a practice of forgiveness that includes the social relationship. I speak as someone who has been on the receiving end of non-social forgiveness. Sophia practiced almost purely non-social forgiveness in the email in which she cut me off. She did say she forgave me: that's the social part. But she said it in the context of simultaneously telling me that I was permanently expelled from every aspect of her life. The words argued against the action, or as I put it in an early journal entry, "She says that it's forgiveness, but it feels like revenge." I wrote that in 2015, and writing these words (in 2021), I have to say it feels the same. I do not now, nor have I ever, felt forgiven by Sophia. Now, for her, non-social forgiveness may be the only realistic option. I don't know enough context to say whether she made the wrong choice. Yet I can say that, for me, those words felt—and they still feel—false. Shunning does not feel like forgiveness.[384]

Pegues argues that this doesn't matter, that forgiveness, properly, is only about the forgiver, not the forgiven. I would say that view flies in the face of a long and multicultural history of the concept. "To forgive" is a transitive verb, and not only in English but in every language in which I know the word. It has an object. We forgive someone. It is something we do in relationship to someone. To say it has no reference to that someone's wellbeing is odd. Or to put it another way, when a person falls on bended knee and says, "Please forgive me," what they do *not* mean is "Please feel better about this in your heart while never giving me any indication that your anger at me has changed at all." On the contrary, they mean, "Help me. Please help us mend this problem between us." That is not always practicable, but it is certainly

---

[384] It may be obvious that I feel her statement was a form of words, not an articulation of the state of her heart. Perhaps it was a purely external forgiveness, an attempt at a civil end. Or perhaps she had, indeed, worked through all her significant resentments at me. That's possible, but it is not what I *feel* to be true. Is my doubt about it a sign of insight into her or a sign that I haven't forgiven myself? The latter is certainly true. Without communication, I cannot evaluate the former. For what it's worth, rereading this section in 2024, I do see her words as less vengeful and more simply expressing the limits of her capacity to address our relationship.

implied in the basic concept of forgiveness. It is certainly a goal and has been throughout human history.

In my experience of feeling forgiveness for others (and I don't claim my experience is universal), it is an internal state that translates into an external willingness to show compassion, to facilitate healing of the other person and the relationship where possible. I have forgiven Ryan. Now, Ryan did very little that ought to require forgiveness. I did far more to him. But in my experience, the nature of forgiveness does not change with the severity of the infraction. Forgiveness is, in essence, a cessation of anger, whether that anger is inspired by a grave crime or a tiny slight. Regardless of Ryan's culpability, I hated him for years. Then, the hatred burned lower, and then it burned out, leaving no significant anger. The little, irrational stings that remain are ripples from the past; they're not living. Because the anger is gone, I can be kind to Ryan without hurting myself. I can reply nicely to his messages. I can accept his desire not to talk in real time about what happened between us. I can be open to whatever he may wish to say and respond without being strongly triggered. That is forgiveness in my experience. As far as reasonable safety permits, forgiveness is able to be magnanimous because it comes from an internal state of ease, not pain.

Pegues says of forgiving someone, "It is not your job to release them and make them feel better about themselves."[385] I understand the value of this sentiment, yet I worry about it too. The value is protecting victims from further harm. My worry is the broad brush it paints with, the ease with which such sentiments can be used to excuse callousness. What I find missing is a sense of proportion. To "release" someone suggests something total: all the weight gone, absolution. To "feel better," however, might mean getting the relief of one conciliatory postcard. These are very different things, yet Pegues lumps them as one. This conflation is significant because, I'd argue, it is within our job description as human beings to make other people feel a little better—not to release them from all their guilt or consequences, and not every person, every time, in every context; that's neither possible nor advisable. But in general, when we have forgiven someone and when we reasonably can, we should certainly help that person feel a little better. We should try to help them heal. It

[385] Pegues.

will surely heal us too. No, it is not a *duty*—and sometimes it is not safely possible. But when it is safely possible, yes, we should consider that part of our *responsibility* as human beings. The alternative is to disregard our impact on each other's welfare, and that is a recipe for perpetual, cyclical, unnecessary hurt.

Forgiveness in Cutoff

Cutoff culture produces a strange relationship with forgiveness. It generally construes it in one of two ways—and they are polar opposites:

1. An action that is potentially self-harming because it reopens a doorway to hurt.
2. Purely an internal state of mind, unconnected to any action.

The idea seems to be that social forgiveness (letting someone back into your life) can be dangerous; therefore, purely internal forgiveness may be the only option. Again, in many cases this is true. Cutoff culture, however, presupposes that this is true in all permanent cutoffs, since one of its tenets is refusal of all contact while the cutoff is in effect. Thus, forgiveness as a social, relational act is inaccessible. This stance is an understandable reaction against an abusive culture: it's an attempt to keep abused people safe. Distrust of social forgiveness can also be a reaction against coercive demands to forgive, an attempt to honor free, authentic forgiveness. The goals are good, but reactionary tendencies often jump to extremes, and extreme responses can create new kinds of damage. Therefore, it pays to rethink forgiveness in the context of cutoff.

The cutter and cuttee do not have equal agency in forgiveness. The cutter is culturally allowed to reach out socially; the cuttee is not. Since sociality is an important dimension of forgiveness, this means that, as a generalization, their experiences of forgiveness will have some significant differences. It pays, therefore, to examine the cuttee's and cutter's situations separately.

The Dynamics of a Cuttee Forgiving a Cutter

In some cases, a cuttee may find the cutoff completely fair: this seems to be the attitude of Steinmetz and Jefferson, who both defend the actions of the people who cut them off. If they ever held anything against them (I don't know if they did), they seem to have completely forgiven them. Steinmetz says of the ex who cut him off, "I am friends with Allie, even if she is not friends with me. And since I am a true friend, the best way I can show my friendship is to let her not worry I'm going to hurt her again."[386] That sounds like a state of forgiveness, an absence of resentment. In general, when we feel we're dealt with fairly, even if that involves harshness or punishment, forgiveness is easier.

To take a trivial example, a few years ago, I received a written critique of some comments I made about teaching practice (my profession), with no opportunity for me to respond. Upon reflection, I found some of those critiques to be fair and some unfair. While the entire critique initially riled me up, after just a couple of days, I had processed the fair critiques and gotten over my anger. As to what I perceived to be unfair—to be honest, I'm still sometimes sore about it. Similarly, I suspect that in most cases where a cuttee has difficulty forgiving a cutter, the cuttee feels the cutoff was unfair (or at least disproportionate to the wrongdoing). Many of us who are abandoned feel the sting of that ostracism keenly. It traumatizes us not least because there's often no accountability, no recognition that the trauma even exists. That generates a lot of anger, and all that can be hard to forgive, especially if it feels undeserved and we have no acceptable way to say so.

Cutoff culture teaches that cuttees are, by default, the ones to blame, that we hurt the cutter, not the other way around. I think many of us internalize this powerfully. In many cases, we probably did harm the cutter, maybe badly. This background reality that we did do harm, reinforced by social condemnation, can lead to tremendous self-flagellation. This, perversely, can make it gruelingly hard to forgive the cutter. That great student of the human heart, James Baldwin, explained why white Americans, as a cultural generalization, have been so cruel to Black Americans, saying, "I think… the hardest thing for any human being to do is to forgive

---

[386] Steinmetz, "She Broke up with Me, and Never Gave Me a Second Chance."

somebody they know they've wronged."[387] For many of us, the most intense rage we will ever feel is rage at ourselves. When that's difficult to face, as it often is, we project it onto the people we've wronged, the ones we associate with our wrongdoing. To me, Baldwin's statement rings true. It rings true in the context of American racism, but that's a topic for a different book. In the context of cutoff, I would go so far as to say the entire reason I have not forgiven Sophia is that I know I wronged her.

To be more specific, I know I've wronged her, but I do not know clearly how or how much. That leaves me between a rock and hard place. I often feel simultaneously unjust and treated unjustly, and I don't know where the line is between the two. That *uncertainty* is the most unsettling thing, the thing that perpetuates a sense of something amiss, something I can't put my finger on or remediate, and that discomfort stokes fear and anger, making forgiveness—of myself and, by extension, Sophia—especially difficult.

For contrast, I was once cut off by a boyfriend I'd dated for about six months and to whom I was moderately close. While I wasn't happy about the cutoff, one thing that made it easy to recover from was that I felt I understood the relationship. I knew what I'd done wrong, and I had a pretty good sense of when I didn't merit his accusations. It took me about a year to get over all my anger at him, and today I have no negative feelings for him (and zero desire to violate his cutoff). I've forgiven him, largely because I forgave myself. I was able to forgive myself because I understood what I'd done or didn't do, so I could think about it, learn from it, resolve to do better next time, and move on.

When we're told someone will never speak to us again, it means we will never receive social forgiveness from them. The very fact of the cutoff suggests that the cutter finds what we've done unforgivable (though the cutter may feel otherwise). In discussing his experience with being ghosted, Arlo invokes a concept of forgiveness that is deeply relational, one that implies mending the relationship. He articulates the pain of this impossibility: "There's no forgiveness possible because of the cutoff. Maybe there's atonement in some spiritual, metaphysical way," but he has

---

387 James Baldwin, Interview, "Civil Rights | James Baldwin Interview | Mavis on Four," (1987) ThamesTv. YouTube, 13:50, uploaded 1 November 1, 2014, https://www.youtube.com/watch?v=3Wht4NSf7E4.

difficulty grasping it: "It feels elusive because it's poorly defined."[388] When we cannot make amends to the person we've hurt, and we cannot be—or know if we are—forgiven by that person, our only recourse is to take whatever steps we can to atone in isolation and forgive ourselves in the end. This is not easy. As Arlo observes, it's even harder when we don't fully understand what we've done.

As I write this in 2022, I have struggled with my uncertainty about Sophia for eight years. I have wondered time and again how to understand my own culpability, and thus move toward improving and forgiving myself and her. But this past spring, quite suddenly, as I was hiking in the California oak woods of the beautiful Sonoma County Regional Park, I came to a realization. While it is true that I will never know exactly what I did to Sophia, I have to conclude that it did not merit lifelong cutoff. I'm simply not that bad. What I did simply wasn't that bad.[389] As I sat there on a shaded bench overlooking a quiet pond, it struck me that, as for what I do understand, I had already addressed it years ago—much of it before she cut me off. I stopped sending accusatory emails, to Sophia or anyone. In fact, I now avoid conducting any serious emotional business by asynchronous communication. I became much more circumspect in my words and assumptions. I became scrupulous in giving the benefit of the doubt, reminding myself I don't know that whole situation, assuming people are struggling with trauma I don't see. I have not had any conflict like the one with Sophia since Sophia, minor conflicts, yes, but nothing like that. I realized I had already forgiven myself for everything I understood I'd done. What was left was a strange, lingering sense that I was accountable for something, like original sin, that I couldn't identify or ameliorate.

There on that bench, I realized I'm not accountable for it. I am not responsible for Sophia choosing to cut me off. I was responsible for apologizing and changing my bad behaviors—and I did. I am not responsible for her need for a lifelong wall between us. And though it may sound counterintuitive, as soon as this thought came to me, I felt forgiveness. I felt a tremendous

---

388 Arlo, in discussion with author, December 17, 2021.

389 My editor notes I'm conflating my deed with my identity. Yes! They are not the same, but they are related, and all part of the mess in my head.

compassion for her, an ease, an emotional understanding. *That's okay, Sophia,* I felt, *you can do what you need to, and I have no wish to hurt you by pushing back.* I found I *wanted* to be kind to her by leaving her alone, not because I owed it but because she *needed* it. That feeling didn't last. It didn't last because eight years of habit dies hard, and frankly, because writing this book requires me to go back and re-live old trauma. Yet I do think it was the fundamental answer.

It may be some folks are thinking, "Well, duh. Isn't the first rule of all self-help articles that you're not responsible for some-one else's choices?" Sure, it is. But as I hope this book has argued (a) reality is more complex: we do influence each other's choices and that carries responsibility, and (b) the emotional awareness and the intellectual knowledge are different things. I'd intellectu-alized many times that I hadn't earned what Sophia dealt, since Day One really, but that day in the park, I felt the truth of it.

The self-forgiveness we are often told to cultivate is important, but it only works if there is something to forgive. Sometimes, peo-ple are cut off for egregious behavior. But many cutoffs happen because that's the only way the cutter knows how to deal with the conflict. Many times, we did not, by any reasonable standard, de-serve lifelong ostracism; it was simply meted out to us, often by people who didn't mean us lasting harm but honestly didn't realize how cutoff hurts because no one ever told them. Once we've worked through our own culpability as best we can, what's left over is not the need to forgive ourselves but the need to *absolve* ourselves. I don't mean absolution in a religious sense but as the general state of realizing we are not responsible for something; it's off our shoulders.

The moment I absolved myself of Sophia's cutting me off, I was filled with forgiveness. It went away—but I know it will be back, with a few more years, a little more time. I still shouldn't contact her, but it's not because I'm reprehensible. It's because she has a right to cutoff, regardless of the reason, and it's because I do not want to hurt her. It has nothing to do with my culpability, not anymore. In sum, for a cuttee striving to forgive the cutter, I think the path often lies in doses of both self-forgiveness and self-absolution, not as cheap evasions of responsibility but as thought-ful journeys into the nature of our responsibilities and where they end.

The Dynamics of a Cutter Forgiving a Cuttee

I think it's harder to generalize about the forgiveness of cutters than cuttees. Cuttees tend to share the common grievance of the cutoff itself. But for cutters, the cutoff is not a grievance; it's a solution. The problems that elicited that solution are diverse and so, too, will be journeys toward forgiveness, impediments to forgiveness, or decisions not to forgive.

In an interview with Lauren Sandler, psychiatrist Karen Swartz gives a snapshot of the different dimensions of forgiveness:

> There are some things that you really want to forgive, you want to move past, you want to have a future relationship with someone. And there are some things that are simply too horrible to forgive and to forget—like violence against a child, abuse. But I think there's a big difference between seeing things as forgivable and having it be the consuming factor in your life. Forgiveness does not always include reconciliation, and having a relationship with someone in the future is about whether they are reliable and dependable and trustworthy, and sometimes you've broken trust in a way that you can never have a relationship again.[390]

Swartz makes a crucial point that forgiveness need not imply letting someone back into our lives (for example, rescinding a cutoff). If someone is not safe to be around, it's prudent to avoid them; that's not the same as actively holding resentments against them. She makes a good point, too, that some heinous acts may be things we can't forgive, though I would state this more provisionally than Swartz does. It is humanly possible to forgive anything; some people can. Some people can't or don't wish to, and it only does harm to urge them to. It's a nitpick, but I'd also question Swartz's use

---

[390] Karen Swartz, in discussion with Lauren Sandler, "The Healing Power of Forgiveness," Johns Hopkins Medicine, July 8, 2014, quoted in Demi Powell, "Johns Hopkins Health - The Healing Power of Forgiveness," Core Spirit, Sep 26, 2019, https://corespirit.com/articles/johns-hopkins-health---the-healing-power-of-forgiveness-w9xqmyvpi.

of the word "want," a word I suspect she meant impressionistically rather than precisely. But to look at it precisely, whether someone *wants* to forgive depends on their own context. Personally, I profoundly agree with Swartz's core point that we should resume healthy relationships with people if we reasonably can, but I'll stop short of telling other people they should always want to do this.

As Pegues and Swartz both note, forgiveness need not imply having a social relationship with someone. Yet forgiveness as a concept does imply sociality. As far as its social aspect goes, cutters' approaches to forgiveness fall into two main categories: the cutter ends the cutoff, or the cutter does not. If the cutter ends (or mitigates or suspends) the cutoff, social moves toward expressing forgiveness are possible. If the cutter does not, they are not, and the cuttee will not know they've been forgiven. Which path a cutter takes depends on many different circumstances, ranging from the severity of the harm done to the cutter's preferred methods of conflict resolution.

As to forgiveness without social contact, Carolyn points to a path for this. Having cut off her brother after decades of emotional abuse, she observes that it's hard to get to forgiveness through the rage, hard but not impossible. Referring to her Christian faith, she says, "God loves everybody just the same, and it's possible for us to do so as well."[391] However, her life experience suggests that you cannot get rid of the rage in isolation. For her, a 12-step program provided a supportive community. For others, she says, it might be a good therapist. Carolyn notes that love, a feeling strongly tinged with forgiveness, can exist even within conflicted relationships: "I can like people who don't like me," she says. "I can love people who don't love me."[392] Carolyn asserts she loves her brother, even though she chose to cut him off and does not anticipate ever rescinding the cutoff.

In some cases, however, forgiveness may be one of the signals that cutoff is no longer emotionally necessary. This was the case with my feelings toward Ryan. Fundamentally, I needed to cut him off because I was angry at him and I could no longer suppress my rage if we stayed in contact. Once the anger was gone, once I had found forgiveness, the cutoff was no longer necessary. Thus, I

---

391 Carolyn.

392 Carolyn.

could reconnect with Ryan and enact forgiving behavior toward him—and, to my delight, receive it.

While the reasons for permanent cutoffs are many, they may loosely fall into two main categories: (1) cutoffs that remain necessary to safety because there is evidence the cutter and cuttee can never be in healthy relationship; (2) cutoffs that persist by habit or because the cutter does not wish to revisit past pain by interacting with the cuttee. An example of the first could be cutting off an abusive parent who has consistently shown poor boundaries. An example of the second could be cutting off a college boyfriend who broke his girlfriend's heart (but wasn't abusive). In the first case, further contact will likely open a door to more harm. In the second case, contact some years down the road likely won't result in ongoing harm, though it may be painful initially. If the people involved are currently capable of healthy boundaries, there's a good chance they'll steer clear doing significant harm again. Every person who cuts someone off needs to make their own decisions about the cutoff, but very generally, I would suggest that (a) if a cutoff is in that second category—if it's not necessary to safety—and (b) if one has reached inner forgiveness, then initiating some contact, however marginal, may be healing. Among other things, it may open the door to a deeper, relational experience of forgiveness, possibly on both sides.

Now, there's an obvious hazard here. If the cuttee was badly hurt by the cutoff, they may not respond positively to contact. Ryan's initial response to me was that he didn't want to be friends. My initial response to a high school friend who had ghosted me was "You have some nerve." Some may respond by initiating a cutoff in return. Such responses can reopen old wounds for the cutter and create new ones. This is a risk each person has to weigh. It's important to consider, though, that in many cases, an initial negative response will be followed by openness to reconnecting, as was true in both the examples above. It's not unusual for a person who's been silenced for a long time to need a moment to give the silencer a piece of their mind. Once they've done so, they'll often feel better and be able to proceed more positively. That said, there's no guarantee.

Yet if one does wish to reconnect, even tangentially, to show forgiveness, the rewards may be deep and lasting, ranging from a sense of ease and closure to a renewed, healthier interpersonal relationship. For those who may contemplate expressing some social indication of forgiveness, here are a few suggestions for what that might look like.

C. Ward Struthers et al. (2008) studied responses to different approaches to showing repentance and forgiveness. They found that victims of harm benefit from signs of repentance on the part of perpetrators and that perpetrators can benefit from showing repentance.[393] As a cutoff itself has likely done harm, acknowledging that reality to the cuttee may help the cutter heal. In some cases, the cutter may regret the cutoff or the way they handled it, and if so, owning that may help the cutter work through feelings of guilt by showing accountability.[394] In other cases, the cutter will not regret the cutoff. It's not inconsistent to acknowledge that the cutoff still caused harm, even if that harm was necessary. It's also worth noting that reconnecting, even marginally, allows the cuttee to express remorse, too, which cuttees are not allowed to do across a cutoff.

Struthers et al. also found, however, that offers of preemptive forgiveness (prior to expressed repentance) can further damage healing: such offers may shame the perpetrator by suggesting a fault they are not ready to acknowledge and, thus, intensify resentment.[395] In other words, stating, "I forgive you" out of the blue can read as condescending or blaming. When initially rescinding a cutoff, it's probably best not to lead with declarations of forgiveness, but to wait until the cuttee expresses regret for their part in the conflict. In comparing explicit forgiveness ("I forgive you"), implicit forgiveness (through an amicable attitude), no forgiveness, and actively holding a grudge, Struthers et al. found that *implicit forgiveness* generated the most prosocial conduct.[396] This suggests that, in most cases, the best approach to showing forgiveness

---

[393] C. Ward Struthers et al., "The Effect of Preemptive Forgiveness and a Transgressor's Responsibility on Shame, Motivation to Reconcile, and Repentance," *Basic and Applied Social Psychology*, 30 (2008): 139, https://doi.org/10.1080/01973530802209178.

[394] Freedman et al. (2022) found ghosters significantly more likely than ghostees to feel guilt in a ghosting situation. Gili Freedman, Darcey N. Powell, Benjamin Le, and Kipling D. Williams, "Emotional Experiences of Ghosting," *Journal of Social Psychology*, May 17, 2022, https://doi.org/10.1080/00224545.2022.2081528.

[395] Struthers et al., 140.

[396] Struthers et al., 138.

when rescinding a cutoff is to simply be amiable, to behave in a way that expresses positive feelings toward the cuttee.

In many cases, the cutter may not wish to resume an interpersonal relationship. Ways of connecting across a cutoff are as numerous as the reasons for cutting someone off. They range from proposing full restoration of the prior relationship to a single communication in the name of tying up loose ends.[397] In general, the stricter the explicit boundaries maintained, the less forgiving the contact will probably seem, but this must be balanced against the cutter's own psychological safety and capacities. Take, for example, a message like this: "I really don't feel able to resume ongoing contact, but I did want to let you know I'm truly sorry if my cutoff has hurt you and I do wish you happiness." Such a message might read like too little, too late at first. Ten years down the road, recollecting it might serve as a great source of comfort because it does imply forgiveness. In many cases, it's probably better than nothing.

In the end, though, we can't know for certain how our overtures will be received. A message intended to be peace-making may read as insincere, condescending, holier-than-thou, etc. We can only make our best guess. In many cases, people who have loved us and been shut out will, indeed, be deeply grateful for an olive branch, even if it takes them a little time to show it.

---

[397] I am struggling to avoid saying "closure." "Closure" has, unfortunately, come to connote demanding someone else to do your own emotional work. My editor (like many) says closure is not something we need communication for: "closure is really something individually felt and in solo moments, like walking in an oak forest, for example. Closure isn't for both parties and both do not need to be there at the time it happens. Sometimes it just occurs in its own time, not on our schedule." (editorial comment, October 31, 2023). There's wisdom in her words. Of course, it's *possible* to have closure without communication, but her observation misses how closure can work as a process. I suspect most conversations requested for "closure" do not immediately bring it. Yet I also suspect a large number of them—if they occur well after the initial injury when emotions are not so hot—do help once more processing has happened. The "aha!" moment may hit while strolling alone in the woods, but that doesn't mean that input from people we've been in conflict with is not important. It often can be for obvious reasons: correcting misconceptions, apology, explanations, implicit or explicit forgiveness, and expressions of good will, for a start.

The Role of Bystanders

Sometimes there can be no forgiveness (or sign of forgiveness) between cutter and cuttee. This is one reason it's important to build wider supportive communities. Sometimes third parties are the only ones available to bring human kindness to deeply wounded people.

In his work in hospice care, Rabbi Kukla has played this role for many, including some who have committed deeply disturbing actions. He tells the story of one elderly woman, whom he calls Ethel, still struggling at the end of her life with her guilt over abandoning her children:

> Near the end [of her life], [Ethel] revealed to me that when she was in her 30s, she had been in an abusive marriage, and her husband and been sexually abusing their two preteen daughters. Desperate and alone, Ethel had fled one night, leaving her daughters alone in their fate, despite her knowledge of their situation. She had spent the rest of her life doing penance for this act of abandonment, immersing herself in feminist justice causes and forming no new intimate relationships. She had never forgiven herself for the betrayal.[398]

Near the end of her life, she attempted to reach out to her daughters through a social worker, but they did not reply. As she was dying, she asked Kukla if he thought her daughters had forgiven her. He said he didn't know. When asked if he thought they should forgive her, he replied, "I really don't know… but I can forgive you."[399] Her response was to sigh in relief. Kukla notes that he himself comes from a background of family estrangement and has chosen not to reconnect with some family members. He says, "I pray that my own estranged family members have a friend in their lives at the end, to forgive them for the things I can't forgive them for."[400] Sometimes forgiveness must come from a person who stands outside the fray, someone who is not the direct recipient of

---

398 Kukla

399 Kukla.

400 Kukla.

the injury and, thus, has more capacity for compassion for all the people involved.

Our culture today is angry and cold, and we can all work to make it a little bit gentler. Though we are not all called to lives of service to the same extent Kukla is, we can all strive to treat the people we encounter as human beings who need kindness.

CHAPTER 14
A KEMETIC RESPONSE TO CUTOFF CULTURE

In interviewing people about their views on cutoff, I had the privilege of talking with licensed social worker Ray Shellmire, who provides culturally sensitive counseling services and activities for the Black community in Portland, Oregon. In particular, he focuses on reconnecting African Americans and others from the African diaspora to their cultural roots through the Kemetic Way, the traditional ethical wisdom of ancient Kemet (Egypt).[401] Though this tradition has particular relevance for African diasporic people, Shellmire is generous in sharing its transformative potential widely. In the Kemetic tradition, Shellmire has the role of a teacher or *seba* (spelled *sbA* and pronounced "seeba" in Medu Neter, the language of ancient Kemet).[402] I sat down with Shellmire to learn about his thoughts on cutoff and its role in African American culture.

Shellmire notes that in African American culture, cutoff is quite common, often viewed as "the thing to do" to address interpersonal problems. "I'm done with you" is a common thread, he says. Shellmire, too, has cut someone off, and he shared his story with me. Young Ray and Leo (not his real name) had been friends

---

[401] Shellmire notes that the word "Egypt" comes from Greek, a European overlay that white supremacist society has leveraged to obscure the Africanness of this impressive, groundbreaking civilization. I will follow his lead in using the African Medu Neter terminology.

[402] Ray Shellmire, in discussion with author, January 21, 2022. All quotes and information attributed to Shellmire come from this discussion.

since junior high. As the years went by, they hung out every day; they were in band together, in sports together. Their friendship seemed tight all the way into college. Ray was a studious eighteen-year-old who kept himself well clear of trouble, so he was dismayed to find the police at his door one day, arresting him for some misconduct he knew nothing about, an experience all too common for Black men in the United States. It turns out Leo had been involved in some criminal activity. When the police asked, "Where are your buddies?" Leo panicked and named Ray, hoping his upstanding friend would serve as an alibi. In reality, his upstanding friend narrowly missed being jailed for a crime he had zero involvement in.

As you might imagine, Ray was furious. "It was like a fire in me that says, 'This dude is bad,'" he told me. So he cut Leo off. He broke away from him due to the pain. Leo apologized, but it was too late. Ray stayed away to protect himself, both physically and emotionally, from a bad influence who he knew had done him wrong.

They hadn't spoken for twenty years, when out of the blue, Leo contacted him.[403] Ray didn't want to talk, but he decided to respond, nonetheless, because he'd realized that separation was "counter to who I truly am."

As they reconnected, Ray learned that Leo had been through some hard times. Since they'd last met, he'd been arrested, struggled with drug addiction, and grieved the loss of his parents. Ray reflected he could have been a support during these troubles, but he hadn't been simply because he wasn't there; he'd cut Leo off. Today, Leo is doing much better and does charitable work with the houseless community. In fact, he inspired Ray to join forces with him in collecting food and supplies for houseless people and creating an open kitchen. Thinking back on his relationship with Leo, Ray concluded, "My instinct around you [Leo] doing [unhealthy] stuff was right, but my spirit around cutting you off was not."

Shellmire sees the prevalence of cutoff in the African American community as a pattern learned from white supremacist cultural colonization. He sees an emphasis on difference, on

---

[403] A strict interpretation of cutoff culture's ethics would call this a violation of Shellmire's boundaries, yet it was the beginning of a healed friendship.

separation, as a strategy for self-protection under white supremacy, but it can be a damaging one. Black vs. white, One True Religion vs. everything else: when these differences are given priority over human similarity, over an underlying message of love and human family, that separation brings "a devastating effect on many levels." Shellmire recognizes the need to protect oneself from unhealthy dynamics but advocates an approach that allows room for growth and change. He encourages addressing conflicts in this spirit: "I need you to be in this for me too.... If you can't do that, I have to set a boundary." That boundary might include low-to-no contact, but where safely possible, it leaves space for reconnection if the other person does change. Thinking of his experience with Leo, he says, "I'm not going to stay in this fear response.... I'm not going to hold things against people for days, years, decades anymore.... And if this [willingness to reconnect] means I'm not gonna be Black, I'm just not gonna be Black."

It should be obvious that Shellmire is not repudiating his African ancestry. On the contrary, he sees the truest African cultural lineage as one of connection and wholeness. He explained to me four main aspects of the Kemetic Way, all based on interconnection, and named for the Gods that represent them:

- The Way of Ausar: collectively generating abundance and prosperity and sharing it;
- The Way of Maat: creating and upholding the sacred and just society;
- The Way of Ankh: being life center and oriented so as to respect, celebrate, and perpetuate life;
- The Way of Atum: communicating, interacting, and living powerfully with creation.

From this worldview, Shellmire says, "We see every living thing as a sibling under one container in creation, emanating from one source." On a practical level, he observes that a task like creating the pyramids *requires* connection with a greater whole, an ability to execute a plan transmitted across many generations. Shellmire credits his immersion in the Kemetic Way with expanding his sense of identity, "beyond one race, one nationality." In this view, "The wind and the water and I are connected. We are the stuff stars are made of."[404] Speaking of his journey toward this deeper sense of connection, he says, "I enjoy this person I have been becoming... because this person I'm becoming is more free; the person I'm becoming is more whole.... It's beautiful... It's like wow!"

Despite the many crises that our world faces today, Shellmire is hopeful that a better age is coming. "In our lifetime," he says, "we're going to see an evolution of humankind." He foresees we'll become more "heart-centered" and adds, "This is not new. This is a return to what made humanity amazing in the first place... It's so powerful when you realize that you are a co-creator."

In the course of our conversation, I mentioned my ongoing struggles with being cut off by Sophia, how difficult it remained for me to be unable to talk things through with her. Slipping seamlessly into counselor mode, Shellmire told me, "They only come back when you see yourself as worthy of their coming back... when you get your inner balance: I am unconditional love, I am unconditionally loving, and I am unconditionally loved." There is no question he saw straight to the core. I as write this (in 2023), I still struggle with imbalance and shame over what happened with Sophia—though it is slowly and steadily getting better. Speaking for myself, I want to be careful of too much faith that Sophia and I can ever explicitly make peace. Regardless of my own psychological journey, she has her own as well, and I am wary of imposing myself on it, even in my imagination. Nevertheless, I cannot help but be swept up in the joy Shellmire radiates in his own sense of connection. Reflecting back on Leo, he said, "This [unconditional love] is why, I think, that friend showed up. It's a magnetic force that just draws things to us.... It's like folding time and space. I lack the words."

---

[404] I love how this formulation inverts Carl Sagan's oft-repeated observation, "We are made of star stuff."

Conclusion

In her remarkable synthesis of Traditional Indigenous Knowledge and Western environmental science, *Braiding Sweetgrass*, Robin Wall Kimmerer (Potawatomi) recounts the story of the Windigo,[405] a being from the stories of her Anishinaabe people, whose insatiable hunger only increases the more voraciously it devours.[406] Kimmerer likens this terrifying and pitiable figure to our dominant capitalist, growth-oriented society, continually desiring and devouring more, lost in self-destruction and destruction of others. Kimmerer writes,

> Cautionary Windigo tales arose in a commons-based society where sharing was essential to survival and greed made any individual a danger to the whole. In the old times, individuals who endangered the community by taking too much for themselves were first counseled, then ostracized, and if the greed continued, they were eventually banished. The Windigo myth may have arisen from the remembrance of the banished, doomed to wander hungry and alone, wreaking vengeance on the ones who spurned them. It is a terrible punishment to be banished

---

[405] I have read statements from various self-identified Native American people in online forums indicating that use of the word is taboo or semi-taboo. Exact practices seem to vary. I mean no disrespect and am following Kimmerer's use (and spelling) from *Braiding Sweetgrass*, a book intended for dissemination among a broad audience, including non-Native people. (I am not citing written sources for this footnote because its authority derives from person-to-person transmission, not a website's authority.)

[406] Anishinaabe refers to a group of Indigenous peoples from the region of the Great Lakes, who share cultural and linguistic traits. The Potawatomi are an Anishinaabe people.

> from the web of reciprocity, with no one to share with you and no one for you to care for.[407]

To be able to share and care is the basis of a healthy life. To be banished from those relations is a dire punishment and, for Kimmerer's people, a punishment of last resort, instigated only after counseling and less extreme forms of ostracism have failed to correct selfish behavior. This hesitation to banish someone makes sense to me, because even banished, the destructive person is still there. In the final estimation, nothing that exists is completely disconnected. There is no such thing as the ultimate cutoff that excises the banished from all earthly interactions. The Windigo can still devour, can still wreak vengeance: these are connections, just negative ones. Nobody wants a Windigo wandering in the woods, menacing the community, insatiable. The most profound safety lies in healing the voracious addictions that drive us apart.

Our current global situation is often described as a *polycrisis*, that is, an explosion of simultaneous crises: climate change, habitat loss, pollution, mass extinction, hunger, poverty, escalating inequality, refugee crisis, environmental injustice, war, colonialism, fascist movements, increasing racism, transphobia, homophobia, xenophobia, political corruption, as well as social media harassment, polarization, addiction, rising rates of mental illness, gun violence, and rape culture (and, in its own small way, cutoff culture). This simultaneous breakdown of so much of our socioecological fabric is not coincidental. The polycrisis is a single crisis. Even where its pieces may appear disconnected or inimical, they're not. For example, cutoff culture arose to combat rape culture, and to some degree it does, but it belongs to the same crisis as rape culture too. Both rape culture and cutoff culture take root in a world that celebrates the devaluation of others. The police officer who dismisses the report of stalking is the Janus face of the blogger who cries "stalker" at a couple of civil emails. Understatement and overstatement of harm both originate in disconnection. The empty space where we do not see each other will be filled by straw people we never see bleed.

---

[407] Robin Wall Kimmerer, *Braiding Sweetgrass: Indigenous Wisdom, Scientific Knowledge, and the Teachings of Plants* (Minneapolis, Minnesota: Milkweed, 2013), 307.

Our lack of consideration and care for each other is embedded in our dominant culture's Windigo thinking. It is the predictable result of five hundred years of empire rewarding greed and self-centeredness,[408] the avaricious desperation of individuals stripped of community. Or to use a Western touchstone, because the West knows the truth of this too, John Donne wrote,

> No man is an island, entire of itself; every man is a piece of the continent, a part of the main. If a clod be washed away by the sea, Europe is the less, as well as if a promontory were, as well as if a manor of thy friend's or of thine own were: any man's death diminishes me, because I am involved in mankind, and therefore never send to know for whom the [funeral] bell tolls; it tolls for thee.[409]

We are not separate from each other. I say with complete seriousness and speaking of physical reality, our existence as independent selves is an illusion. It is equally true that we, as individuals, do exist. I am me and you are you. This is obvious and important. But there is no wall that divides us from the rest of the world, no wall between me and the air I breathe or the bacteria that digest my food or the mites that eat my dead skin. There's no wall between the sound waves of the dog's bark and my ears and brain. No wall between these signals of black on white that strike your retina and, through this marvelous telepathy, impress some imperfect copy of my thoughts on your own. If you speak back to me, there is, likewise, no wall; some version of your thoughts

---

408 In his memoir, *Becoming Story*, Greg Sarris writes, "The Kashaya Pomo elders refer to Europeans as *pala-cha*, miracles: instead of being punished for killing people and animals, chopping down trees, damming and dredging the waterways, the Europeans just kept coming." (Berkeley: Heyday, 2022), 211. We didn't escape our punishment, though; we've just kept forging new links of transgressions until, as Marley told Scrooge, "It is a ponderous chain!" Charles Dickens, *A Christmas Carol*, "Stave 1: Marley's Ghost," accessed May 22, 2024, https://dn790007.ca.archive.org/0/items/achristmascarol00046gut/46-8.txt.

409 John Donne, "Meditation XVII," *Devotions upon Emergent Occasions* (1623), *Wikisource*, April 14, 2012, https://en.wikisource.org/wiki/Meditation_XVII.

becomes a piece of my brain. There is no wall between my mind and yours, many hazy cheesecloth layers, but no wall.

The mantra of our capitalist society is that we are responsible only and totally for ourselves, but it is nonsensical to say that I am solely responsible for me and you are solely responsible for you. You can affect me, and I can affect you. With power comes responsibility. I hold some responsibility for you, and you for me. We say this isn't true, but in practice, we understand it well. In leftwing equity discourse, it's why we provide trigger warnings and decry microaggressions: if we weren't responsible to each other, these acts would have no place in our ethics. The belief that another being's suffering isn't mine is an illusion. A hurt world hurts us all.

To live in this hurt world is to live with trauma. We cannot afford to indulge in cultural systems that, by their nature, increase our collective trauma. On the contrary, it is vital that we transform our culture to better support healing and mental wellness. Among other things, that means questioning cutoff culture.

Being cut off from someone we are attached to with little-to-no hope of any reconciliation or even being on civil terms is inherently traumatic. This does not mean it traumatizes every individual in every case. Yet it creates conditions that are predictably associated with trauma: it breaks community bonds, breaks trust, prevents communication, removes supports, hinders closure, and implies enmity. By implying enmity, it implies threat, which sets the conditions for a fight or flight response. These adrenaline-fueled fear and anger responses impede clear thinking, which can increase the risk of stalking or revenge behaviors. Permanent cutoffs in serious relationships do harm.

Let me say it one more time: people do have a right to cut others off. This is one dimension of our right to self-protection, both physical and psychological. To rob us of this right would invite distress and abuse. It follows, too, that we have a duty to respect others' right to cut us off by leaving them alone. I do not agree that this duty, in all cases, places an ethical prohibition on absolutely any contact ever, including such acts as a check-in to see if time has healed or a polite offering of peace years later. But it does mandate a cessation of any but, at most, infrequent and rather brief attempts at contact.

However, our culture should view the decision to permanently cut someone off as extreme—because it is. Cutoff is an extreme form of ostracism, and to be ostracized is a primal denial of the human need to be socially accepted. Today, we treat permanent cutoffs as a norm, a default for addressing difficult relationships. A couple breaks up: it's expected that they'll permanently reject all contact. A person is sucking up your energy: cut them out of your life. This normalization, this trivialization, of an extreme act is not healthy.

We should support the need for cutoffs, and we should respect that a person may need to cut someone off for reasons that do not make sense to an outside observer. But as cultural norms, we should foreground other recourses first: talking it out honestly, therapy, support from friends and family, distancing a relationship (e.g. from dating to social media contacts), setting boundaries around type and frequency of contact, taking a temporary break from contact, setting conditions for resuming contact (e.g. no talk of money), and sanctioning minimal contact through a third party are all less extreme options for addressing breakdowns in relationships. They will not always work, but they will work often and with less trauma and easier healing than a permanent cutoff. They will help us get along with each other's imperfections.

We could talk all day about what we ought to do. We ought to be kind and considerate, use "I" statements, listen deeply, and mirror back what others have said to verify we understand. We ought to be straightforward but tactful, avoid passive aggression, set boundaries politely, practice self-care while being forgiving and carefully think before we speak, not rant, not snap, not make assumptions, and more besides—we ought to.

And we will fail, because we are living in fractious and traumatized civilization just beginning what the depredations of global capitalism have ordained will be a painful transition to whatever the next civilization will be. We are surrounded by trauma, we drink it daily, and we mete it out. We will yell and snark and say unfair things and walk away when we should listen. We will strive to do good, and we will sometimes do ill. The only thing we can do about that is to try to make humane allowances. Here's the good news: when we do so, we not only help individuals we're in conflict with; we help the world. Every time we do so, we replace condemnation with compassion, fear and anger with relief. We lessen the cumulative trauma.

Since Sophia cut me off, I've had a lot of dreams about her: dreams where I've been afraid of her, pleaded with her, told her off, passed her by with an air of removing my pearl from before swine. I've had dreams where she excoriated me with blazing hatred, where we've painstakingly moved back into minimal civility, where she ran away the instant she saw me. But a while back—for the first time in eight years—I had a dream where we were just friends. Not good friends, not on intimate terms, but not walking a tightrope either, just amicably talking over random stuff. I wish that could be real life; it probably never will be. Yet in my dream, I had a confidence that all of it was real. "I am unconditional love, I am unconditionally loving, and I am unconditionally loved," as Ray Shellmire puts it. What a great sensation of safety it is to *feel* in community, to face storm and thunder of this age of ours together.

SELF-HELP EXTRAS

Appendix A

Tips if You Wish to Cut Someone Off

In his 1946 essay "Politics and the English Language," George Orwell offered six rules for effective writing, including items such as avoiding overused metaphors and needlessly long words. His sixth rule famously concludes, "Break any of these rules sooner than say anything outright barbarous."[410] I am not here to prescribe what you should do. In the spirit of Orwell, I will offer some principles based on my own experiences and research. Reject any of them rather than violate your own sense of safety, conscience, or ethics.

1. *Don't ghost someone unless you need to for safety.* Provide some announcement of the cutoff.

2. *State your boundaries clearly.* Do not rely on metaphor or generality. For example, "I will not respond to any contact from you" is clearer than "You will never be welcome in my life again." Clear boundaries include stating whether you intend your cutoff to be permanent or not. If you're not sure how long the cutoff needs to be, that's fine. You can say you will let the person know if you are ever open to contact again or that they can ask about it in X years.

3. *Be invariably polite.* This may, indeed, delay the cuttee's emotional detachment from you, as politeness can be interpreted as encouragement for reconciliation. But combined with clear boundaries, it may not be much encouragement, and it may help

---

[410] George Orwell, "Politics and the English Language," *Horizon*, April 1946, reproduced by UNZ.org, 2003, p. 264, https://archive.org/details/PoliticsAndTheEnglishLanguage.

prevent escalation of unwanted pursuit and greatly speed mutual healing as time goes by. Moreover, it just shows decency.

I include in "being polite" not showing anger. Anger can be an especially corrosive last impression of a relationship. Anger is also normal, and it's not healthy to completely suppress it, but in the social act of cutting someone off, it may do the least harm to you and the cuttee to contain the anger and maintain civility. Therapists, friends, and others can help with processing anger later, without involving the cuttee.

4. *Don't use permanent cutoff if something less extreme will accomplish the same goal.* For example, if your goal is to break up with your partner and not be close to them anymore, and if they are not abusive, temporary no contact and/or other boundaries can often achieve this.

5. *Bear in mind that permanent/indefinite cutoff is often traumatizing and think carefully before choosing it.*

How to Avoid Cutting Someone off by Accident

A friend of mine has found people sometimes think he's ghosted them when he hasn't. He just gets caught up with family and work and sometimes lets communications go unanswered. He says, "To me those silences don't matter. When I see a friend again, it's like no time has passed, but they sometimes think I've stopped being their friend."

I told him what I'd tell anyone in this fix: if misunderstandings seem likely, tell people explicitly how to read and respond to your (lack of) communication. It's perfectly fine to say, for example, "I often don't reply to messages when I'm busy. It's honestly not personal. If I don't reply and you want to get in touch, feel free to ping me. I'm much more likely to reply with a little reminder." In our complex and rapidly shifting world, where silence can mean anything from "I've been busy" to "you're never allowed to speak to me again," setting straightforward, honest expectations is more important than ever and can save a lot of heartache.

Appendix B
Surviving Cutoff

I've been advised to cut this section. It's a full chapter of self-help, and didn't I say this book is not self-help? I cannot cut it, though, because if I were one of my readers, these pages would be what helped me most. This is a help-each-other book, but in a culture that often discourages helping others, the present reality is that if you have experienced cutoff trauma, it may be difficult to find effective help, so tools for helping yourself are vital.

This chapter shares some strategies and realizations I've learned through my own experience, and what's true for me may not be true for you. I am not a mental health professional. I offer these observations only as the reflections of one person who has lived through this.

Is It Trauma?

Our culture's default position is that cutoff is not a valid reason to experience trauma, and this can mean we fail to recognize that we ourselves are experiencing trauma—or if we do recognize it, we feel crazy. Moreover, it's true that cutoff does not always cause trauma. A good initial question can be: is trauma what you're feeling?

Maté calls trauma, "an inner injury, a lasting rupture or split within the self due to difficult or hurtful events."[411] A key word is "lasting." If you feel annoyed, frustrated, or even deeply angry and obsessed about the cutoff for a week or two and then the pain and anger consistently recede, that may not be trauma. This was my friend Meg's response to a friend cutting her off. Meg did not experience it as trauma. However, if you feel your life negatively

[411] Gabor Maté, with Daniel Maté, 20.

impacted in that wound changes your life—not just your relationship with that person but your *life*—in a lasting, negative way, that sounds like trauma to me. If it impacts your ability to trust or how you see human relations, in general, that sounds like trauma to me. But you are not me. If *you* think it is trauma, it is probably trauma. Trust yourself.

Surviving the Initial Trauma

Nothing can shortcut the pain of cutoff trauma, but here are some strategies for navigating those initial, agonizing weeks, months, or even years.

Some Emotional Validation: It is okay to feel wrecked. It is normal. What you are experiencing, in many cases, is harder than a loved one's death. It is trauma layered over grief; it is shock; it feels like betrayal, and it will take time to work through. There is nothing wrong with you or strange about you for feeling traumatized.

A Practical Suggestion: Do not contact the person who has cut you off or anyone close to them (and not to you) without permission from a mostly disinterested third party, for example, a therapist, clergy, support group, or a clear-sighted friend. I'm going to call this person (or people) your *gatekeeper*, because you can empower them to decide which communications get through the gate.

I figured this out the hard way. Like most of us, I tried to address my cutoff pain by myself at first; I tried to make reasonable choices by myself. But it is difficult to be reasonable while operating out of trauma. Trauma contributes to sustained stress: stress without quick relief. Sapolsky notes that sustained stress impedes judgment and executive function; it makes it harder to make rational decisions and to change our patterns of behavior.[412] Under such circumstances, it can help to lean on a calmer, disinterested person's judgment.

If I had committed from the start to following a gatekeeper's advice about when and how to contact Sophia, I would not have sent her the angry letter that I will regret all my life. After writing that letter, I did commit to always having a gatekeeper. I am still living under that commitment. It has protected me, and likely Sophia, from being retraumatized by at least two other improper

[412] Sapolsky, 130–31.

communications. It has prevented a potentially ugly escalation into restraining orders and the like.

Now the second proviso—don't contact anyone close to the cutter (and not close to you) without permission of a disinterested gatekeeper—is a realization I arrived at late, after reaching out to Tammy and being rebuffed. Contacting third parties is less dire, but it can still save multiple people pain just to get another person's okay before trying it.

Choosing a Gatekeeper

I personally will not choose a gatekeeper who is ideologically opposed to the idea of all contact ever. I choose people who value both boundaries and (re)connection. The point is not to affirm that I have no agency; it's to help me use my agency sensibly. I have chosen people whose judgment I trust, who are not directly involved in the cutoff, and who have my best interests at heart. I asked my friend Derek to be a gatekeeper after he helped me be more sensitive to Sophia's feelings. My therapist and my pastor have also acted as gatekeepers. It's important to avoid choosing an enabler who will merely endorse what I want. I have a friend who is very much "on my side" and harsh in her judgments of Sophia. I love her like a sister, but I will not use her as a gatekeeper because I doubt her impartiality in the same way I doubt my own. I am fortunate to have a strong intuition for whose judgment I trust, but for those who have more difficulty trusting others, a mental health professional may be a solid choice: they bring the added safety of being licensed to help with psychological distress.

Sharing with a Gatekeeper

Whenever I feel tempted to contact Sophia, I share my thoughts with a gatekeeper. How am I considering attempting contacting? What do I want to say? Why? What am I hoping will be the result? I listen to their reflections and answer their questions. In my experience, this may take half an hour to an hour per instance.

Committing to the Gatekeeping

Gatekeeping only works if I commit to obeying a gatekeeper's judgment. If they say, "This is not a good idea," that doesn't mean I instantly, wholly abandon it. But I hold off, consider, revise what I wanted to say, when, how, etc. If I'm still considering contact, I'll consult with them about my revised idea. Since 2017, I've attempted no contact with Sophia. The few times I've been tempted, my gatekeeper has said no, and I have listened. Sustained stress can impair reason. I have emotionally railed against every single prohibition my gatekeepers have set, and I have never once regretted following their judgment.

Gatekeepers May Get It Wrong; It's Okay:

In 2017, my therapist made the wrong call. She said, "This message looks good," and Sophia harangued me for it as if I were a stalker (or that's what it felt like). But even in this case, there was a benefit to relying on someone else's judgment: I was not alone! I cannot overstate the comfort being able to say of my final message, "My therapist thought it was fine. My *therapist* thought I should send it." This is a balm against our society's relentless refrain that you must be a crazy stalker. To act in concert with someone else's reasoned judgment is incredibly psychologically stabilizing.

It's a reality that cutoff trauma can increase our risk of engaging in stalking or harassing behavior. It is vital not to stalk people, harass them, or engage in other behavior that is likely escalate the situation. Such actions only intensify trauma, for ourselves, for the person who cut us off, and sometimes for bystanders too. One of the most powerful gifts we can give ourselves and others is insurance against these missteps, and the best insurance is a clear-sighted comrade to tell us when contact is not a good idea.

Surviving on the Internet

Don't seek advice in articles or videos on the internet. They will often tell you are at fault and that your pain is irrelevant. This will compound the trauma. As far as you can, simply avoid the urge to search for consolation this way.

The following advice is a load of hooey: "Begin by accepting the relationship is over." No, no, no, no. This is how a grieving process ends, not how it begins. Acceptance is (typically) the final stage of grief. When the doctor pronounces someone dead, we don't immediately say, "Well, grieving widow, you better accept they're gone." Cutoff is no different. That acceptance advice is donkey doo. Grief begins with anger and disbelief. Just let it. There's really no alternative. That said, see above about the help of a gatekeeper. You may not believe that relationship is over. In some cases, you may be right. But that's a separate issue from when or if attempting *contact* is a good idea.

To get sympathy on social media, mention "trauma," not "cutoff": "Hugs" on social media can help us feel less alone, but mentioning being hurt by a cutoff is likely to get us ignored or attacked. Once I stopped discussing "cutoff" in casual online contexts and began referring to my "trauma," people's responses instantly became an order of magnitude more sympathetic. There's no need to share specifics. If someone asks, it's perfectly legitimate to say, "I'm not in a good place to talk about it."

Resist the urge to vent about the cutter online: This is just good internet hygiene. The more neutral-positive we can keep our communications, the more positive energy we spread, the less negative energy we attract, and the less pain will come back to bite us.

Surviving the Quest for Therapeutic Support

Approach traditional therapy with caution. By all means, use it if it helps, but be aware that there is a perception field around cutoffs. Most therapists are not trained to recognize cutoff trauma or address it. Thus, getting help from traditional therapy can be hit and miss. If feels like it's compounding the feelings of invisibility and isolation, perhaps that particular therapist was not the right fit.

Explore help from abandonment specialists and support groups. Disclosure: I have not done this myself. By the time I was aware these supports existed, I was several years into my coping process and had other supports in place. From all I have seen, these resources can be helpful. I am not aware of any therapist or group that specializes in cutoff. However, many therapists note on their professional profiles if they specifically address abandonment. I recommend Susan Anderson's website, Abandonment.net, for more resources.

Surviving with Coping Mechanisms

Numerous coping mechanisms exist for managing grief and trauma. A therapist or support group can recommend healthy coping mechanisms. I will list some I have used or am aware of. Here, again, there is no one size fits all. Of those I have used, my own typical experience is that there is some benefit, often not much. The exception is mindfulness, which I will discuss more below.

To calm the body/mind: Consider physical exercise, music, gardening, walking in nature, and mindfulness exercises. (See a cautionary note about silent mindfulness below.)

To get your mind off it: Stay active with other trusted friends and relationships, pursue hobbies, or develop new interests.

To process it: Attend therapy/support groups, talk with trusted friends (if they can be supportive), write down your thoughts, or visualize your pain as a bundle you can lay down and walk away from, create music playlists.

Some Words about Writing to Process the Trauma

Being a writer, I've used this one a lot! To date, I've written a novel manuscript, two and half short stories, that 8,000-word letter to Sophia, tens of thousands of words of journaling and notes, and this book. Does it help? A bit. In general, I find it soothes in the moment but not in the long term, and, thus, feels somewhat addictive. This addictive feeling has lessened, though, as time has gone on and my healing overall has progressed. Let me emphasize, this is *my* experience; yours may differ.

However, one significant benefit of recording my thoughts is being able to look back on my healing process. When I re-read *Mercy*, the novel manuscript I wrote in 2015–2017, I am amazed at what a different place I was in. The concerns, mindsets, and feelings of that time are radically different from my processing now. Whenever I feel like I'm stuck in this forever, seeing black-and-white evidence of that progress is truly comforting.

Some Words on Anger and Mindfulness

Being mindful refers to being intentionally, distinctly aware of something, usually oneself: one's thoughts, emotions, and responses, what they are and where they are coming from. Though Western traditions of mindfulness exist, Western society today primarily draws on practices from the East, from Hindu and Buddhist traditions. I am more familiar with mindfulness through my Buddhist practice and will address it from that vantage point.

Mindfulness exercises are the only daily coping mechanism that has appreciably helped me, and they have helped almost miraculously well. There's a caveat, though: attempting silent mindfulness, in particular, as a way to process trauma can also backfire because the mind has no subject to grasp. It can, therefore, become an echo chamber for distressed rumination that intensifies troubling thoughts and emotions rather than alleviating them. With good intentions, Western society often invokes mindfulness in unwise ways. These days, it's common in schools, workplaces, books, and articles to praise mindfulness as a means of self-care. Modern Western society is highly individualistic, and we often to transfer that individualism onto our mindfulness practices, casting it as a solitary activity with the single goal of helping ourselves to feel calmer. That's a good goal but narrow. In Buddhist practice in Asia, mindfulness is typically practiced in community and with the guidance of a teacher. It can certainly help the self, but it also helps us to be more aware of others, to increase our capacity for compassion. Mindfulness is rooted in an awareness that we're all in this together. We all need some help, and we can give some help too.[413]

I began my mindfulness practices about four and a half years after I was cut off, and I don't know how my experience would differ if I had begun it much earlier. After four years, I was over the initial grief and shock but profoundly ground down by both the cutoff itself and our culture's unsupportive response to my pain.

---

413 My profound thanks to Reverend Kosho Finch for this teaching. I have attempted here, imperfectly, to distill several years of his Dharma Talks, as well as the interview he kindly gave me for this book, March 10, 2023, and additional details emailed June 27, 2024.

My journey toward a mindfulness practice began in earnest with conversation with my third therapist, which helped clarify for me that my immediate problem had become anger. Now, anger had been a persistent factor ever since the cutoff, and it was initially understandably directed at Sophia for cutting me off. Five years later, it was like the match had been set to the kerosene. I was still lividly angry at Sophia, but also at her friends, her husband, her sister, at myself, at society, at my online communities, at the internet, at capitalism, at my place of work. Once, when my union was preparing to go on strike, I spoke on their behalf at a board meeting. I led with, "I'm angry nearly all the time." This got a validating chuckle from my union comrades—but it was true. I was in the grips of undifferentiated anger.

Once I was able to identify that as the problem, solutions were easier to pursue. The anger itself was not a cutoff problem; it was an anger problem. I realized I needed to prioritize strategies to calm the anger.

The first strategy I attempted was limiting the anger to a certain allowable time of day. I knew I couldn't just turn it off. I also knew I tended to wake up angry and calm down as I got into my workday. I had recently started a small morning mindfulness practice, and I decided, with my therapist's blessing, to give myself the time from waking up till my mindfulness practice (about an hour) to be as angry as I pleased. After that, throughout the day, I would actively try to push the anger away. If I felt it mounting, I'd try to distract myself with other thoughts. This was far from a perfect endeavor. I spent my share of afternoons composing tirades in my head; on occasion, I still do. But the reduction of overall anger in my life was radical and almost instantaneous. In fact, the combination of mindfulness and confining anger to the morning worked so well that I only needed to maintain the conscious confinement effort for about three weeks. After that, I wasn't routinely waking up angry.

I have kept up my daily mindfulness practice since then, and I regard it as a necessity for my mental health. It's not intensive, not usually more than fifteen minutes every morning (and, yes, I've missed a few). I'm not very good at it but, on the whole, I'm getting better. I have a range of different exercises, which include a walk around my neighborhood observing nature, chanting mantras, reading the short Heart Sutra, and silent mindfulness. Crucially, however, I do this practice in conjunction with study through my local Buddhist temple, and that community support and teacher's guidance are indispensable. In Buddhist teaching, one takes refuge in the Buddha, the Dharma (the teaching), and the Sangha (the *community*). As Buddhism has understood for some 2,500 years, connectedness to community is vital.

Anger is a very common response to cutoff, but it is not everyone's principal response. My friend Anna shared that her primary experience of emotional devastation is sorrow. Mindfulness can help calm a range of emotions. At the same time, I invite a contextual, individualized approach. If a different strategy works better for you, use it.

Learning How to Die (Metaphorically!)

Important: Throughout this section, I refer to death *only* symbolically, never as a literal option. If you are considering suicide or if you are worried you may physically harm someone else, please seek professional help immediately. Suicide and crisis hotlines assist with these and other mental health crises. In the United States, you can dial 988 twenty-four hours a day for free, confidential emotional support.[414]

Healing is possible.

Indeed, healing is natural. Some of the best news in the world is that, to an extent, it just happens. Time does heal. The shock wears off. The old relationship begins to recede into the past. The new reality becomes the daily habit. Grief progresses.

Cutoff is a pickle here, though, because its nature tends to thwart time's healing. A natural and common, though not universal, stage in healing is the desire to reconnect, to reconcile. Cutoff prohibits this, which means that every time we start to reach this stage, we can be reinjured. The short, sharp shock of thwarted reconciliation pulls the wounds open again. It can be a vicious cycle. What's the way out?

In some cases, reconciliation can eventually happen. A seemingly permanent cutoff proves not to be permanent. In fewer cases, a close relationship can even be rekindled. But a large percentage of the time, the cutoff will be permanent and/or the close

---

[414] Thanks to Ray Shellmire for providing this information. For more information on 988 services, see https://www.fcc.gov/988-suicide-and-crisis-lifeline. or 988lifeline.org.

relationship will be permanently lost. Finding peace in cutoff does require acceptance, but acceptance is the end, not the beginning. With the impeded healing described above, it's not surprising it's a journey likely to take years, or that many don't fully reach that acceptance in this life.[415] Many people who have experienced cutoff liken it to dying or being killed. Discussing his pain at being ghosted, Arlo says, "It feels like a death except I know it's not one. I don't know how to categorize it."[416] In keeping with our social norms, Anderson's book does not explicitly address cutoff, but in an email communication with me, she noted, "In abandonment, I nickname cutting someone off as 'emotional murder.'"[417]

What do you do when there is no going back? What do you when it is impossible to reconcile or even make any civil, social peace with a person you once loved? What do you do when there is no happy ending, when the story of that particular relationship is a tragedy: tragic flaws and tragic consequence, and no hope of anything else? Like Hamlet, you may have to die (metaphorically!).

My Own Journey to Death (and Rebirth)

As I came to grips with the realization that a) my friendship with Sophia was irrevocably over and b) we could not even part on good terms, I devoted tremendous thought and energy to how to reach closure with this: years of thought, years of energy. About four and half years in, that I began to realize I needed to die (metaphorically). About a year earlier, my mother had said, "Sophia has

---

415 For example, Kramer (2003) found that in vulnerable elders, 59% of the sample cited family conflict as a concern at the end of their lives. B. Kramer, "Family Conflict at the End of Life: Lessons Learned in a Model Program for Vulnerable Older Adults," *The Gerontologist*, 43 (2003): 280.

416 Arlo.

417 Susan Anderson, email message to the author, March 19, 2021. My mother echoed this sentiment. Of course, she's biased in her concern for me, but I'll share her words because I find them eloquent: "I realized that cutoff is a form of murder that eludes judicial examination… Like any murder, there may be other repercussions, given that the killer has not forgotten the victim nor, in this case, has the victim forgotten the killer. There could be ghosts of the victim in recollections or regrets…." email message to the author, December 28, 2021.

killed you in her mind, and you need to kill her too." (Because we live in that sort of world, I will specify she meant *in my mind*, not literally.) My mother was right about the symbolically life-ending nature of the situation, but she was wrong about direction of the killing. It was not Sophia I needed to kill but myself. My life as a person in close relationship with Sophia had to be over. The life that had been ravaged by that tragedy had to end. To move on, I had to be reborn as someone else.

But how? The situation, in this life, was not healable. Yet I could not simply let myself linger Fisher King-like in festering woundedness for the rest of my (literal) life. Moreover, I could not pretend that this trauma had not transformed me in an ongoing (literally) lifelong way. How could I understand this? What metaphor, what narrative, existed to explain this? After several months of groping, it came to me somewhat suddenly that the metaphor I needed was *karma*.

Reverend Finch, sensei of Henjyoji Shingon Buddhist Temple, of which I am a member, defines karma as "intentional, volitional action," a short definition with a precise meaning.[418] It is "intentional" in that it is not inadvertent: stepping on someone's foot by accident does not generate karma. It is "volitional" in that it is willful: if someone leaps out at you and, in a panic, you punch them, that may be to some degree intentional (you know you're punching them), but it is not thought out; it's automatic. Because the punch is not volitional, it does not generate karma. However, choosing to punch someone in anger would generate karma. The "action" of karma includes physical actions, speech, and thought.

Karma is a neutral concept. It accrues with both our bad and good actions. Reverend Finch explains, "Everything you do, think, or say plants a seed in your mind. The seed will germinate given the proper conditions." Depending on the action, the fruit may be sweet or sour; it may help or hinder our spiritual journey. As with Hinduism, Buddhism traditionally holds that karma continues beyond a given lifetime. Since people typically don't have memories of their past lives, we cannot see all of our karma, but spiritual practice can help us better understand ourselves and the traces of our karma in our lives. Certainly, we can consider our actions in this life and reflect on our intentions. Reverend Finch, however,

---

[418] Reverend Kosho Finch in discussion with the author, March 10, 2023.

stresses that Buddhism teaches not to blame other people for their own misfortunes. We don't know why others' misfortunes happen. It is not our job to draw conclusions about their karma.[419]

In my own life, I see my karma in obstacles I helped create for myself in the past but have to navigate in the present. It describes the scars of trauma. As a lifelong agnostic, I don't have much investment in the idea of karma across literal reincarnations. I'm not invested in denying it, but I have no active belief in it. The metaphor of karma across lifetimes, however, proved to be the key that I needed.

Being a person who understands life through stories, I found immeasurable help in a strange little niche (at least, it's "niche" in the US), the Japanese light novel series *Honoo no Miraju*, unfortunately officially translated as *Mirage of Blaze*, by Mizuna Kuwabara.[420] To skip the details of this forty-volume, monstrous work of genius, I will merely note that I came to see myself as like someone who has lost the war and died in battle, a complete loss, a failure, and is then reborn. Other lives follow, other problems. The legacy of that failure leaves deep, persistent scars, but the war itself recedes into the past; the enemies of that life no longer have to be enemies. My cutoff trauma was the war I died in. Then, I became alive again, still navigating the transformations in me but in a new a life as different person, and the old life in the past.

I would be lying if I said this rebirth was total. Sometimes, I am that old person, right back where I was. But understanding myself as living with my karma was a turning point in my journey. It broke me out my frozen pain and gave me a way to understand what "moving on," as people so often counsel, might actually mean.

I wish that someone had offered me this metaphor, in therapy, in conversation. It wouldn't have helped at first; grief must be

---

419 Reverend Kosho Finch. In Western popular culture, "karma" sometimes refers to people who have hurt us getting their comeuppance, their "karma," through natural consequences. See, for example, Taylor Swift's song, "Karma." But the concept of karma is more helpful if we think about our own: the patterns we find in our lives and what we can learn from them.

420 The title of this profoundly Buddhist work could be more idiomatically translated as *The Blazing Mirage*, where the blaze, as I interpret it, represents our passions and the mirage their fundamental impermanence.

grieved. But my grieving process proper—accepting the loss of the friendship—was over in a couple of years, and by then, I was ready to be reborn, yet no one was there to tell me that was what I had to do. By sharing my experience, I hope to make this idea accessible for others. There are also other models of rebirth. It's not a coincidence that many people fleeing abusive relationships "find religion," and become born again in the Christian sense, either literally as born-again Christians or through other types of faith community. This can be another way of becoming a new person. Twelve-step programs offer the idea of surrender to a higher power. I'm sure there are many other pathways.

This is what it can mean to "move on," to begin to "let go." This is a step—just a step—toward acceptance. For me, it meant killing myself and learning to live again. To reduce this hardest task to platitudes, as if ending your own self were as trivial as remembering your morning jog, is profoundly destructive. The advice to let go is not wrong per se, but its understanding of humanity is. Don't fall for it. It isn't you who's crazy; it's the idea that human beings should be superhuman, that grief can be skipped, trauma switched off. What's crazy is the idea that if you can't do those things, then you're sick and absurd. You're not sick and absurd. You're not superhuman, and you don't have to be.

I am reminded of something the late, astounding Carrie Fisher said in her witty and touching memoir, *Wishful Drinking*. Speaking of her lifelong struggle with bipolar disorder, she asserts,

> One of the things that baffles me (and there are quite a few) is how there can be so much lingering stigma with regards to mental illness, specifically bipolar disorder. In my opinion, living with manic depression takes a tremendous amount of balls. Not unlike a tour of duty in Afghanistan (though the bombs and bullets, in this case, come from the inside). At times, being bipolar can be an all-consuming challenge, requiring a lot of stamina and even more courage, so if you're living with this illness and functioning at all, it's something to be proud of, not ashamed of.

> They should issue medals along with the steady stream of medications one has to ingest.[421]

I have neither grappled with bipolar disorder nor served in Afghanistan, and I don't wish to make false equivalencies, but I think this sentiment could apply, in spirit, to any experience of living with trauma. It is a battle. It is a war, with oneself and in the world. And if I could, I'd gladly give you a medal for surviving.

---

[421] Carrie Fisher, *Wishful Drinking* (New York: Simon and Schuster, 2009), 159.

Afterword

Cutoff Culture as a Manifestation of Neuroliberalism

If I were starting to write this book today, I might center it on a term I recently learned: "neuroliberalism." Coined by Engin Isin in 2004,[422] its narrow definition refers to the ways governments leverage psychology to achieve desired outcomes within a market-driven society, for example, offering an incentive to get consumers to switch to a green energy scheme. More broadly, however, I would frame it as the psychology of neoliberal economic ideology: the values and beliefs about the human psyche that follow neoliberal logics.[423] Under this broader definition, cutoff culture is one example of neuroliberal ideology.

Neoliberal economics, our current global system, advocates the dominance of capitalist markets with minimal intervention to redistribute wealth (e.g. low taxes, few social services, and few

---

[422] Isin, Engin, "The Neurotic Citizen," Citizenship Studies 8, 2004, 217–235. Though Isin discusses the action of governments, in our current government-corporate complex, this would logically have to include the actions of large corporations as well. See also Whitehead, Mark, Jones, Rhys, Lilley, Rachel, Howell, Rachel, and Pykett, Jessica, "Neuroliberalism: Cognition, Context, and the Geographical Bounding of Rationality," Progress in Human Geography, vol. 43, no. 4, 2018, pp. 632-649, https://doi.org/10.1177/0309132518777624.

[423] My reading of neuroliberalism, influenced by Antonio Gramsci, posits that neuroliberal actions occur not only in the intentional maneuvers of governments but also in the hegemonic grip of neuroliberal ideology, which permeates every level of our society. The cultural results are not necessarily planned; many are incidental.

regulations to hinder capital accumulation).[424] Its basic logic—famously summed up in the movie *Wall Street*—is "Greed is good": the idea that individuals' welfare is best served by encouraging self-serving consumption and competition within markets. In advertising, this shows up as "You're worth it"; i.e. you deserve (to buy) the product. In neoliberalism, selfishness is a virtue.

Neuroliberalism can be seen as a set of beliefs about human relations that provides an ethical justification for neoliberalism. It is the ideology of maximum self-responsibility: we have no right to expect help from anyone and no obligation to help anyone either (with few exceptions, like our minor children).

To be transparent, I am ardently opposed to neoliberalism as an economic philosophy. It is the economics of imperial oppression and ecological collapse. I am also deeply concerned about its partner, neuroliberalism, as a seemingly self-evident set of values for how people should relate to each other. I would like to see a more relational ideology replace it. That said, in many situations, I agree with specific decisions that reflect neuroliberal values. It depends on context of the decision.

Neuroliberalism justifies selfishness through the ideology of "self-care." Negative impacts on others are generally acceptable if they result from discarding social responsibilities in order to take care of oneself. Examples include cutoff, withdrawal of emotional support, and refusal of material aid (e.g. "I just can't take in my aged parents"). Conversely, negative impacts on others are generally *not* acceptable (or at least are problematic) if they result from asking others to take on a social responsibility. For example, asking for communication after a cutoff is suspect. So is asking for another's "emotional work." So is expecting your grown child to let you move in.

Under neuroliberalism, forgiveness exists not for the offender, the relationship, or the community, but purely for the forgiver's peace of mind. Under neuroliberalism, closure does not involve social interaction but only one's own mental processing. In therapy, neuroliberalism downplays *what happened* and emphasizes *how*

---

[424] Neoliberalism styles itself as wanting few regulations: small government. But in practice, it supports intensive regulation to benefit capital accumulation, such as subsidies to oil companies or interest-bearing debt imposed on poor nations.

you can change your thoughts about it.[425] In feminism, neuroliberalism says, "Don't apologize or feel guilty; it's all right to put yourself first (for once)." By the way, I agree this is healthy in many cases; women are often exploited in the name of serving others' needs. In images of masculinity, the neuroliberal paragon is Ayn Rand's John Galt (who might today be a Silicon Valley CEO): the charismatic, driven entrepreneur whose personal life goals justify exploitation of other people and the planet. At work, neuroliberalism says burnout should be solved by better time management and self-care (not more time off or reasonable productivity expectations). In relationships, neuroliberalism says a relationship is a transaction in which both parties want something, and if someone isn't getting that they want, it should end. The common theme is prioritizing individual wants and self-responsibilities over reciprocal responsibility and care. This ignores our species's inherently social nature. When deprived of dependable social supports, we languish.

My uncle, who was a Methodist minister, used to tell a story about the afterlife. (I don't think he invented it, but I learned it from him.) He said hell is a place where people are seated at a banquet, but their arms are tied with sticks so that they can't bend at the elbow. They can see and smell all this wonderful food, but they can never eat it. Heaven is also a place where people are seated at a banquet with their arms tied with sticks, but they are feeding each other.

---

[425] The economic version of this is "Let's not waste time on how socioeconomic systems kept you poor; you can't change that. Let's focus on how you can change your attitude to become more successful at making money within those systems."

Acknowledgments

This book is the work of many minds, notably my amazing editor, Jennifer Brennock, as well as Monte Lin, Melissa Ousley, Kristen Hall-Geisler, and Ali Shaw from Indigo Editing.

My thanks, too, to the experts who helped with this project: Kipling D. Williams, Susan Anderson, Ray Shellmire, Rebecca Bailey, Reverend Kosho Finch, Pastor Jeanne Randall-Bodman, Brenda H. Lee, and Lucia O'Sullivan, and to everyone who shared their experiences, particularly Jeff Reifman and "Ryan."

I owe a special debt of gratitude to those who contributed to this book knowing I am sometimes critical of their views. To willingly participate in a project that challenges one's views is a rare and courageous act. My respect and thanks go to Jennifer Brennock, Ferrett Steinmetz, "Meg," "Delia," "Lyn," and "Cole."

To "Anna" and Z. A. and to my mother, Patricia Spicer, I am blessed to have your caring and your thoughtful feedback on my drafts. Thanks also to my family for putting up with years of complaints about cutoff and especially to my partner, Glenn, for his support and willingness to share his own experiences in the book.

Finally, thank you to my professors and classmates in the Master's in Degrowth Ecology, Economy, and Policy at the Autonomous University of Barcelona. This book is very much in alliance with degrowth values.

www.ingramcontent.com/pod-product-compliance
Lightning Source LLC
Chambersburg PA
CBHW062206270326
41930CB00009B/1658

* 9 7 9 8 9 9 1 2 0 7 6 0 7 *